Faith Development and Fowler

Faith Development and Fowler

edited by

CRAIG DYKSTRA and SHARON PARKS

Religious Education Press
Birmingham, Alabama

Library of Congress Cataloging-in-Publication Data

Faith development and Fowler.

  Includes bibliographies and index.
  1. Faith—Psychology. 2. Developmental psychology.
3. Christian education—Philosophy. 4. Fowler,
James W., 1940-   . I. Dykstra, Craig R.
II. Parks, Sharon.
BT771.2.F25 1986   248   86-17766
ISBN 0-89135-056-X

Grateful acknowledgement is given as follows:

For permission to quote from "East Coker" in *Four Quartets* by T. S. Eliot, © 1943 by T. S. Eliot; renewed 1971 by Esme Valerie Eliot. Reprinted by permission of Faber & Faber Ltd. and Harcourt Brace Jovanovich, Inc.

For permission to quote from "The Dry Salvages" in *Four Quartets* by T. S. Eliot, © 1943 by T. S. Eliot; renewed 1971 by Esme Valerie Eliot. Reprinted by permission of Harcourt Brace Jovanovich, Inc. and Faber and Faber Ltd.

To Doubleday & Co., Inc. and Faber and Faber Ltd. for permission to quote from *Collected Poems,* "The Abyss" by Theodore Roethke, © 1968.

To the Westminster Press for permission to quote from *Christ in a Pluralistic Age* by John B. Cobb, Jr. © 1975.

To Silver Burdett Company for the use of "Faith and the Structuring of Meaning" by James Fowler in *Toward Moral and Religious Maturity* © 1980.

To Harper & Row Publishers, Inc. for the use of Figure 5.2 from *Stages of Faith,* © by James Fowler, 1981.

Religious Education Press, Inc.
Birmingham, Alabama
10 9 8 7 6 5 4 3

Religious Education Press publishes books exclusively in religious education and in areas closely related to religious education. It is committed to enhancing and professionalizing religious education through the publication of serious, significant, and scholarly works.

PUBLISHER TO THE PROFESSION

Contents

Introduction

The term "faith development" is a relative newcomer in the lexicon of important concepts we use in the field of religion to organize our insights into human growth and transformation. It has been introduced to us primarily by the work of James W. Fowler, whose faith development theory has quickly become one of the most widely known and influential theories of human development having to do with faith and the religious life. Its influence has been particularly strong among those who are responsible for thinking through and carrying out the ministries of education and care in religious communities. This book is a collection of essays written largely by theorists in these fields. Its purpose is to engage Fowler's theory in an extended critical conversation, evaluating its strengths and weaknesses, proposing ways in which it might be further enhanced and developed, and suggesting some of its appropriate uses in and implications for these "practical" fields.

WHY READ THIS BOOK

It is worth asking right at the start why anyone should read a book like this one. The book is admittedly a little unusual. It is fairly rare, particularly in such fields as religious education and pastoral care, that an entire volume be focused on just one theorist's ideas. In order to justify such attention, the object of attention would have to be unusually significant. Is Fowler's theory of faith development that important? We believe that it is, but it is important for us to say why.

Our answer is that Fowler addresses concerns that are central and abiding in religious education and pastoral care and in our own lives of faith. Furthermore, Fowler addresses these concerns in a way that draws together perspectives, insights, and resources that are particularly salient in the current scene. In other words, Fowler's theory is more than just one of any number of interesting and potentially useful academic analyses. It is an expression of a wider cultural and intellectual mood. It is a consolidation and crystalization of a whole way of seeing things that is already in some sense "out there." Fowler, we think, tells many of his readers, but in a way that they could not have put it themselves, what they in some sense already "knew" to be the case. If this hunch has any truth in it, it may help to account for the fact that Fowler's theory has been so readily and happily received by so many. It also provides the rationale for a book like this. For some critical engagement of Fowler's theory, its assumptions and implications, may do more than just raise questions about what *he* has thought and said. It may also help each of us to raise questions about what we ourselves assume and believe about faith, about growth in faith, and about ministry.

A CONCEPTION OF THE LIFE OF FAITH

In order to carry out the fundamental tasks of care and education in communities of faith, and even to understand our own lives, we require some overall conception of the life of faith. We need to have some clarity about what the qualities and characteristics of living in faith are. Our conception of the life of faith provides basic clues for what we can and are called to hope for ourselves and for one another. It helps us to articulate who we think we are, what we think we are doing, and where we think we are going. It helps us to see both where we have been and where we are heading as well as where others may be along the way. We all know that human beings grow and change and become what they were not. So a conception of the life of faith invariably includes some markings of its major turning points and transitions, mapping out the contours of the journey.

Perhaps this is the central concern that Fowler's theory addresses, the need for a fundamental conception of the life of faith. But if this is what the theory provides, should we not pause to ask whether this need has not already been filled in other ways? Do the various religious faiths not have their own internal conceptions of the life of faith, their own versions of the sacred journey? Why do we need another? Why do we need a faith development theory when we already have so many other sketches of the "pilgrim's progress" (Bunyan) and the "stages on life's way" (Kierkegaard), to take two examples from Christian literature? Do we need another because the others have become inadequate? Or have they just been forgotten? Is Fowler's theory a replacement for the shopworn? Or is it an approach to be set alongside the others, needed because we live in a new age with its own set of concerns and issues, insights and modes of discourse?

Whatever our answers to these questions, it does seem that the contemporary work on "faith development" is a part of an ages-long search for a conception of the religious life, and, like its predecessors, one that both deals with issues that mark the contemporary life out of which it emerges and makes use of the resources of the contemporary culture.

PLURALISM

One issue that pervades our own time is the issue of pluralism. Since the Enlightenment, but even more pressingly in the twentieth century, the plurality of religious visions has become increasingly apparent and the parochial nature of particular conceptions has come under intense criticism. There is significant difference of vision both within religious communities and among them. At the same time, the need for mutual understanding, acceptance, and appreciation in a world become small and dangerous is profound. It is simply not possible in our world to be satisfied with exclusivistic understandings of faith that are incapable of comprehending the power and richness of other religions and the maturity in faith of persons whose beliefs and traditions differ from our own. But sheer relativism—the view that one way of living and believing is just as good as any other—is no answer either. We know that life without any real standards or discriminating values is bound ultimately for chaos and violence.

We all find ourselves facing these issues in different ways and out of different experiences. Fowler has said that his own experiences as a child watching his Methodist minister father deal with a great variety of people, as a teenager participating each summer in the life of a Christian conference center, and as an adult assisting Carlyle Marney in the development of his interracial, ecumenical, and intercultural Interpreters' House were formative. So also were his college studies in history and the sociology of religion, his involvement in student politics, and his doctoral studies in religion and society. The combination of a powerful nurturing in a particular faith community and subculture together with an introduction in young adulthood to the many ways there are of seeing and being in the world often leads to a kind of "vertigo of relativity," and Fowler's case was no exception. A kind of skepticism develops when one encounters one system of meaning after another and they all seem plausible. It is the very plausibility of them all that seems to undermine each in turn.

Finding a way to make sense of the meaning and dynamics of faith in the light of the fact of pluralism and the inadequacy of relativism is central to the point of faith development theory. Fowler's theory attempts to provide one way of holding together some of what may be universal about human faith experience, while also recognizing the particularity of various ways of being in faith.

Fowler's basic clues to a way of resolving the tensions inherent here came most decisively from the work of H. Richard Niebuhr. In an unpublished lecture given in 1984 at Harvard Divinity School, Fowler, speaking of his rereading of Niebuhr during his graduate studies, said: "I had read Niebuhr earlier, but I somehow had not been ready for the richness, the subtlety, the catholicity of Niebuhr's thinking. . . . Niebuhr had seen everything I had seen in terms of the vertigo of relativity, and yet had emerged from that with an astonishing capacity to affirm the sovereignty of God and to see that relativity need not lead to relativism, but that all of our constructions of meaning, all of our worldviews are in some sense relative to that ground of being and meaning which they to some degree try to apprehend and bring to clarity for us." Fowler's doctoral dissertation was on Niebuhr, and was later published as *To See the Kingdom: The Theological Vision of H. Richard Niebuhr.* Although the work of Wilfred Cantwell Smith, Paul Tillich, and others have been important influences on Fowler's understanding of faith in a pluralistic context, Niebuhr remains fundamental, and an understanding of Niebuhr illuminates in important ways what Fowler's theory is about.

THE PSYCHOLOGICAL APPROACH
TO HUMAN DEVELOPMENT

A second theme that is prominent in our time is that of the psychological and developmental understanding of the human self. Every culture, just like every religious faith, needs some conception of human life. Ours is one in which people have for some time been, and are now increasingly, experiencing significant and rapid social change as well as a dramatic extension of the human life cycle. Both factors call forth theories of change and development. At least in Western culture, the social sciences, particularly psychology, have been providing the primary language of interpretation for doing this. It should be no surprise that these resources are mobilized for the interpretation of change and development in faith and in the understanding of religious experience.

The late nineteenth and early twentieth centuries saw the development of a new empirical psychology. William James was a key figure here, and his classic, *Varieties of Religious Experience,* was an early and influential attempt to categorize and understand the psychology of human religious experience. From a different angle, but with a similar psychological emphasis, came the work of Sigmund Freud, who interpreted religious experience as a way in which the human psyche deals with the internal and external pressures of one's social environment. Out of such investigations grew the whole new field of psychology of religion which provided the predominant paradigm for understanding and interpreting religious (as well as moral) experience and development.

None of this was lost to the churches. In response to these studies, another new field—religious education (which, in turn, later spawned the field of pastoral psychology)—arose to put these studies to practical use and, in many cases, carried them along further. All of this was supported by a generally optimistic cultural ethos and a liberal theology that believed in the ongoing progress of humanity and in the power of religion and religious experience to sustain it. But, after a healthy marriage between social scientific inquiry and liberal theology, which produced volumes of study on religious and moral growth, religious experience, and systematic education for the moral and religious life, a separation took place. The world situation changed dramatically, and a new theology (what we now call neo-orthodoxy) grew out of a world at war. Trust in human religious experience, in the possibilities of moral and religious growth, and in psychology to interpret what was most fundamental to the divine-human relationship was shattered. Psychology of religion and liberal theology were no longer adequate, and religious education had to search for new ground on which to stand.

By the 1960s, however, the great neo-orthodox hegemony in Protestant theology had fallen apart. On the Catholic side, Vatican II released new vitalities in theological study and in religious education. At the same time, new psychological influences were coming to attention. Erik Erikson's *Childhood and Society* was published, and his eight stages of psychosocial development were easily accessible to religious educators. The ego psychologies of Anna Freud, Karen Horney, and Harry Stack Sullivan were also having a major impact, especially on pastoral care and counseling. Jungian psychology was gaining increasing attention. One of the most striking new factors, however, was the work of Jean Piaget. With his cognitive-structural approach to developmental psychology, a major new way of doing psychology appeared. Piaget was being translated and read, and the implications of his work on moral and religious development were being explored, especially among religious educators. The significance of the cognitive-structural approach for moral and religious development became more clear and widely recognized, however, when Lawrence Kohlberg formulated a life-span theory of moral development out of Piaget's work and began to articulate its philosophical base and implications.

Just as the combination of personal experience and academic study worked both to raise the issue and suggest the resources for Fowler's grappling with the issue of pluralism, so too with the matter of religious experience and psychology. During his year at

Interpreters' House, Fowler spent a great deal of his time listening to the life stories of nearly three hundred people. Not only were there sustained encounters with clergy, but also with professionals in business, journalism, and other fields, as well as with groups of community organizers in black communities. As he listened to them tell about their lives, he began to recognize two key patterns: the power of early childhood in the formation and malformation of people's lives and the close connection between people's faith and their personal identity. He began to notice, too, how people's faith tends to address different issues at different eras of the life cycle. He found that Erikson's work was a particularly helpful interpretive tool. Consequently, when he later returned to Harvard Divinity School to teach, the themes of faith and identity and of religious growth and human development were prominent in his classroom and in his thought. His students there made him aware of Kohlberg's work, and study with Kohlberg and others at Harvard in cognitive-structural development theory led directly to the formulation of his own cognitive-structural theory of faith development and empirical studies to test it.

THEORY, BIOGRAPHY, AND CULTURAL MYTH

It is sometimes said that theory is biography writ large. This tends to be particularly evident in theories of human development, since they are inevitably shaped by the theorist's own life experience no matter how informed by other perspectives. One sees in Fowler's theory an attempt to incorporate and account for both the theological and the psychological: his own Christian biblical tradition and contemporary pluralistic human experience. Behind it all is the concern of a pastor for the immediate struggles of the particular people with whom he deals, the concern of a scholar to link his insights up with the theories of others and to prove his point in the academic arena, and the concern of a teacher to communicate his ideas in a way that is widely accessible as well as practically useful. It may also be said that theories are sometimes cultural myths writ small. That is, some accounts of human nature and development, especially those which are highly synthetic in nature and which deal with basic issues that permeate a cultural situation, reflect and articulate a common cultural experience (including, in our present case perhaps, a need for continuity in times of cultural discontinuity, a need for traditional religions to understand themselves in relation to and communicate with other religions and peoples, and even a tendency for consumeristic cultures to overvalue "development").

Fowler's theory can be seen from both perspectives, and we have tried to indicate in brief compass some of the ways in which this may be true. Understanding the theory in these terms may help to account for both some of its forcefulness as well as some of its limitations. It is through our own life experience that we come to real insights. There is no other way. What we see, we must see from our own perspectives. And if a theory is to have any passion in it, it will come from the way it speaks from and to its author's own life. Likewise, if a theory is to have power, it must speak to its hearers in their circumstances and in a language that has some broad currency. But this is always a treacherously difficult business, especially when one attempts to speak about something as deep in human experience as faith and to account for it in generic, universal terms. Can we really speak meaningfully of the meaning and experience and development of faith in human life as a whole from the point of view of our own experience in faith, even from the point of view of our own culture's experience? Or is such an enterprise doomed from the start? But we cannot not say anything, can we? In any case, speaking about these matters cries out for dialogue, for discussion.

OVERVIEW OF THIS COLLECTION

The discussion in this book is divided into five parts. The first of these is a basic overview of Fowler's faith development theory. The only essay not entirely written originally for this volume, "Faith and the Structuring of Meaning," is a revised and updated version of an essay first published in 1980. This essay provides the best brief introduction available to the major dimensions and insights of Fowler's theory. It is published here to introduce Fowler's work to readers who have not read him already, especially his major work, *Stages of Faith* (1981), and to provide readers who have studied his theory with a helpful survey of the most important themes. All readers will be interested to note, however, that this revision contains new descriptions of each of the stages of faith which are based on Fowler's continuing empirical research.

Part II is entitled "Evaluating Faith Development Theory." All of the essays in this volume contain evaluations of various aspects of Fowler's theory, but these in particular raise critical questions about the basic structure of the theory, particularly in relation to Fowler's understanding of the nature of faith itself. Craig Dykstra analyzes Fowler's understanding of the meaning of faith and proposes an alternative, describing the difference it would make if it were adopted. The basic issue here is whether faith is really a human universal or a mode of life that is grounded in a more or less conscious and chosen responsiveness to the activity of God in the world. The two alternatives have quite different implications for the relation of human development studies to our understanding of growth in faith. J. Harry Fernhout argues that Fowler's description of faith tries to cover too much territory, and that he actually works with three different understandings of faith which he does not adequately discriminate. Fernhout concludes that the theory thereby becomes conceptually unmanageable and ultimately lacking in an organizing center, and that it ultimately becomes impossible to distinguish faith development from general human development.

John M. Broughton claims that Fowler's theory moves in a direction that is in inherent contradiction with its own intentions, leading to rationalistic, conformist individualism rather than to faith. According to Broughton, faith development theory is most fundamentally an expression of modern, bureaucratic culture and ideology which has been captivated by its political and economic interests. Maria Harris, writing explicitly from the point of view of a feminist religious educator, takes a close look at the metaphors for knowing, experience, and time embedded in Fowler's understanding of faith and development. She articulates the questions that get raised when some other metaphors are given more prominence. The ones she calls to our attention are the metaphors of art, sisterhood, and sabbath, all on the basis of the underlying metaphor of completion.

Part III is entitled "Enhancing Faith Development Theory." In this section the emphasis changes to ways in which Fowler's theory might be enhanced or enriched by plumbing deeper into issues that the theory has already raised, by expanding into new but adjacent territory, or by rethinking some of its research assumptions and procedures. Sharon Parks argues that faith development theory would be enhanced by a more thorough understanding of the nature of the imagination and its relation to human spirit and the Spirit of God. She believes that such an exploration can provide a way to overcome the problem of the relationship between structure and content that cognitive-structural theories have difficulty addressing, but that moral and religious perspectives must engage. Stuart D. McLean shows how attention to the way development is affected by the fact that we live in multiple communities of faith and to root metaphors for understanding the self in social context at each stage of faith development can enrich Fowler's theory. He does this by arguing that these two areas of exploration have been dealt with helpfully by one of Fowler's own major sources, H. Richard Niebuhr, and that Fowler would do well to follow Niebuhr here as he has elsewhere. C. Ellis Nelson and Daniel Aleshire take a look at Fowler's research methods, articulate their strengths, and suggest some ways they might be improved. They highlight the complexity of this area of research and the difficulty of getting good data, but conclude that the concerns they raise do not necessarily invalidate Fowler's claims. Rather, they point in directions where more work needs to be done.

In Part IV, "Faith Development Theory and Ministry," two essays from the field of pastoral care and counseling and one from religious education examine some of the potential usefulness of Fowler's theory for their respective fields. K. Brynolf Lyon and Don S. Browning show how Fowler's theory can be related to understandings of emotional development and helps to make "faith" a useful interpretive category in pastoral care. Particularly interesting here is the way they bring Fowler's work into conversation with another major school of psychology that is now of special interest among pastoral psychologists, object-relations theory. Carl D. Schneider explains the usefulness of Fowler's stage theory for making diagnoses in pastoral counseling and claims that Fowler's work is a major advance over previous attempts to develop a pastoral diagnostic framework. He also sees some problems, however, especially in the theory's lack of attention to the contents of people's personal images—an area where psychoanalytic perspectives have proven particularly effective. To show this, Schneider provides an analysis of "Mary's Case" (reported in *Stages of Faith*) in which he comes to some different conclusions from Fowler's. Craig Dykstra turns our attention to religious education. He articulates some basic questions that are important to religious educators and shows at what points Fowler's theory is most helpful in answering them. He argues that while faith development theory cannot be—and does not intend to be—the core of an approach to religious education, it can be an important conversation partner if we know what to look for and how to use it.

The final part of the book, Part V, gives the stage back to James Fowler. Fowler challenges some of the claims his critics have made and articulates what he finds helpful and stimulating for his own thinking. He responds to the issues raised by these essays and discloses his view of the future directions of faith development theory and research.

The essays that comprise this book were written over a period of several years. They have been part of an ongoing conversation which has collected new participants along the way. Much of what is found here is the result of face-to-face conversations and re-workings of papers that had to be revised in the light of what we learned from each other. Significant disagreements among the authors still remain, as any reader will see. We really would not want it to be otherwise. This creates a good deal of the excitement of this volume. Our hope has been to stimulate careful and critical reflection on this matter of faith development, and to ask you to join in the discussion.

The initial stimulus for all of this was, of course, Fowler's own writing. As some of the early work began to appear, it of itself engendered widespread conversation. The major event in the genesis of this book, however, was a conference held at Auburn Theological Seminary in New York in March, 1982, and organized by its president, Barbara Wheeler. The liveliness of that discussion, in which we together with James Fowler and several others represented in these pages participated, made it clear to us that what we were doing needed to be shared with others. The conversation carried on long after that conference and came to include others whose interest in this theory we came to know. One important occasion was the first Faith Development Institute, held at the Candler School of Theology in Atlanta in the summer of 1982. There we were graciously hosted by James Fowler and his staff.

We wish, then, to thank all of those who have participated in these discussions over the last several years, and particularly those whose writings appear in this volume. We also wish to make public our sincere appreciation to James Fowler for being so willing to keep in conversation all along the way, even when criticism has been sharp as well as appreciative. Finally, we wish to acknowledge Auburn Theological Seminary for the financial and organizational support which it provided and without which this volume would never have been possible, and, above all, to convey our deepest appreciation to Barbara Wheeler for her full partnership with us in every aspect of this endeavor from beginning to end.

CRAIG DYKSTRA
SHARON PARKS

PART I

An Overview of Faith Development Theory

Chapter 1

Faith and the Structuring of Meaning

JAMES W. FOWLER

"The meanest man must have his canvas, and it must be one which reflects somehow his own sense of significance in a world that is significant. Above all, it must be integral, unified, even if it should suffer from being pale." So writes Ernest Becker in the conclusion of one of the most insightful chapters of *The Structure of Evil.*[1] The chapter is about *homo poeta,* man the meaning-maker, the singular animal burdened with the challenge of composing a meaningful world. *Faith* has to do with the making, maintenance, and transformation of human meaning. It is a mode of knowing and being. In faith, we shape our lives in relation to more or less comprehensive convictions or assumptions about reality. Faith composes a felt sense of the world as having character, pattern, and unity. In the midst of the many powers and demands pressing upon us, enlarging and diminishing us, it orients us toward centers of power and value which promise to sustain our lives, and to guarantee "more-being."[2]

Although it is by no means fully conscious, and is often largely unreflective and tacit, I believe faith to be a human universal. Most often, it comes to expression and accountability through the symbols, rituals, and beliefs of particular religious traditions. The major religious communities are the living repositories of the faith expressions of countless peoples in the past and present.

*This chapter is an updated and revised version of "Faith and the Structuring of Meaning," *Toward Moral and Religious Maturity,* ed. James W. Fowler and Antoine Vergote (Morristown, N.J.: Silver Burdett, 1980), pp. 41-85. Used with permission.

These elements form traditions. They can serve to awaken and express the faith of people in the present.[3] But faith is not always religious in the cultural or institutional sense. Many persons in our time weave and paint their meaning-canvases in communities other than religious, and often with symbols or stories which have no direct relationship to traditions of group piety or religious worship.

Faith is an extremely complex phenomenon to try to operationalize for empirical investigation. It has more dimensions than any one perspective can contain. An examination of two major dimensions of faith's dynamic may help us to appreciate that complexity and to be clearer about faith. In this approach, I aim to treat faith as a generic *human* phenomenon—a way of leaning into or meeting life, whether traditionally religious, or Christian, or not.

FAITH AS RELATIONAL

Faith begins in relationship. Faith implies trust in another, reliance upon another, a counting upon or dependence upon another. The other side of faith as trust is faith as attachment, as commitment, as loyalty. Erik Erikson points to the developmental foundations of faith when he observes that the first major task faced by the child's infant ego is that of achieving mutuality in a relationship marked by trust with the primary giver of care (usually the mother).[4] As the infant comes to trust and rely upon the consistency and care of the parent, it also comes to feel a sense of trustworthiness, of *rely*-ability in the self, which becomes the anticipation of a later ability to commit the self and to invest loyalty. Writers such as Martin Buber, George Herbert Mead, Harry Stack Sullivan, in addition to Erikson, have clarified how imperative for the development of the self is this fundamental "faithfulness" in the relation of the child to primal others.

But I turn to the philosopher Josiah Royce[5] and to the theologian H. Richard Niebuhr[6] for the most helpful clarifications of the foundational quality of faith as relational in human life. Royce and Niebuhr show us that all viable and lasting human communities have either a tacit or an explicit faith structure which is triangular in form. In communities, a self (S) is bound to others (O) by shared trust and loyalty.

But our ties to others are mediated, formed, and deepened by our shared or common trusts in and loyalties to centers of supra-ordinate value (CSV). Thus,

Consider a few examples. Although I will never know personally more than a few hundred other citizens of my nation, I am bound to them all in some quality of trust and loyalty through a shared commitment to the principles of justice and right which inform the Constitution and Declaration of Independence. In another context, the faith structure of the university centers in free inquiry and a commitment to truth. Though I may never know personally many of my colleagues in other schools or departments of the university, I presume—until proven otherwise—that they share with me a loyalty to and trust in the central values underlying the university. Other examples could be offered endlessly: the tacit covenant to truth required in the use of language; the covenantal aspect of marriage; the presumption of fidelity to duty and to standards of excellence in the professions and business; and so on and on. The interesting thing is that this triangle of faith, which is the hallmark of viable and lasting human relationships at every level, is made visible to us as much in its breakdowns or failures as when it is in good working order. Theodore White's book on Watergate is aptly titled *Breach of Faith*. When we fail the public trust in politics, are unfaithful in marriage, or fail to live up to the standards of our profession, not only do we betray

our covenanting partners—tacit or explicit—but we also betray
the center(s) of supraordinate value to which we are presumably
loyal. And such breaches reveal, painfully, that we live by structures of trust and loyalty—by triadic relations of faith.

A moment's reflection will show that each of us belongs to a
number of faith-relational triangles. In each of the roles we have
assumed, in each institutional context in which we work, in each
significant relationship we enjoy, we "keep faith" with some others and with the value commitments we share with them. Certainly, in examining this triangular faith structure of relationships, we are in touch with a major source of the forms and colors
with which we paint on the canvas of meaning which nurtures
homo poeta.

As a culmination of our look at faith as relational, let me point
to the broadest and most inclusive relationship in faith. This is
the faith triangle that includes—when it is intact—all the others
of which we are part. This is that most inclusive triangle in which
the self relates to the canvas of meaning itself. In other writings, I
have referred to this largest canvas of meaning as our sense of an
ultimate environment. In Jewish and Christian terms, the ultimate environment is expressed with the symbol "Kingdom of
God." In this way of seeing, *God* is the center of power and value
which unifies and gives character to the ultimate environment.[7]

We have not come to terms with faith as relational until we
have examined it as an activity of knowing and being in which
the self makes a bid for relationship to a center of value and
power adequate to ground, unify, and order the whole force-field
of life. In the study of faith development, we recognize, of course,
many moments—some of which may last the remainder of a
lifetime—in which persons do *not* feel themselves related to any
value or power adequate to unify and order their experience. For
some persons, the images they form to express a unity and order
in the ultimate environment are at best neutral toward their lives
and human events generally, or at worst they are hostile and
destructive. Nonetheless, even as negativity or as void, a person's
unconscious assumptions or conscious convictions regarding
power and value in the ultimate environment have important
implications for the character and quality of the relational commitments in the range of his or her other triangular relationships.

An important double action is at work here. In the weaving and painting of our meaning-canvases, the materials, forms, and colors often come directly from our experiences of faith and unfaith in the more everyday relationships of our lives. Conversely, our commitments in these smaller faith triangles have everything to do with the way we see them in relation to larger and more comprehensive frames of felt meaning.[8]

Faith, we have seen, is an irreducibly *relational* phenomenon. It is an active mode of knowing and being in which we relate to others and form communities with those with whom we share common loyalties to supraordinate centers of value and power. Faith is an active mode of knowing and being in which we grasp our relatedness to others and to our shared causes as all related to and grounded in a relatedness to power(s) and value(s) which unify and give character to an ultimate environment.

FAITH AS A KNOWING

Faith is a way of being, arising out of a way of *seeing* and *knowing*. The attentive reader will have caught our use of such verbs as "compose," "construct," "maintain," "form," "attach," "invest," "commit" to characterize aspects of the dynamic relationships involved in faith. In this approach to faith, we stand in the structural-developmental tradition pioneered by J. Mark Baldwin and John Dewey, and brought to heightened clarity by Jean Piaget, Lawrence Kohlberg, and their associates. In this tradition, *knowing* means an acting upon and "composing" of the known.[9] Knowing occurs when an active knower interacts with an active world of persons and objects, meeting its unshaped or unorganized stimuli with the ordering, organizing power of the knower's mind. Knowing is adequate or "true" when the mental ordering of the elements of reality correspond to their relationships as experienced and known by other reliable knowers. When the "object" of knowing is thus accurately known, when it is not "subjectively" distorted, we speak of "objectivity."[10] Piaget, in the latter part of his career, has focused with special acumen on the child's and adolescent's way of composing the reality of the world of objects and of relationships between objects. His work has disclosed integrated patterns of thought, formally describable, which characterize a sequence of increasingly more adequate mental systems of knowing ("stages"). Armed with this Piagetian theoretical approach, Kohlberg[11] and later Selman[12] have renewed the constructivist approach in a more thorough reworking of Piaget's earlier investigations. Kohlberg has investigated the child's, adolescent's, and adult's ways of constructing situations of moral dilemma and choice and of forming solutional approaches to them.

An important aspect of moral thinking and knowing is the capacity to construct the point of view of other persons and groups. Kohlberg and Flavell did pioneering work, extending Piaget's investigations of perspective-taking.[13] But it is Robert Selman who has developed the best theoretical work, based on empirical studies, on social perspective-taking.

Recently, Robert Kegan has made a new extension of the Piaget and Kohlberg paradigms. In an impressive doctoral dissertation, Kegan rigorously sought to extend Piaget's primary focus on knowing as active structuring or organizing to account for the dynamics of personality or ego development.[14] The cgo, Kegan argues, is to be understood as the total *constitutive activity of knowing* (with its evolving characteristic patterns) by which the self constitutes and, therefore, knows other persons and the self as related to others. Ego, he insists, is the construal of the self and others in relationship. In an approach that seeks to unify an understanding of the ego's total constitutive activity (including even the "dynamic unconscious" of depth psychologies), Kegan throughout points to the ways we construct both the "world" and ourselves in the "knowing" that is ego.[15]

Later we will return to an assessment of aspects of Kegan's bold thesis. Our purpose now is to show that *faith itself is a powerful expression of constructive knowing.* Here we have in view the composition (constitution) and interpretation of the *persons, values, communities,* and *images of ultimate environments* to which we are related in trust (or mistrust) and loyalty (or disloyalty) in faith.

In the previous section, we traced the relational character of faith at several levels. We spoke of interpersonal faith, of faith as involved in the relation of person and group or groups. We noted a triangular faith structure in all viable social institutions or associations. And, finally, we sought to evoke an awareness of one's relatedness to an "environment of environments," a unifying, integrating vision centering in an image or images of supraordinate value and power that can unify one's experiences in the confusing welter of the force-field of life. From a constructivist (structural-developmental) standpoint, *each* of these levels of relationship involves *constitutive-knowing* (the knowing that composes or establishes both the known and the knower in relation to the known).

Up to a point, the structural features of constitutive knowing disclosed to us by Piaget, Kohlberg, Selman, and now Kegan, for each of their respective domains, serve us well in understanding the constitutive-knowing that is faith. Faith does involve knowing the world of physical objects and the laws of their relatedness, movement, and change. Faith does involve constructions of the self and others, in perspective-taking, in moral analysis and judgment, and in the constitutions of self as related to others which we call ego.

But when we conceptually address the last relational step of faith—that of relatedness to an ultimate environment—certain decisive problems emerge from the effort to extend the Piagetian approach to constitutive-knowing so as to encompass the domain of faith.

At one time I would have named three such problems. The first of these I would have seen as arising from the fateful way Piaget (and following him, Kohlberg) separates *cognition* (the "structural aspect of knowing") and *affection* (the "energetics or emotional dimension of knowing"). Clearly, from what we have said about faith, it is a knowing which involves both reason and feeling; both rationality and passionality. While Piaget and Kohlberg acknowledge the inextricable unity of cognition and affection in actual behavior and choice, neither of them has dealt adequately in his theory with that unity. Kegan's work, however, has helped me reformulate the cognitive-affective problem. He argues that the problem we confront here is not one of how theoretically to integrate thought and feeling. Rather, the challenge is to recognize that meaning-making, as a constructive movement, is prior to and generative of both reason and emotion. We must, Kegan asserts, see meaning-making as the self's total constitutive-knowing activity, an activity in which there is no thought without feeling and no feeling without thought. So long as we widen and deepen our understanding of cognition (and the structures of constitutive-knowing) in this broader sense, then this problem of the Piagetian bifurcation of cognition and affection is, in principle, overcome.

But there remain two other significant sets of issues which any adequate accounting for the character of faith as a "knowing" in structural-developmental terms must address. Neither Piaget nor Kohlberg intends to provide a theory of ego or personality development. Both, therefore, have approached the task of identifying the forms of reason or logic characteristic of different "stages" in human thought without making a critically important distinction: They have not attended to the differences between constitutive-knowing in which *the identity or worth of the person is not directly at stake* and constitutive-knowing in which it is. This has meant that Kohlberg has avoided developing a theory of the moral self, of character, or of conscience. Strictly speaking, his stages describe a succession of integrated structures of moral logic. He has given very little attention to the fact that we "build" ourselves through choices and moral (self-defining) commitments. His theory, for understandable theoretical and historical-practical reasons, has not explicated the dynamics of the inner dialogue in moral choice between actual and possible selves.[16]

There is a problem involved in Kegan's 1977 proposal that we extend Piaget's structural paradigm to include *all* the self's constitutive-knowing. It arises from a lack of clarity about how he makes the move from a theory of knowing which strives for *objectivity* and rational certainty in knowing to one in which the self's identity and worth and more—its very constitution—are at stake. Kegan does in fact call attention to two parallel philosophies of knowing in recent European thought: the objectifying, technical reason which has as its ideal the elimination of all subjectivity (positivism), and the kind of knowing which emphasizes subjective freedom, risk, and passionate choice (existentialism). And he acknowledges Piaget's primary focus of attention on the former. But then he moves toward an inclusion of the second within the first without adequately accounting for how various subfunctions of knowing, such as perception, feeling, imagination, and rational judgment are related and are to be distinguished from one another.

In both faith-knowing and the kind of moral-knowing which gives rise to choice and action, the constitution or modification of the self is always an issue. In these kinds of constitutive-knowing not only is the "known" being constructed but there is also a simultaneous confirmation, modification, or reconstitution of the *knower in relation to the known.* To introduce this freedom, risk, passion, and subjectivity into the Piaget-Kohlberg paradigm (as we must in faith development) requires that we examine the relationship of what we may call a *logic of rational certainty* (Piaget's major concern) to what we may call a *logic of conviction.* (I use the term "logic" here in a metaphorical sense, designating two major kinds of structuring activity which interact in the constitutive-knowing that is faith.) This relationship between these two "logics" is not one of choice between alternatives. A logic of conviction does not negate a logic of rational certainty. But the former, being more inclusive, does contextualize, qualify, and anchor the latter. Recognition of a more comprehensive "logic of conviction" does lead us to see that the logic of rational certainty is part of a larger epistemological structuring activity and is not to be confused with the whole.

I am asking you to focus on the logic of conviction as a more comprehensive mode of knowing. It transcends while including the logic of rational certainty. To do so brings the recognition of another layer of problems. Faith, as a generative knowing, "reasons" holistically—it composes "wholes." In faith, the self "knows" itself and the neighbor in relation to an ultimate environment. A spread of meaning, a canopy of significance is composed to backdrop or fund more immediate, everyday action. The Piaget paradigm took form and has been refined as a logic of objects and of relations between objects. To be sure, Piagetian formal operational logic does involve the construction of nonempirical, imaginative constructs, some of which (say, in theoretical physics) operate with the same remoteness from the possibility of direct empirical validation as do faith constructions. But we must recognize a critical distinction between the "fictive" or "imaginative" constructions of theoretical physics and those of faith and theology. This distinction arises primarily from our earlier point about the degree to which the identity and value of a self or selves are at stake in our acts of constitutive-knowing. I can live with curiosity and intrigue about the question of the nature and character of "black holes" in space. But in my unknowing, I am not paralyzed in my choices of lifestyle and commitments. At certain points in my life, and in the lives of all of us, however, situations arise in very practical contexts, and with fateful life-defining potential, that are of another sort. These are situations in which rational analysis and systemic mapping yield a clarification of options, but provide no criteria for highly consequential value choices. In these situations, we choose and act (and/or find explanations and rationales for our acts) with reference to our assumptions or convictions about the character of power and value in an ultimate environment. Our choices and explanations of choices in these situations reflect operative attachments to meaning-giving images and centers of value and power.

This latter domain—the domain of faith and of logic of conviction—involves recognizing the role played in faith of modes of knowing we call ecstatic[17] and imaginative.[18] As is becoming generally recognized, the mind employs the more aesthetically oriented right hemisphere of the brain in these kinds of knowing.[19] To my knowledge, none of the Piagetian cognitive-constructivists, including Kegan, have given any significant attention to the bihemispheric, bimodal forms of thought involved in the constitutive-knowing that is faith. To move in this direction requires coming to terms with modes of thought that employ images, symbols, and synthetic fusions of sense and feeling. It means taking account of so-called "regressive" movements in which the psyche returns to preconceptual, prelinguistic modes and memories, and to primitive sources of energizing imagery, bringing them into consciousness with resultant reconstruals of the experience world.[20] To deal adequately with faith and with faith's dynamic role in the total self-constitutive activity of ego means trying to give theoretical attention to the transformation in consciousness—rapid and dramatic in sudden conversion, more gradual and incremental in faith growth—which results from the re-cognition of self-others-world in light of knowing the self as constituted by a center of value powerful enough to require or enable recentering one's ultimate environment.[21]

We must underscore that the effort to attend to these more

affective, imaginative, and holistic modes of knowing does not *negate* the part played by the operations of the logic of rational certainty. It does not mean a capitulation to unbridled fantasy or subjectivity, nor does it mean a relinquishing in faith of the critical role of rational reflection. Rather the challenge is to see how rational knowing plays the crucial role of conceptualizing, questioning, and evaluating the products of other modes of imaginal and generative knowing. As Lynch writes: "And for what shall we be held more accountable than for our images?"[22] We are trying to grasp the inner dialectic of rational logic in the dynamics of a larger, more comprehensive logic of convictional orientation.

Our discussion of faith as a knowing has led us on a somewhat circuitous route. Faith, we have claimed, is a mode of knowing and construing. It is that part of the total constitutive-knowing of selves in which we compose a holistic sense or image of an ultimate environment. Our compositions of an ultimate environment derive unity and coherence by virtue of our attachments, our convictional investments, in power(s) and value(s) of supraordinate significance.

Going beyond Piaget and Kohlberg, and building on Kegan, we have claimed that the constitutive-knowing by which self-other relationships are constituted does not involve just an *extension* of the logic of rational certainty. Instead, it involves a transformation in which a logic constitutive of objects must be seen as integrated with and contextualized by a logic of conviction. This means that what we are calling faith is a core process in the total self-constitutive activity that is ego. Ego development so understood must take account of the integration of and interplay between a logic of rational certainty and a logic of conviction that characterizes the epistemology of faith.

INQUIRY INTO FAITH DEVELOPMENT:
THE SEARCH FOR STRUCTURES

A summary, composite definition of faith as we are discussing it might go this way. Faith is:

The process of constitutive-knowing
Underlying a person's composition and maintenance of a comprehensive frame (or frames) of meaning

Generated from the person's attachments or commitments to centers of supraordinate value which have power to unify his or her experiences of the world

Thereby endowing the relationships, contexts, and patterns of everyday life, past and future, with significance.

So understood, faith is an aspect of the total constitutive activity of the *ego*. It functions to provide orientation, hope, and courage. It grounds sustaining strength, purpose, and experiences of shared commitment which find the self and others in community.

In a constructivist perspective, faith is understood to have its own structural characteristics. That is to say, underlying the wide variety of *contents* which come to be expressive of the faith of persons, there are formally describable *patterns* or *structures* of thought, of valuing, and of constitutive-knowing. In fifteen years of research, we have generated a provisional constructivist theory of faith development in which structural "stages" are characterized by relatively equilibrated integrations of such patterns. In the course of faith development, periods of equilibration alternate with transitional phases in which, under the impact of new experiences, of changed environments, and of new ways of knowing in other domains, the structural patterns of faith-knowing undergo relinquishment and transformation. We believe that the equilibrated stage-like positions we have identified constitute a developmentally related sequence. We believe that the order of appearance is sequential and that the sequence will prove to be invariant. Each new stage builds on and incorporates into its more elaborate structures the operations of previous stages. An eventual aim of our research is to test whether further refinements of our descriptions of these stages, through the analysis of future longitudinal and cross-cultural research, can demonstrate the salience of generic or universal structuring potentials of the human psyche.[23]

Our research procedure has been described in detail elsewhere.[24] Briefly, we employ a structured, semiclinical interview of one to three hours (somewhat briefer with children). Respondents are asked to tell about aspects of their life-histories and to express in detail their views, convictions, and experiences regarding a series of existential life-issues with which faith must deal. This list is uniformly pursued and probed in each interview. Respondents are encouraged to share concrete experiences and crises out of their own lives and to address the faith issues experientially whenever possible. Though respondents often voluntarily answer in specifically religious terms, religion as an issue and context is not explicitly introduced until the last quarter of the interview. An effort is made for congruence between values and attitudes against self-reports of performance and choice in actual life situations.

These interviews are transcribed. Analysis for structural features is carried out by trained scorers. The formulations of position and outlook vis à vis the faith issues are regarded as the *contents* of the person's faith. A thematic or content analysis can be carried out and systematized in order to understand the person's faith or belief system. Structural analysis, however, aims to go "under" the content elements to identify the deeper structural operations of knowing and valuing which underlie, ground, and organize the thematic content. Stage assignments are based on structural analysis. For a description of the sample on which the stage theory has been constructed, see Appendix B of the author's *Stages of Faith* (1981).

Based on our research, we have formulated seven structurally distinct faith stages. As with other constructivist theories, movement from one of these stages to the next is not an automatic function of biological maturation, chronological age, psychological development, or mental age. While each of these factors plays a significant role in the "readiness" for stage transition, transition itself occurs when the equilibrium of a given stage is upset by encounters with crises, novelties, and experiences of disclosure and challenge which threaten the limits of the person's present patterns of constitutive-knowing. A change of social, political, or economic environment can contribute to stage change. Of course, a person can overdefend existing faith structures by screening out and "not-knowing" dissonant data. In extreme forms, this becomes the "closed" or "authoritarian" mindset. But when there is sufficient ego strength and faith to sustain a vulnerability to the threats to one's meanings, through constructive accommodation new patterns of constituting and maintaining a meaningful world can emerge. The role of supporting communities and usable models in the development of faith can only be alluded to here. Fuller treatments of the relation of stage-change to conversion and to the theological realities of revelation and grace have been dealt with elsewhere.[25]

STRUCTURAL STAGES IN FAITH DEVELOPMENT

In *Life-Maps*[26] and *Stages of Faith,* I have given detailed descriptions of the stages, with illustrative passages from interviews scored at each stage. I refer the interested reader to those accounts for comprehensive introductions to this theory. In this context, I will limit myself to a necessarily schematic presentation.

Primal Faith. Faith begins with a prelanguage disposition of trust and loyalty toward the environment that takes form in the mutuality of one's interactive rituals of relationship with those providing consistent primary care. This rudimentary faith constructs preimages of powerful and trustworthy ultimacy, in order to offset the anxiety that results from the separations and threats of negation that occur in the course of infantile development.

Intuitive-Projective Faith. The structures of an emotional and perceptual ordering of experience, which result from the relations and events of earliest childhood, now constitute tentative and labile, but nonetheless powerful, vectors in the child's first conscious efforts to give meanings to experiences. The lack, yet, of stable logical operations, coupled with limited abilities to differentiate and coordinate one's own perspective from and with others, gives free reign to the imagination and gives to the child's experience an episodic character. In this stage (which orients to mystery and to visible signs of power), deep and long-lasting images can be formed, which can result, for better or worse, in impressing a permanent cast on the emotional and cognitive funding of faith. (Correlates with Piaget's *preoperational* stage and with Kohlberg's *punishment and obedience* stage.)

Mythic-Literal Faith. Though the emotive and imaginal funding of the previous stage is still operative in this new stage, new logical operations make possible more stable forms of conscious interpretation and shaping of experience and meaning. Cause and effect relations are now clearly understood. Differentiation of one's own perspective from those of others is a dependable acquisition. The young person constructs the world in terms of a new "linearity" and predictability. Though still a potent source of feelings, the previous stage's store of images gets "sealed over," and its episodic, intuitive forms of knowing are left behind. One does not yet, however, construct the interiority (the feelings, attitudes, and internal guiding process) of oneself or others. In making sense of the larger order of things, therefore, this stage typically relies on the external structures of simple fairness. It most frequently constructs an ultimate environment on the analogy of a consistent, caring, but just ruler or parent. Goodness is rewarded; badness is punished. In the effort to gather its meanings in their interrelatedness, this stage employs narrative. Story (and stories) is as close as it comes to reflective synthesis. In its use of symbols and concepts, it remains largely concrete and literal. (Correlates with Piaget's *concrete operational* stage, and with Kohlberg's *instrumental exchange* stage.)

Synthetic-Conventional Faith. The dominant clue to the structuring of this stage focuses in the emergence, typically in early adolescence, of "mutual interpersonal perspective-taking." "I see you seeing me; I see the me I think you see." And conversely, "You see you according to me; you see the you you think I see." Identity and interiority, one's own and others', become absorbing concerns. *Personality,* both as style and substance, becomes a conscious concern. Values, commitments, and relationships are seen as central to identity and worth, at a time when *worth* is heavily keyed to the approval and affirmation of significant others. Amid the mirrorings of self from significant others, we struggle to find a balance with our own feelings of selfhood. In trying to become what will be found worthy by those—present and future—who matter, we seek for values and beliefs to call forth our trust and to direct our loyalties. This stage holds together a vital but fragile dance in which we try to shape the movements of our life to give expression to a way of being forming from within, while at the same time trying to maintain connections and exchanges with all those to whom our becoming seems integrally connected. Beliefs and values which link us with them take form in a tacit, largely unexamined, unity. From within this stage, we construct the ultimate environment in terms of the personal. God is one who knows us better than we can know ourselves—knows who we are and who we are becoming—and, in connecting deeply with others and ourselves, we are somehow linked with the depth, or height, of ultimacy. Selfhood derives from important relations and roles. (Requires Piaget's *early formal operations* and correlates dominantly with Kohlberg's *interpersonal concord* stage.)

Individuative-Reflective Faith. This stage requires breaking the balance of the last stage's dance. Its tacit system of beliefs, values, and commitments must be critically examined, and be replaced or reorganized into a more explicit meaning system. The sense of self, derived from one's important roles and relationships, must be regrounded in choices (and exclusions), and in a qualitatively new authority and responsibility for oneself. Roles and relations, once *constitutive* of identity, now being chosen, become *expressions* of identity. "System" becomes a generative metaphor for this stage. Control becomes its goal. In its new-found power to bring so much that is constitutive of self, others, and world to consciousness and presumed control, this stage of faith is vulnerable to the self-deception that forgets mystery, including the mystery of its own unconscious. It relates to symbols with a strategy of demythologization. It critically examines symbol and mythos and converts their "meanings" into conceptual formulations, little suspecting that much is lost in the process. (Requires Piaget's stage of *full formal operations* and correlates dominantly with Kohlberg's *social system and conscience maintenance* stage.)

Conjunctive Faith. What the previous stage struggled to bring under consciousness and control, the present stage must allow to become porous and permeable. This stage arises from an awakening to polar tensions within oneself and to paradox in the nature of truth. It seeks to find ways to unify seeming opposites in mind and experience. While it knows that symbols are symbols and is capable of reducing them to abstract meanings, it has learned that truth, while robust, must be given the initiative if it is going to correct and transform us. Therefore, faith, in this stage, learns to be receptive, to balance initiative and control with waiting and seeking to be part of the larger movement of spirit or being. It develops a second or willed naivete, an epistemological humility in face of the intricacy and richness of mystery. Moreover, it comes to prize a certain givenness to life, as opposed to always

choosing one's way or group. It comes to value the stranger as one by whom new truth—or liberation from self-deception—may come. It uses multiple names and metaphors for the holy. This is to avoid idolatry and to honor paradox. This stage has little use for the tribalism of homogenous groupings, and no use for ideological holy war. (Requires an extension of Piaget's *formal operations* toward *dialectical thinking;* correlates with either Kohlberg's *prior rights and social contract* or his *universal ethical principles,* though it is not limited just to these two options, as we soon shall see.)

Universalizing Faith. From the paradoxical awareness and the embrace of polar tensions of the previous stage, the structuring of this stage is grounded in the completion of a radical process of decentration from self as the epistemological and valuational reference point for construing the world. Such a one has begun to manifest the fruits of a powerful kind of *kenosis,* or emptying of self. Often described as "detachment" or "disinterestedness," this *kenosis* is actually the fruit of having one's affections powerfully drawn beyond the finite centers of value and power that bid to offer us meaning and security. An identification with or participation in the Ultimate brings a transformation in which one begins to love and value from a centering located in the Ultimate. (Represents a radical transvaluation of valuing and a re-seating of ethical and religious cognition. Nothing in Piaget correlates with it; Kohlberg's description of a *stage 7* begins to move toward it.)

WHAT'S IN A FAITH STAGE?

Following Piaget and Kohlberg, we think of a stage as an integrated system of operations (structures) of thought and valuing which makes for an equilibrated constitutive-knowing of a person's relevant environment. A stage, as a "structural whole," is organismic, i.e., it is a dynamic unity constituted by internal connections among its differentiated aspects. In constructivist theories, successive stages are thought of as manifesting qualitative transformations issuing in more complex inner differentiations, more elaborate operations (operations upon operations), wider comprehensiveness, and greater overall flexibility of functioning.

At its present level of elaboration, the faith stage theory can be schematically presented in terms of seven operational aspects which are integrated and reintegrated at each of the six levels or stages. Figure 1 presents a graphic suggestion of the transformations each aspect undergoes in the transitions of faith development and of the organismic interconnectedness of the aspects in each stage.

Figure 1. (A-G represent structural aspects of faith in each stage.*)

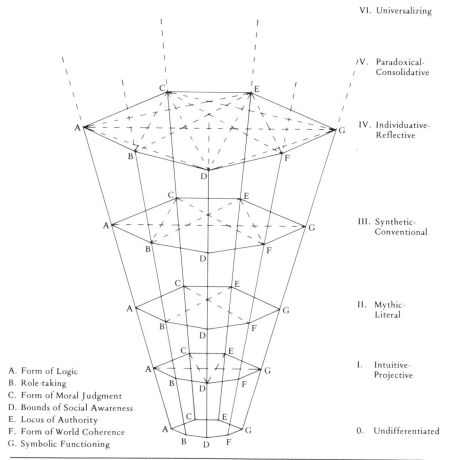

VI. Universalizing

/V. Paradoxical-
    Consolidative

IV. Individuative-
    Reflective

III. Synthetic-
     Conventional

II. Mythic-
    Literal

I. Intuitive-
   Projective

0. Undifferentiated

A. Form of Logic
B. Role-taking
C. Form of Moral Judgment
D. Bounds of Social Awareness
E. Locus of Authority
F. Form of World Coherence
G. Symbolic Functioning

---

*The lines connecting the aspects of each stage are merely suggestive and are not to be taken as representations of empirically established relations.

As will become plain, we are indebted to the pioneering constructivist theorists for elaborating the stages and structural transformations of Aspects A, B, and C. The inclusion of Piaget's, Selman's, and Kohlberg's stages here show the correlations we find empirically between them and the other aspects we investigate. Moving from left to right (from A to G in Table 1), we are trying to suggest how, in the knowing that is faith, the "logic of rational certainty" (A) and its derivatives (B and C) are contextualized by and integrated with aspects of a logic of conviction (D, E, F, and G). If, as our data suggest, something like the integrated operational system depicted here can be demonstrated at each stage, then of course the actual process of transition from one stage to another will *not* necessarily occur either in a movement from A to G, or in an even and simultaneous transformation of all the aspects. Rather, transition will be uneven and ragged, with first one sector leading and then another catching up or creating "drag" on the total process.

Starting now with *Aspect A,* the "Form of Logic," let us characterize briefly each of the elements indicated in Table 1. Our descriptions of the "Form of Logic" build upon Piaget's theory of cognitive stages. This aspect focuses upon the patterns of reasoning and judgment available to the developing person at each cognitive stage. For the equilibrated operational pattern of a given faith stage *fully* to emerge, the correlated level of Piagetian cognitive operations must have been developed. This underscores again that the holistic knowing that is faith must not be understood as irrational or a-rational. Kohlberg and Selman (whose stage theories of perspective-taking and moral judgment are Aspects C and B respectively) claim that the Piaget cognitive levels are *necessary but not sufficient* for the correlated levels of perspective-taking and moral judgment. This is true in faith stages as well, though we must qualify the assumption of temporal priority implied in this claim. Because of faith's qualification of the logic of rational certainty within a logic of conviction, it would be a mistake to assume that cognitive development, as Piaget understands it, always leads temporally in faith stage transitions.[28] When examining charted descriptions of faith stages 4 through 6, readers knowledgeable of Piaget's theory will find that we have identified further adult substages in formal operational thought,

TABLE I ·

Aspect Stage	A. Form Of Logic (Piaget)	B. Role-Taking (Selman)	C. Form of Moral Judgment (Kohlberg)	D. Bounds of Social Awareness
0	*	*	*	*
I	Preoperational	Rudimentary Empathy (Egocentric)	Punishment—Reward	Family, primal others
II	Concrete Operational	Simple Perspective-taking	Instrumental Hedonism (Reciprocal Fairness)	"Those like us" (in familial, ethnic, racial, class and religious terms)
III	Early Formal Operations	Mutual Interpersonal	Interpersonal expectations and concordance	Composite of groups in which one has interpersonal relationships
IV	Formal Operation. (Dichotomizing)	Mutual, with self-selected group or class—(Societal)	Societal Perspective Reflective Relativism or Class-biased Universalism	Ideologically compatible communities with congruence to self-chosen norms and insights
V	Formal Operations. (Dialectical)	Mutual with groups, classes and traditions "other" than one's own	Prior to Society, Principled Higher Law (Universal and Critical)	Extends beyond class norms and interests. Disciplined ideological vulnerability to "truths" and "claims" of out-groups and other traditions
VI	Formal Operations. (Synthetic)	Mutual, with the Commonwealth of Being	Loyalty to Being	Identification with the species. Trans-narcissistic love of being

*Undifferentiated combination of basic trust, organismic courage, premonitory hope with admixtures of their opposites—preconceptual, prelinguistic mutuality.

FAITH STAGES BY ASPECTS

E. Locus of Authority	F. Form of World Coherence	G. Role of Symbols
*	*	*
Attachment/dependence relationships. Size, power, visible symbols of authority	Episodic	Magical-Numinous
Incumbents of authority roles, salience increased by personal relatedness	Narrative-Dramatic	One-dimensional; literal
Consensus of valued groups and in personally worthy representatives of belief-value traditions	Tacit system, felt meanings symbolically mediated, globally held	Symbols multidimensional; evocative power inheres in symbol
One's own judgment as informed by a self-ratified ideological perspective. Authorities and norms must be congruent with this.	Explicit system, conceptually mediated, clarity about boundaries and inner connections of system	Symbols separated from symbolized. Translated (reduced) to ideations. Evocative power inheres in *meaning* conveyed by symbols
Dialectical joining of judgment-experience processes with reflective claims of others and of various expressions of cumulative human wisdom.	Multisystemic symbolic and conceptual mediation	Postcritical rejoining of irreducible symbolic power and ideational meaning. Evocative power inherent in the reality in and beyond symbol *and* in the power of unconscious processes in the self
In a personal judgment informed by the experiences and truths of previous stages, purified of egoic striving, and linked by disciplined intuition to the principle of being	Unitive actuality felt and participated unity of "One beyond the many"	Evocative power of symbols actualized through unification of reality mediated by symbols and the self

suggesting ongoing cognitive development. These stylistic variants or substages of formal operations we find necessary in the description of stage-typical patterns in the construction of and reflection upon comprehensive frames of meaning.

Aspect B, "Role-Taking," owes most to the previously mentioned research of Selman on social perspective-taking. In the faith stage theory we rely explicitly upon Selman's account of structural stages in perspective-taking up to and through our stage 3. Beyond stage 3 we have found it possible and necessary to extend Selman's approach, applying it to persons' abilities to construct the perspectives of their own chosen groups or classes (stage 4), and then of groups, classes, or ideological and convictional traditions other than their own.

Aspect C, the "Form of Moral Judgment," represents an inclusion, with slight modifications based on our data, of Kohlberg's stages of moral reasoning. As will become apparent below, there are significant parallels between moral judgment stages and faith stages.

Aspect D, "Bounds of Social Awareness," focuses on the extent of inclusiveness and accuracy of construal of the reference groups in relation to which persons ground their identity and define their moral responsibility. Parallel in some ways to role-taking, this aspect differs in that it attempts to account for the typical range of persons and groups "who count" in one's composition and maintenance of identity and of a meaningful world at each stage.

Aspect E, "Locus of Authority," centers on the patterns of constitutive-knowing and commitment by which persons, ideas, institutions, experiences, and processes of one's own judgment are invested with meaning-sanctioning authority. To whom or what does a person look for validation or legitimation of his or her most significant felt meanings? How is that "locus" constituted? How is it justified? With this aspect we are well into the elements of a logic of conviction. In the domain where the construction and worth of the self are at stake, trust in and loyalty to sources of authorization cannot be accounted for solely within a logic of rational certainty. In fact, trust in and loyalty to the logic of rational certainty as a comprehensive principle of authority may *itself* involve a faith commitment involving risk, judgment, and conviction.

We have pointed out that faith reasons in "wholes." *Aspect F,* the "Form of World Coherence," represents a focus on each stage's particular way of composing and holding a comprehensive sense of unified meanings. This aspect describes a sequence of stage-typical *genres* employed by persons to conceive or represent patterns of coherence in their ultimate environment. In the movement through its successive stages we see, in this aspect, in a sensitive way, the reconciliation or integration of the logics of rational certainty and of conviction.

Much work remains to be done with *Aspect G,* "Symbolic Functioning." It is in this aspect, particularly, that we must take account of the bihemispheric functioning of thought and imagination in faith. It is with reference to this aspect that "regression in the service of faith development," illumined by psychoanalytic investigators,[29] and the integration of unconscious elements into consciousness described by Jungian students of faith and individuation,[30] must be incorporated faithfully. In this aspect, particularly, the dynamics of a logic of conviction must be seen as operative with powerful transforming potential for the orientation and functioning of the total psyche. The theoretical and empirical engagement with this aspect at present constitutes one of the most vital yet difficult growing edges of this project.

REFLECTION ON SPONSORSHIP
FOR FAITH DEVELOPMENT

In conclusion, I want to share some very general implications of this perspective for religious education. In order to do so, I shift somewhat from the role of theorist and empirical investigator and speak as a theologian and educator.

First, the theory presented here stimulates us to look at faith development in a life-span perspective. Some of the most interesting and powerful faith stage transitions occur only in adulthood. Faith, as seen here, involves an ongoing process, of forming and reforming our ways of being in and seeing the world. One who becomes Christian in childhood, for example, may indeed remain Christian all of his or her life. But one's *way* of being Christian will need to deepen, expand, and be reconstituted several times in the pilgrimage of faith. Churches, synagogues, and other communities of faith need to expect and provide support for ongoing adult development in faith. I am convinced that the faith community which sponsors ongoing adult development will find it quite natural to nurture its children and newcomers in developmentally appropriate and dynamic ways.

Second, to our initial surprise, my associates and I found that something on the order of 90 percent of our interviews with adults ended with the respondent—following two and a half hours of intense conversation—saying something like this: "I really appreciate this experience; I *never* get an opportunity to talk about these things." We have found that the faith development interview, especially with adolescents and adults, is already an intervention. In the course of the interview, people become involved in the important work of bringing their faith to words. Sometimes, they are doing this for the very first time. On other occasions, they engage in a process of critically reformulating their faith and values outlook. From this experience, I have come to believe that it is most important to provide occasions for people to express in words, in action, in contemplation, "the faith that is in them." Articulation means bringing experience and commitment to word and act. It enables persons to be more responsive and intentional in their own faith growth. It alerts them to unrecognized conflicts, indicating readiness for growth, and enables them to attend to experiences of revelation and disclosure. Commitments are consolidated, integrated, and evaluated in the process of articulation. And, if this articulation is carried out in groups, there is a mutually strengthening impact among the members.

Third, faith development sponsorship must avoid viewing the stages as constituting an achievement scale or a program by which to rush people to the next stage. The potential fullness of each stage needs to be recognized and realized. Each stage has a potential wholeness, grace, and integrity. Yet, a strong nurturing environment will provide persons with support in facing those challenges of faith in life and action—as well as in reflection—which keep persons open toward new horizons in faith growth. I believe that we are genetically potentiated for growth in faith throughout the life cycle. And I also believe that each stage represents genuine growth toward wider and more accurate response to God, and toward more consistently humane care for other human beings. We stand under an imperative toward ongoing growth.

Fourth, the language, rituals, and teachings of particular communities of faith are of critical importance for faith development. The philosopher Santayana says, "You cannot be religious in general." This theory helps us see that "transmissive" models of education never succeed in transferring the knowledge and faith of the teacher into the mind and heart of the child. The child's faith always depends upon his or her own constructions of images and insights. But religious language, rituals, and ethical teachings do *awaken* the child to the domain of faith; they channel her or his attention toward the transcendent. They provide experiences of shared attention and celebration of the holy. As such, to use Horace Bushnell's beautiful language, they are "gifts to the imagination."[31] Therefore, the stories, language, and liturgy of our particular faith communities must be made available and tangible for the child's participation and constructive appropriation. The young child does not, of course, develop conceptual mastery of these things. Rather, he or she encounters images which awaken and form the faith imagination of the child, providing affective, volitional, and conceptual directions by which to grow in faith.

Fifth, respecting an individual's present "place" of faith, faith development theory helps us avoid trying to provide comprehensive answers for the questions a person is not yet asking. It helps us avoid playing broken records when he or she is ready to compose and sing new songs. It helps us understand the power of predictable conflicts and tensions she or he experiences in the midst of particular stage transitions. It should enable us to allow space to struggle and to provide models which may help in his or her constructions of the next place in faith.

Sixth, faith development theory helps us overcome the tendency to think of faith as separate from everyday life. The seven aspects of the faith stage, as set forth in Table 1, help make explicit the recognition that faith serves to organize the totality of our lives and gives rise to our most comprehensive frames of meaning. We can see that faith development, understood in this way, involves what Martin Buber calls the "sacralization of all life." It stands against the compartmentalizing of a person's or community's life.

Finally, Alfred North Whitehead wrote, in *Religion in the Making,* that religion involves the transition from God the Void to God the Enemy, and from God the Enemy to God the Companion. Faith development theory helps us recognize that there are times in faith when God seems to approach us as Nothingness or as Slayer. We do not make the transition from one stage to another without disruption, pain, confusion, and a sense of loss. All growth involves pain. To see this does not mean that we can avoid the pain of growth. But it does suggest that we can reimage faith growth so as to embrace the necessary pain and disruption as essential elements in it, thus diminishing the anxiety and fear pain brings.

Saint Augustine wrote, in his *Confessions,* "Thou hast made us for Thyself, and our hearts are restless until they find their rest in Thee." The restlessness which so characterizes our frenzied lives of work and consumption has a source deeper than can be cured by our ambitious activities. The search for intimacy and sensation in contemporary cultures bespeaks a loneliness deeper than even our closest ties of friendship and love can overcome. Faith development theory, for all its technical language and abstract concepts, is an expression of the story of our search for communion with Saint Augustine's "Thou." Faith communities must discover anew how to meet people as *whole* beings, embracing their hearts as well as their minds, their bodies as well as their souls. We must enable people to name and recognize their hungers and their real depth. Forms of spirituality, community celebration, testimony, and shared action in faith can then emerge which will sustain a humanizing common life. Such faith communities are indispensable for the human family's well-being. Our restlessness for divine companionship, if denied, ignored, or distorted, dehumanizes us and we destroy each other. Recognized and nurtured, it brings us into that companionship with God which frees us for genuine partnership with our sisters and brothers, and for friendship with creation.

NOTES

1. Ernest Becker, *The Structure of Evil* (New York: Macmillan, 1968), p. 210.
2. See Richard R. Niebuhr, *Experiential Religion* (New York: Harper & Row, 1972), esp. ch. 2.

3. See Wilfred Cantwell Smith, *The Meaning and End of Religion* (New York: Macmillan, 1963), esp. ch. 7.

4. Erik H. Erikson, *Childhood and Society,* 2nd ed. (New York: W. W. Norton, 1963), ch. 7.

5. Josiah Royce, *The Sources of Religious Insight* (New York: Macmillan, 1912), ch. V.

6. H. Richard Niebuhr, *Radical Monotheism and Western Culture* (New York: Harper & Row, 1960); *The Responsible Self* (New York: Harper & Row, 1963).

7. See Jim Fowler and Sam Keen, *Life-Maps* (Waco, Texas: Word Books, 1978). For a theological examination of the vision of the Kingdom of God, see James Fowler, *To See the Kingdom* (Nashville: Abingdon Press, 1974), esp. chs. 3 and 4.

8. For example, a man who experienced a profound disturbance in the relationship with his mother in infancy will likely have either a deep-going inability to trust others at all levels in later life, or a powerful religious experience which opens a relationship with God which transforms his ability to trust and make commitments to other persons. See the chapters by Loder, Vergote, Rizzuto, and Jaspard in *Toward Moral and Religious Maturity,* ed. James Fowler and Antoine Vergote (Morristown, N.J.: Silver Burdett, 1980). See also James Loder, *The Transforming Moment* (San Francisco: Harper & Row, 1981) and Ana Marie Rizzuto, *The Birth of the Living God* (Chicago: University of Chicago Press, 1979).

9. See William F. Lynch, S.J., *Images of Faith* (Notre Dame, Ind.: University of Notre Dame Press, 1973).

10. See Jean Piaget, *To Understand Is to Invent* (New York: Viking Press, 1974).

11. See Lawrence Kohlberg, "Stage and Sequence: The Cognitive-Developmental Approach to Socialization," in *Handbook of Socialization Theory and Research,* ed. D. Goslin (New York: Rand McNally, 1969), pp. 347-480.

12. See Robert L. Selman, *The Development of Conceptions of Interpersonal Relations,* Vols. I & II (Publication of the Harvard-Judge Baker Social Reasoning Project).

13. See John H. Flavell, *The Development of Role-Taking and Communication Skills in Children* (New York: John Wiley & Sons, 1968).

14. Robert G. Kegan, *Ego and Truth: Personality and the Piaget Paradigm* (Doctoral dissertation, Harvard University, 1977). See Kegan's chapter in Fowler and Vergote, *Moral and Religious Maturity,* which builds on and further develops Kegan's position. My dialogue with Kegan here is based primarily on the earlier work. For Kegan's most fully developed statement, see his *The Evolving Self* (Cambridge, Mass.: Harvard University Press, 1982).

15. This point finds resonance, though in quite another frame of reference, in the chapters by McDonagh and Hauerwas in Fowler and Vergote, *Moral and Religious Maturity.*

16. See ibid.

17. See Andrew Greeley, *Ecstasy: A Way of Knowing* (Englewood Cliffs, N.J.: Prentice-Hall, 1974).

18. See Lynch, *Images of Faith;* and Ray Hart, *Unfinished Man and the Imagination* (New York: Herder and Herder, 1968). See also Sharon Parks, *The Critical Years* (San Francisco: Harper & Row, 1986).

19. See Robert E. Ornstein, *The Psychology of Consciousness* (San Francisco: W. H. Freeman, 1972); and Julian Jaynes, *The Origin of Consciousness in the Breakdown of the Bicameral Mind* (Boston: Houghton Mifflin, 1976).

20. W. W. Meissner, S.J., "Notes on the Psychology of Faith," *Journal of Religion and Health* 8 (1969) 1, pp. 47-75.

21. See chapter by Loder in Fowler and Vergote, *Moral and Religious Maturity.*

22. Lynch, *Images of Faith,* p. 18.

23. See Richard Anthony, "A Phenomenological Structuralist Approach to the Scientific Study of Religion" (Paper presented at an American Psychological Association symposium on "Methodological Issues in the Psychology of Religion" [1976]).

24. See James W. Fowler, *Stages of Faith* (San Francisco: Harper & Row, 1981), Appendix A.

25. See Fowler, *Stages of Faith,* pp. 281-303, and James W. Fowler, *Becoming Adult, Becoming Christian* (San Francisco: Harper & Row, 1984), pp. 71-75, 138-141.

26. Fowler and Keen, *Life-Maps,* pp. 25-97.

27. Fowler, *Stages of Faith,* pp. 117-213.

28. By extension, at this point, we can see why Kohlberg's claim that moral stage transition would "logically" occur prior to, and as a necessary condition for, faith stage transition is theoretically mistaken. See Lawrence Kohlberg, "Education, Moral Development, and Faith," *Journal of Moral Education* 4 (1974) 1, pp. 5-16. For my response, see Fowler, "Moral Stages and the Development of Faith," in *Moral Development, Moral Education, and Kohlberg,* ed. Brenda Munsey (Birmingham, Ala.: Religious Education Press, 1980).

29. See Meissner, "Notes on the Psychology of Faith"; and Erik H. Erikson, *Young Man Luther* (New York: W. W. Norton, 1958).

30. See Gregg Raduka, "Fowler's Stages of Faith Development from the Perspective Taken by Carl Jung in His Published Works," (Doctoral dissertation, University of Maryland, College Park, 1979).

31. Horace Bushnell, *Building Eras in Religion* (New York: Charles Scribner and Co., 1881).

PART II

Evaluating Faith Development Theory

Chapter 2

What Is Faith?:
An Experiment in the Hypothetical Mode

CRAIG DYKSTRA

The understanding of faith that is at the center of any theory of faith development is critical. James Fowler is fully conscious of this in the way he works out his position. Many of his early publications dealt with the matter of what faith is, and this is necessarily the topic of the first part of his most extensive statement of his theory, his book *Stages of Faith.* It is important, I believe, to be clear on why this is so. The reason that a definition of faith is central to a theory of faith development and must come first has to do with the fundamental structure of the argument in such a theory. In Fowler's theory, the argument has this form: "*Since* faith is . . . , faith can be described developmentally in the following ways."

Allow me to propose a thought-experiment. Instead of beginning the discussion of faith development theory either by stating a definition of faith (or by criticizing definitions of faith already given by someone else), it might be useful to experiment with another way of doing things. I believe that in much of the discussion about faith development theory that has gone on to this point, there is a hidden hypothetical. My hunch is that it will be useful to get it out in the open. This, I believe, may help us all to see more clearly what is going on in the whole matter of faith development theory and critical arguments about it today.

In *Stages of Faith,* Fowler begins early with a number of sentences that begin with the phrase "faith is." "Faith is," he says, "a coat against nakedness."[1] "Faith is a human universal."[2] "Faith is a person's or group's way of moving into the force field of life. It is our own way of finding coherence and giving meaning to the multiple forces and relations that make up our lives. Faith is a person's way of seeing him- or herself in relation to others against a background of shared meaning and purpose."[3] There are many other such statements, all of them designed to portray the nature of faith for readers, and to do so in such a way that (1) the nature of this reality can become clear to us, and (2) the understanding of faith that emerges can fit with what comes later about faith as a structural developmental phenomenon.

I think Fowler is largely successful at this. When Fowler describes faith, we recognize in his descriptions something with which we ourselves are familiar. We also find that his descriptions of the *stages* of faith coincide with something of what we know about ourselves and about other people. These are major reasons why we find Fowler's theory of faith development so appealing. He describes for us realities with which we are already familiar.

In spite of all this, however, Fowler's theory of faith development has come under some criticism, and much of it has had to do with this central matter of Fowler's understanding of faith. Interestingly, the critics' arguments often take a form similar to that of Fowler's. They, too, will say: "*Since* faith is . . . , *therefore* . . . ." In these cases, however, what faith is is defined differently from the way Fowler defines it, and the conclusions about the relationship between faith and development are (either slightly or significantly) different.[4] My point in saying all of this is not that the discussion back and forth should not go this way, but that it is important that we recognize that this is the form the discussion often takes. When we see this, we can also see that in all of these positions and counter-positions there is a hidden hypothetical. It seems to me that the entire discussion would be advanced if this were made plain. If we could all put the arguments in hypothetical form, if we could start with *if* rather than *since,* then we could all be a great deal more clear about what is at stake. We could ask both Fowler and his critics first to state their positions in the hypothetical mode, and then to argue for the validity of both the understanding of faith that governs the theory and the conclusions about the relationship between faith and development that are derived from it. We could ask theorists and critics both to begin, at least, by saying: "*If* faith is . . . ; *then* . . . can be said about the developmental nature of faith or about the relationship between faith and human development."

There are several advantages to proceeding in this way. First, it makes it possible to examine theories of faith development (and criticisms of them) both logically and empirically. We are given a way to ask clearly: "What assumptions or presuppositions are operating in this theory?" "What arguments are given for them, and are they adequate; or are there none?" "What is the basic logic of the theory?" "Is it valid?" "What empirical evidence is important to sustain the hypothesis?" "Is the evidence provided compelling?" And so on.

A second advantage is that it makes possible some very clear comparative work between theories about growth or change in faith. It makes it possible to say: "If faith is A, then X. But if faith is B, then Y follows instead." We are able, when we put theories in this form, to compare the assumptions, presuppositions, arguments, logic, and evidence provided in each theory and make responsible judgments about their relative worth and power.

A third and, I think, major advantage of proceeding in this way is that we are provided a great deal more flexibility in our critical responses to faith development theories. To take the case at hand, it provides us an honest way, for example, to evaluate whether and to what degree Fowler is right about what faith is without having to disagree with his whole theory if we conclude that his understanding of faith has some problems. We might conclude that his understanding of faith is (1) wrong, (2) incomplete, (3) one of several possible but essentially compatible options, or (4) one of several possible but essentially incompatible options among which we must choose. But in any of these cases we would still have some flexibility of response.

For example, if one of the alternatives we were forced to choose was alternative (1) or (4), we might still be able to affirm many (or even all) of Fowler's conclusions about the relationships he charts between "faith" as he understands it and "faith development" as he describes it. We would simply conclude that to the degree he is talking about a reality at all (and we might well conclude that), that reality is not "faith," at least as we define it, but it is still an important reality to know about and take into consideration. Or, if one of the alternatives we chose were (2) or

(3), we could profit from and use as much of what Fowler has to say about both "faith" and "faith development" that we could agree with, given our own position on what faith is. And then we could add to that what we ourselves have to say about faith and faith development, perhaps helping Fowler to refine his own theory along the way. We could say: *"Insofar as* faith is . . . , then . . . follows concerning faith development. But to the degree that faith is also . . . , then . . . also follows with regard to faith development." Finally, if the alternative we were to conclude is best was (5), namely, that Fowler's definition of faith is essentially right and complete, there would still be room to evaluate Fowler's conclusions about what follows from this understanding of faith for faith development. He might be essentially right about "faith," and still wrong in some respects about "faith development."

I realize that all of this is rather formal and abstract. My intent is not to leave it at this. I hope that Fowler and his critics will experiment with this form of discussion, but my main task in this chapter is to use it myself. First, I want to lay out some of how I think Fowler's theory looks when it is put in this form and discuss some of the implications which derive from that. Second, I want to suggest an alternative hypothesis about the nature of faith and supply some reasons for choosing this alternative. Third, I want to develop some of the implications for the relationship between faith and human development if my alternative were to be taken seriously. And, finally, I want to discuss briefly the degree to which my alternative may or may not be compatible with Fowler's understanding of faith development.

"FAITH" IN FOWLER'S THEORY

In order to put Fowler's argument about faith and development into the hypothetical mode, we will have to start by trying to summarize what Fowler takes "faith" to mean. I will try to do this by laying it out in my own way, having culled through what I believe to be the essential ingredients from his various writings. Whether I have gotten this right, both the reader and Fowler will have to judge.

It seems to me that, according to Fowler, faith has the following central features:

(1) Faith is a human activity (not a thing people have, but a way of knowing and being that they are engaged in);
(2) Faith is an activity that takes place through relationships;
(3) The most significant aspects of these relationships are the aspects of trust and loyalty;
(4) Faith involves some object(s). In faith, we trust *in* and are loyal *to* something;
(5) In faith, we are related in trust and loyalty not only to persons and groups, but also to the "supraordinate centers of value and power" (i.e., the "gods") to which the people and groups whom we trust and are loyal to are also related;
(6) Through these relationships of trust and loyalty, our "world" (both proximate and ultimate) is shaped, meaning is made, and our own selves are constituted;
(7) This activity of world-shaping, meaning-making, or "constitutive knowing" is the core activity which defines faith.

Now, to begin to put all this in the hypothetical mode: *If* faith is all of this, *then* certain things follow which make it possible to formulate the idea of "faith development."

First, it follows that faith is a human universal (that is, everyone has faith of some form within the range of this definition). Faith is a human universal because human beings cannot live without living in a "world," without some sense of meaning, without some constitution of the self. Nor can we live without living in some relationships of trust and loyalty to something. Without relationships of trust and loyalty, without a "world" and some sense of meaning and self, we die spiritually, psychologically, and even physically. These are the very things that make us human beings at all.

Second, it follows from this definition of faith that faith is something which is continually undergoing change. We know that faith, understood in these terms, changes because we all experience, empirically, changes in our "world" and in ourselves. Over time, the way we see things, what things mean to us, relationships of trust and loyalty, commitments to centers of value— all these change.

The statement of the main thesis of Fowler's theory of faith development, in a hypothetical mode, then, would look something like this: "If faith can properly be defined in the terms set forth above, then faith is both a human universal and a phenomenon which undergoes change (the nature of which may very well be developmental in character)."

It seems to me that this hypothetical statement is valid: the "then" clause follows logically from the "if" clause. But notice that in order to make the statement both valid and significant for faith development theory, we had to add a parenthesis which itself has a hypothetical hidden in it. It is contained in the word "may." The fact that the central features of faith undergo change does not yet mean that they *develop*. The idea of development normally requires that the changes which take place move through an ordered, and usually hierarchical, progression. Thus, the idea of "faith *development*" does not follow necessarily from this understanding of faith in and of itself. Fowler is making a specific claim about the kinds of changes that are central to faith and about the nature of those changes, namely, that they are developmental.

While his theory is a theory of faith *development* (that is, in his view, faith itself develops through a hierarchical, ordered progression), Fowler does grant that *some* of the changes that take place in faith are nondevelopmental in nature. These are changes in what he calls the "contents" of faith.[5] He argues, however, that not all the changes that take place are nondevelopmental. Rather, he claims that the most significant changes are developmental in nature, and that these have to do with the structural dimensions of our knowing and being. This is where he calls upon the insights of Piaget, Kohlberg, and other structural-developmental theorists to help him describe the structural and developmental progression of changes in faith (again, as he defines faith in the "if" clause). Furthermore, he argues that the developmental changes that take place at the structural level have an effect on the "contents" of faith. Therefore, even changes in the "contents" cannot be fully understood apart from structural changes.

I have no particular problem with Fowler's decision to explore this hypothesis. His particular effort is aimed toward following the hunch that there *are* developmental changes in faith itself. It is by following this hunch that Fowler has been able to make the many substantial contributions he has. It is simply important to remember that this, too, should be understood for what it is: the following of a hunch or the investigation of a hypothesis, rather than an assumption of what is the case. There is, after all, another possibility. It is possible that all of the changes in faith (even as he understands faith) are nondevelopmental.

The more important problem, from my point of view, is the first hypothetical. Fowler never really *argues* for his view of the nature of faith. It is true that Fowler does work hard to distinguish what faith is from other possible candidates for study, namely, religion and belief.[6] But he never really considers other possibilities for how faith might be understood, possibilities which would distinguish faith from religion and belief just as Fowler's does. Why is this? Answers to this question will be partly conjecture on my part, but I can think of several reasons why he might not.

First, he has taken an understanding of faith which was dominant in his own theological studies—especially of H. Richard Niebuhr and Paul Tillich. In other words, there may be biographical reasons. Second, this understanding is one which is still very much alive in contemporary religious and theological studies, and the alternatives are not nearly so dominant. This is a point made, though not specifically in reference to Fowler, by George Lindbeck in his book, *The Nature of Doctrine.* Lindbeck calls the position under which Fowler's understanding of faith falls the "experiential-expressivist" theory of religion and points out that "for nearly two hundred years this tradition has provided intellectually brilliant and empirically impressive accounts of the religious life that have been compatible with—indeed, often at the heart of—the romantic, idealistic, and phenomenological-existentialist streams of thought that have dominated the humanistic side of Western culture ever since Kant's revolutionary 'turn to the subject'. . . . The habits of thought it has fostered are ingrained in the soul of the modern West, perhaps particularly in the souls of theologians."[7]

More important than either of these two reasons, however, are others which have to do with the way that this understanding of faith makes faith development theory itself possible. That is, a *structural developmental* theory of the nature of growth or change in faith *requires* precisely the kind of understanding of faith that Fowler in fact presents. Without this understanding of faith, or something very much like it, it would not be possible to move from the "if" clause to Fowler's "then" clause. And a theory of faith *development* requires just the "then" clause that I have attributed to Fowler. If certain features that are packed into Fowler's definition of faith were not there, a structural developmental theory of growth or change in faith would itself be impossible from the outset.

Lindbeck tells us that there are at least four characteristics of all experiential-expressivist theories:

> (1) Different religions are diverse expressions or objectifications of a common core experience. It is this experience which identifies them as religions. (2) The experience, while conscious, may be unknown on the level of self-conscious reflection. (3) It is present in all human beings. (4) In most religions, the experience is the source and norm of objectifications: it is by reference to the experience that their adequacy or lack of adequacy is to be judged.[8]

The advantages for Fowler of an understanding of faith consistent with this kind of theory of religion are obvious. Faith, in this model, becomes a category that is not limited to any particular religion. It is generic. Hence, faith, structurally and dynamically speaking, means the same thing in every religion. Only the "contents" change from faith to faith. Furthermore, faith need not be limited to "religious" faiths. Though the various religious faiths may express (to be sure, in different ways and perhaps more or less adequately) the experience(s) which are at the heart of "world," self, and meaning, such experiences are not limited to religious people. So faith can be universal, by definition. Everyone has faith, even if it is "unknown on the level of self-conscious reflection." Only if this is the case can universal, generic, structural, and, hence, developmental, categories be used to talk about faith growth or change in faith itself. Otherwise, changes in faith are dependent on and refer to "contents," which cannot be accounted for in terms of structural development.

A second advantage of this kind of understanding of faith for Fowler is that the criterion for the adequacy of any religion or religious expression does not lie within its own "contents" but lies instead at the level of the structures of experience: of the experience of the most important (as Lindbeck puts it) or of the most ultimate (as Fowler puts it) that are available to us. Because the criteria are experiential, and because experience can (according to structural-developmentalists) be described in an essential manner structurally, developmentally, and hierarchically, Fowler can claim (as he does) that the highest stage of faith development describes normative faith. The structural *level* of one's faith, rather than the "contents," becomes the primary norm. It is normatively more important to be at, say, stage 5 (regardless of one's religion or lack of it) than to be, say, learning the beliefs, values, and ways of living of the Jewish or Christian or Muslim faith increasingly more deeply.

In sum, the most significant reason why Fowler does not consider other kinds of understandings of faith is that he needs the one he has got in order for the "then" clause to follow from the "if" clause and make any sense. Fowler *cannot* define faith any differently and still have a structural developmental theory of growth or change in faith. His very predisposition to construct a structural developmental theory of growth in faith pushes him toward this kind of understanding of faith.

AN ALTERNATIVE PROPOSED

There are, then, very good reasons for Fowler to provide the understanding of faith that he does in his theory. And his turns out to be one way of working out a hypothesis on faith and development that is strong and well-integrated. But we announced at the beginning that this essay would be an experiment, and it is time to move toward an alternative hypothesis.

That there are a number of alternatives available is suggested in a very important statement about "faith" in John Cobb's book, *Christ in a Pluralistic Age.* Cobb says:

> Faith has meant and rightly means many things. Sometimes it means a vision of reality or a structure of existence. Sometimes it refers specifically to the Christian vision of reality or the Christian structure of existence. Receptivity to the personal presence of Jesus is faith, as is the assuredness of the one who knows himself or herself justified. Faith in a different sense is "the substance of things hoped for." Faith as confidence in the future grounds meaning in the present and is intimately related to faith as the Christian vision of reality and

the Christian structure of existence. In other contexts faith is used to mean faithfulness, life affirmation, confidence, commitment, trust, and ultimate concern. Indeed, an exhaustive list of meanings is impossible. Sometimes faith is treated as a genus of which Christian faith is one species. Sometimes faith is seen instead as that which is unique to Christianity. Sometimes it is defined as a relation to another; sometimes, as a property of the individual. *As long as no one of these meanings of faith is exalted into the one thing required* in an absolutist and particularizing sense, a pluralistic approach should be open to accepting them all and sorting out their complex interconnections with one another and their varying relations with Christ and with other religious traditions.[9]

It is obvious from this quotation that there are many candidates for the "if" clause (the clause which defines "faith" in a theory of growth in faith). And because there are many to choose from, it is very important that we know we have a choice and that we proceed by consciously making a choice and by making that clear to those who read our theories. This would be a way of taking seriously Cobb's advice that no one definition of faith be made absolute.

The alternative that I want to put forward is not one that arises out of an attempt to say what faith is in any generic sense (that is, in a sense that would be true for all people or even for all religions). Rather, it is an attempt to say what faith means from a Christian perspective—and perhaps it is from only a particular form of Christian perspective. This approach has some problems, I realize. It might make scientific study of (as well as ecumenical and interfaith dialogue about) faith and faith development a good deal more difficult. But it has the advantage of not presuming that what faith means to a Christian, to a Jew, to a Muslim, and to a social scientist is in every case the same. Whether or not that is the case would have to be resolved through actual dialogue among diverse people, rather than be settled in advance by definition. And this, though more difficult, is what, in my view, is most needed. By stating one's understanding of faith from the standpoint of one's own faith, one both informs others and invites others to do the same. At the same time, in taking this approach I do not mean to say in advance that my understanding of faith is the only possible one or that whatever anybody else calls "faith" is not really faith. In fact, as I will hope to show, it is possible for us to define faith from a particular faith perspective while still not restricting faith to that perspective. This approach does allow for the *possibility,* however, that what different people and groups mean by "faith" may be so diverse that it would be impossible to talk about faith or faith development in any general or generic sense at all. Again, we would have to talk to each other and find out.

The choice I am about to present for my own "if" clause is one that is influenced by what Cobb goes on to say in the paragraph following the quotation I have already given. Cobb continues: "Still, faith is too important a theme of Christianity to be left simply in this relativistic sea. Recognizing that any definition has an arbitrary element, but guided by the historical importance and changing content of faith, we can establish that a central and normative theological meaning of faith is 'the appropriate, primal response to what the divine is and does'."[10] My definition differs only slightly from this. I would suggest that *faith is appropriate and intentional participation in the redemptive activity of God.*

Some of the essential features of these two definitions should be noted. First, both definitions correlate faith with the divine. (I use the specific term, "God," while Cobb uses the more general term, "the divine." I will say why in a moment.) This means, in both cases, that faith is dependent upon God and cannot be a reality without God. Faith is not here a way of "composing the world" or of "creating meaning." Rather, it is a way of being related to what *is,* not just what *we take to be,* the reality which is the ultimate source of meaning and the ground of all existence. If there is no such God, then faith is an illusion. And if it is not *God* to whom we are related, then what we have is not faith. This means that faith is not necessarily, by definition, a human universal. It may be quite possible for many people (even most) *not* to be so related to God at all. Faith may be something that is rare. In any case, faith, in this definition, is not a generic and structural feature of being human. It is a possibility in human existence, but not a necessity.

Because faith is understood here as a possibility, but not a necessity, an interesting advantage arises. This way of understanding faith helps make some sense of the notion of idolatry as an opposite of faith. In the understanding of faith that Fowler adopts, idolatry is a form of faith. We may trust in and be loyal to what is not truly God, but that is still faith in Fowler's terms. This is because, for him, faith is in no way necessarily correlated with God. Thus, he is in the odd position of having to say that in idolatry we still "faith" (to use the word as a verb). In the understanding I have presented this problem does not arise.

A second essential feature in both of these definitions is that faith is seen as an activity, as in Fowler's approach. But there is a difference. Here faith is an activity of responding appropriately to who God is and what God is doing. It is, therefore, an activity which we may or may not engage in. This helps to make sense of such an idea as "unfaithfulness." The Hebrew and Christian scriptures, for example, are full of references to "faithless generations" and "faithless persons." What can this mean? It does not mean that they are not engaged in the human activity of "making meaning" and "composing ultimate environments." It usually means that they are in some sense disobedient. And what they are disobedient to is not their own values and images, but to God. In other words, faith is an activity that we may fail at—if we undertake it at all.

A third essential feature of faith in this definition is that it requires particular kinds of knowledge. In order to undertake the activity of faith, we need to know something. We need to know who God is and what God is doing in order to be able to respond. We also need to know how to respond, which involves learning the skills and habits and ways of thinking and behaving and feeling that are involved in a way of living that is an appropriate response. About all of this we may be either ignorant, unskilled, or wrong. Or we may know and be able, but only partly or inadequately. To deal with ignorance, error, faulty understanding, or lack of competence or skill, it is not enough that certain humanly generic structures of knowing and being are operative. A particular kind of learning and training needs to be undertaken. As Lindbeck notes, pagan converts to Christian faith "submitted themselves to prolonged catechetical instruction in which they practiced new modes of behavior and learned the stories of Israel and their fulfillment in Christ. Only after they had acquired proficiency in the alien Christian language and form of life were they deemed able intelligently and responsibly to profess the faith, to be baptized."[11] The reason for this is that faith, by this definition, is not the creation or expression of meaning so much as it is the appropriation of meaning from outside ourselves.

In order to learn—of God and the way of life that is an appropriate response to God—we need something which we ourselves cannot provide. In order to know God and what God is doing, and to know how and be able to respond, we need to have some access to the source of all that. This means that faith is dependent on God's own action of revelation. God must be present to us in some way. God must make what God is doing known to us somehow, and enable and empower us to participate with God in redemptive activity. At least to this extent, faith must be understood as a gift, rather than as an achievement or as the development of our own capacities and structures. It is not quite right, then, to say, as even I have, that faith is our own activity or response—at least if we allow that to exhaust the matter.

All of this raises, indirectly, the issue of the relation of faith to meaning. In Fowler's understanding, faith is in a sense both the quest for and the construction of meaning. For Fowler, the work and goal of faith development is meaning. Here the relationship is understood differently. Meaning becomes, not the goal, but a by-product. And meaning is not so much constructed as appropriated. We are not the ultimate creators of meaning. We live in a world shot through with meaning. Thus the concern of faith, as I understand it, is not meaningful living so much as it is living in appropriate response to God (which, by the way, turns out in fact to be meaningful living). Participation in the redemptive activity of God is not so much a matter of making sense out of our existence as it is a *modification* of our existence. It is finding new life and following a new way, one which we have not created and could not find were it not for the fact that God has given it to us and made it possible.

My definition, in distinction to Cobb's, names the divine as God, specifies the nature of God's action as redemptive and lifts up the participatory nature of our response. Cobb puts his definition the way he does, I think, in order to insure that his definition not "limit faith to its Christian form" and at the same time allow "for great diversity of judgment as to what the appropriate, primal response to the divine may be and for the possibility that it may differ markedly from time to time."[12] I believe that my definition leaves open these same possibilities, while at the same time making it clear that there is only one "divine" and that this divine is one who redeems rather than destroys. It also suggests that the kind of response that is appropriate to faith is a response of active participation with God in God's activity for the sake of the world.

There are some presuppositions behind all this that need to be clarified. The ideas of redemption and of God as redeemer presuppose our need for redemption and involve an assumption that we cannot redeem ourselves. We need redemption because we, as human beings, live in ways that tend to destroy others and ourselves. We live primarily under rules of destruction, rather than of abundant, creative life. Faith means turning from an old way to a *new* way of life. To put it a little differently, in faith we are *saved* from an old way of life and put into a different way of being and living in this world. Enslaved by self-deception, competitiveness, aggressiveness, protectiveness, callousness, selfishness, by manipulation, depersonalization, idolization, ridicule of and flight from others, and by the fear of death—all of which characterize our daily existence—we cry out for a new way. And, in fact, by God's grace we find that a new way has opened. Faith is participating in this new way, this redemptive activity of God, in our concrete situations in life. Implicit in the word "participation" are such dimensions as trust, loyalty, belief, fidelity, and commitment. Also involved, and highlighted here, is action.

One further difference in my definition is that I include the word "intentional." I do this in order to highlight that the self is an active subject in faith. Faith is not something that just happens to us. It is something that we as agents to some extent both choose and will (though it is not simply a matter of our choosing and willing, either). This requires a degree of consciousness and thoughtful (even critical) reflection on our part in relation to faith. Nevertheless, though reflective consciousness is a necessary dimension of faith, as I understand it, there are dimensions of intentionality which are prereflective and preconscious. Faith, in order to be intentional, need not (indeed, is not and cannot) always be entirely conscious and reflective. There are, even in this definition, dimensions of faith which are hidden from us but which still form part of who we are as intentional agents in faith.[13]

IMPLICATIONS FOR FAITH DEVELOPMENT

Enough may have been said about this understanding of faith to allow us now to put it in the hypothetical mode and examine what its implications are for the relation between faith and human development. *If* faith is appropriate and intentional participation in the redemptive activity of God, *then*. . . . Then what?

First, if faith is this, then growth or change in faith involves growth and change in what one knows and how one is able to, and in fact does, live. It is this rather than growth or change in what Fowler calls "structures." The difference between Fowler and me on this point is difficult to grasp since both of us talk about faith as involving knowing and as ways of living. But the difference is crucial. In my understanding, what we know and appropriate and the way we live are not just the "contents" of faith, while faith itself is the structure in and by which this content is appropriated. Rather, faith is the appropriation itself, and the "structures" are general human capacities for appropriation. Growth in faith, as I understand faith, does not necessarily come with the development of these capacities. Stephen Toulmin argues that the basic concern of structural-developmental studies is with the development of gross capacities to function. The emergence of new structures is the development of that "through which the developing organism becomes *able* to deal more effectively with its environment, and its 'stages' are accordingly defined in terms of the achievement of such . . . *capacities.*"[14] The presence of capacities does not determine whether and how they will be used, however. Hence, as Toulmin goes on to say, "we shall do better to assume that whatever general 'native capacities' a child [or adult] possesses are capable of realizing themselves in a wide range of different specific ways (or none) depending on the particular cultural context within which he has the opportunity to exercise them."[15] The heart of faith, in my definition, is not the "general 'native capacities' " one has, but what one does with them. This is what one would be primarily interested in in attending to growth or change in faith under my definition. Some may use these capacities for appropriate and intentional participation in the redemption activity of God and others may not. Even though general capacities may be universal, such participation may not be.

Second, if faith is what I have suggested, growth or change in faith will not necessarily be progressive. Rather than involving movement through a series of irreversible stages, growth or change may involve regressions. For various reasons we may participate *less* appropriately and intentionally at a later point in our lives than we did earlier. And insofar as there are "stages" of growth or development, they will be of a different sort than the ones Fowler describes. There may be realms of knowledge which need to be appropriated in faith, and some realms may have to be experienced and appropriated before others.[16] There may be different levels of participation in redemptive activity, and it may be that some must be engaged in before others. It is movement into these realms and levels that would constitute any stages and progress in them. In both of these, however, particular kinds of practices will be necessary in order to grow in faith. Certainly among them (for most faiths) will be worship, the study of "sacred" texts, engagement in certain disciplines (such as meditation or fasting), dialogue with and fellowship among members of a community of people who share that faith, and activities of service to the world. Though these practices are in part expressions of the faith that is growing, they are not just that. They are also experiences *through which* growth in faith takes place; and they are necessary ones for that growth. Through such practices, people's knowledge of, capacities for, and patterns of response to God are being formed. One further point on this subject: It would be wrong to expect that any account of growth or development in faith so understood would be able to describe an endpoint or highest stage. Since the focus here is on participation itself, rather than on capacities for participation, and since participation in the redemptive activity of God is an inexhaustible activity, there is no end to growth in faith.

Third, if faith is what I have described it to be, the criteria for growth in faith will have to arise from within faith itself. That is, an account of what "appropriate and intentional participation in the redemptive activity of God" consists of will have to be given, and this is a theological task rather than a social scientific or general phenomenological one. This is a reversal of what Fowler's understanding of faith implies, where general structures of human consciousness provide the criteria for faith development.

Fourth, if intentionality is an essential feature of faith, then what one looks at to discern growth in faith is the whole constellation of the self, not just structural features. It is impossible here to go into anything like the kind of analysis that a full discussion of intentionality (and its related concepts, character and agency) would require. Suffice it to say that what I mean by intentionality is not discrete, isolated "intentions," but the total orientation of the self that gives it whatever coherence and integrity it has. Intentionality also suggests the idea that who we become is to a major extent our own responsibility. And what we are responsible for is to bring all that we are and experience and do into conformity with God and God's will. For Christians, to have faith means ultimately to be formed "in Christ" and to live "in Christ." And, as Stanley Hauerwas puts it, "to be formed in Christ . . . is to be committed to bringing every element of our character [of our selves] into relation with this dominant orientation. This is our integrity, when everything that we believe, do, or do not do, has been brought under the dominion of our primary loyalty to God."[17] What one would look for, then, if one wished to analyze change or growth in a person's faith, would be the patterns of intentionality that constitute a person's fundamental orientation in life. The kind of interview schedule that Fowler has provided proves to be a very helpful tool in this effort. But the aim of its use would be different. By the use of such questions, one would be trying to discern the *narrative* of a person's life and see how the different themes, events, and experiences in it hold together. And one would analyze that narrative in order to discern what patterned orientation or fundamental intentionality is imbedded in it, rather than the structural capacities that can be abstracted from it. The result, rather than stage assignment, would be a "faith biography" that revealed and represented that person's faith life in its wholeness and complexity.

There is one other implication of this understanding of faith for how we conceive of growth in faith that I would like to mention. This has to do with how we understand the relation between faith and the development of psychological structures such as those identified by Piaget and other developmental psychologists. In the understanding that I have presented, faith itself is not a structural developmental phenomenon. To the extent that it is developmental, it is developmental in a different sense. Nevertheless, insofar as faith is an activity, people must have the "native capacities" to carry out this activity if they are to be able to carry it out at all. If faith involves knowing, people need to have the capacities to know at the level that faith requires. If faith involves worship, study, and service, people need to be able to do these things. If faith involves intentionality, it is necessary that people have the cognitive, social, and emotional capacities to form and carry out that intentionality. All of these involve forms of cognitive and psychosocial development, dimensions of which may very well be linked. Thus the study of human development is still significant for the study of growth or change in faith insofar as it can help us see what people are able to carry out in faith. Infants and young children simply do not have the cognitive and psychosocial capacities for faith in the sense we have defined. These capacities must be there before faith, in our sense, can possibly emerge. But what capacities are in fact needed has to be determined by a theological description of faith. Developmental studies can tell us when and how they emerge (and even suggest what some of the capacities are that those who study growth in faith might well attend to). But whether, for example, formal operational thinking is a prerequisite for "mature" faith or not is something that will have to be decided only by looking, from within faith, at what faith requires. Theories of human development cannot themselves be the framework on which theories of faith development are hung.

COMMON GROUND

Our final question has to do with the degree to which this approach to understanding faith and growth in faith is compatible with Fowler's faith development theory. Throughout the discussion I have been highlighting the differences. The different understandings of faith we put in our "if" clauses lead to different consequences in our "then" clauses. And there have arisen some substantive differences. What the two of us mean by faith is, it seems to me, so different that what Fowler calls "faith development" is not what I mean at all when I try to think about what it means to grow in faith.

Nevertheless, there is at least room for mutual edification. In one essay, Fowler says that education in the church needs to be understood as "education for creative discipleship" and that this is something different from "education for faith development."[18] Since "creative discipleship" is very close to what I mean by faith, Fowler's understanding of both the distinction and the connection between the two is worth exploring. Fowler states the connection of "faith development" and growth in "creative discipleship" in terms of readiness. He says, we "cannot afford to neglect the question of what human beings bring, by way of readiness to respond, to the encounter with the record of revelatory event and to tradition. . . . Life-span research into what we have come to call 'faith development' has begun to shed light on the quality and shape of the imagination's capacity to respond to revelatory events at different developmental stages."[19] To me, it is the response itself, rather than the readiness, that is faith. But I agree with Fowler that his theory can help us to understand that readiness.

Faith, as Cobb says, "has meant and rightly means many things." Perhaps the use of the hypothetical mode will help us all to be more clear about which of these meanings we work with. Then we can find more accurately the specific places where we agree and disagree on the issue of growth and development in faith and perceive more carefully our reasons for them.

NOTES

1. James W. Fowler, *Stages of Faith* (San Francisco: Harper & Row, 1981), p. xii.
2. Ibid., p. xiii.
3. Ibid., p. 4.
4. See, for an example, Loder's portion of the article, James E. Loder and James W. Fowler, "Conversations on Fowler's *Stages of Faith* and Loder's

The Transforming Moment," *Religious Education* 77 (March-April 1982) 2, pp. 133-39.

5. See Fowler, *Stages of Faith,* ch. 23.

6. See ibid., ch. 2.

7. George Lindbeck, *The Nature of Doctrine* (Philadelphia: Westminster Press, 1984), p. 21.

8. Ibid., p. 31.

9. John B. Cobb, Jr., *Christ in a Pluralistic Age* (Philadelphia: Westminster Press, 1975), pp. 87-88; italics mine.

10. Ibid., p. 88.

11. Lindbeck, *The Nature of Doctrine,* p. 132. For further discussion of the kind of learning that faith, according to the type of definition I have presented, requires, see Lindbeck, pp. 32-42, 62, 68-69, 100, and 128-34.

12. Ibid.

13. For a discussion of intentionality and agency which is consistent with my position, see Stanley Hauerwas, *Character and the Christian Life* (San Antonio: Trinity University Press, 1975), ch. 3. For a discussion of pre-reflective intentionality, see Edward Farley, *Ecclesial Man* (Philadelphia: Fortress Press, 1975), ch. 4.

14. Stephen Toulmin, "The Concept of 'Stages' in Psychological Development," *Cognitive Development and Epistemology,* ed. T. Mischel (New York: Academic Press, 1971), p. 49; italics mine.

15. Ibid., p. 58.

16. See Diogenes Allen, *Between Two Worlds* (Atlanta: John Knox Press, 1977) for an exposition of such a scheme.

17. Hauerwas, *Character and the Christian Life,* p. 223.

18. James Fowler, "Future Christians and Church Education," in *Hope for the Church,* ed. T. Runyan (Nashville: Abingdon Press, 1979), p. 105.

19. Ibid., pp. 110-11.

Chapter 3

Where Is Faith?:
Searching for the Core of the Cube

J. HARRY FERNHOUT

James Fowler's theory of faith development has gained wide acclaim as an important contribution to the study of human development. The keystone of Fowler's theory is his articulation of the nature of faith. For this reason, any serious assessment of this theory must include a critical evaluation of what Fowler means by faith.

Fowler asserts that faith is "an extremely complex phenomenon. . . . It has more dimensions than any one perspective can contain."[1] On occasion, Fowler tries to capture faith's complexity by adopting H. Richard Niebuhr's analogy of a cube: Even when three sides of the cube are visible, there are still three sides hidden, not to mention the inside.[2] Fowler acknowledges that the complexity of his view not only makes it difficult to pin down what faith is precisely, but also provides his critics with plenty of ammunition. He lightheartedly quotes Harvey Cox's admonition, "There is something to offend everyone in this way of talking about faith."[3]

In this chapter I will argue that in explaining what faith is, Fowler has given a lot of attention to the sides of the cube, but has not thoroughly dealt with the substance of its center, namely, that which makes it solid and uniquely a *faith* cube. Further, because Fowler's account of faith lacks a solid core, the sides of the cube (the characteristics which define and/or delimit faith) tend to expand and contract. Because of this, the faith cube becomes difficult to distinguish from other cubes, especially from the complex "cube" of ego or identity. Further, because faith has so many seemingly movable sides, its complexity becomes conceptually unmanageable. In sum, Fowler's is an "everything and nothing" view of faith. The flexible sides of the cube incorporate wide-ranging aspects of development, but the core of the cube is hollow.

These problems have significant implications for Fowler's theory of faith *development.* Those whom Fowler calls "psychological critics" of his theory also find his concept of faith too broad and inclusive and his account of faith development to be indistinguishable from ego development. Lawrence Kohlberg, for example, contends that Fowler's broad definition of faith leads to "confusions," making the empirical study of the relation of religion (Kohlberg's term) and morality very difficult.[4] Whether Kohlberg is right or wrong on this specific point, he and others are responding to genuine difficulties in Fowler's theory.

AN ORIENTATION TO THE PROBLEMS

Fowler's *Stages of Faith* is subtitled "The Psychology of Human Development and the Quest for Meaning." It is "the quest for meaning" which gets at the heart of what Fowler's faith development theory is about. The theory addresses the psychology of human development from the particular angle or perspective of the human quest for meaning. Thus, to grasp what Fowler means by faith, it is crucial to understand the nature of the quest for meaning.

Fowler asserts that the human quest for meaning has to do with the fact "that from the beginning of our lives we are faced with the challenge of finding or composing some kind of order, unity, and coherence in the force fields of our lives."[5] In this statement the influence of a structural-developmentalist perspective on human development, as articulated particularly by Piaget and Kohlberg, is readily apparent. Structural-developmentalists regard human beings as meaning-making beings. The need and the capacity to make sense of and give order to experience in a noninstinctual way constitutes human uniqueness.

Fowler's appreciation for the structural-developmentalist perspective on meaning-making is particularly evident in his essay "Moral Stages and the Development of Faith." This essay makes

it clear that Fowler understands the human quest for meaning in
very broad terms. He claims that

> as members of a species burdened with consciousness and self-con-
> sciousness, and with freedom to name and organize the phenomenal
> world, we nowhere can escape the task of forming tacit or explicit
> coherent images of our action-worlds. We are born into fields of
> forces impinging on us from all sides. The development of perception
> means a profound limiting and selection of the *sensa* to which we can
> consciously or unconsciously attend. The development of cognition—
> understood here in its broadest sense—means the construction of
> operations of thought and valuing in accordance with which the *sensa*
> to which we attend are organized and formed. Composition and
> interpretation of meanings, then, are the inescapable burden of our
> species.[6]

In other words, the totality of a human being's attending to his or
her perceptual world is a process of meaning-making.

Fowler describes faith as "*an apparently genetic* consequence of
the universal burden of finding or making meaning."[7] But this
raises an important question: How are we to understand the
connection between faith and the quest for meaning, understood
in the extremely broad terms indicated above? Is faith, for example, to be equated with the human quest for meaning, or is it an
aspect of this quest?

At times Fowler seems to suggest that faith is coextensive with
the broad process of meaning-making. He asserts that faith
"points to a way of making sense of one's existence," of "giving
order and coherence to the force-field of life."[8] Faith is described
as a way of leaning into life. Seen in this way, it is extremely
difficult to discern a distinction between faith and meaning-making in general. Faith becomes just another word for meaning-
making.

But there is more to Fowler's understanding of faith. Fowler
maintains that in the overall process of meaning-making, we
consciously or unconsciously "invest trust in powerful images
which unify our experience, and which order it in accordance
with interpretations that serve our acknowledgment of centers of
value and power."[9] There are three important elements here: trust
in powerful images; acknowledgment of centers of value and

power; and the unification or ordering of experience. The last element reiterates faith as the ordering of life. But the other two elements indicate that, for Fowler, faith also means something more specific. Within meaning-making as a whole, faith has to do with the "investment of life-grounding trust and of life-orienting commitment."[10] This trust and commitment are invested in centers of value and power, transcendent in that they are beyond personal control and provide life-orientation.

Such trust in and commitment to a center of value or power shape a person's assumptions concerning the nature of reality. Faith includes the activity of forming comprehensive *images* (world pictures) of reality. If humans, in the meaning-making process, come to know reality by constructing mental schemes and structures that try to assimilate, grasp, and order experience, then faith has to do with the construction of an ultimate schema that seeks to grasp the whole of experience. Thus, Fowler says:

> Let us designate those images by which we holistically grasp the conditions of our existence with the name *images of the ultimate environment.* And let us point out that such images of the ultimate environment derive their unity and their principle of coherence from a center (or centers) of value or power to which persons of faith are attracted with conviction. Faith, then, is a matter of composing an image of the ultimate environment, through the commitment of self to a center (or centers) of value or power giving it coherence.[11]

Fowler draws together the various elements of faith discussed thus far in one of his composite definitions of faith:

> Faith, we may say, is
> —a disposition of the total self to the ultimate environment
> —in which a trust and loyalty are invested in a center or centers of value and power
> —which give order and coherence to the force-field of life
> —which support and sustain (or qualify and relativize) our mundane and everyday commitments and trusts
> —combining to give orientation, courage, meaning, and hope to our lives, and
> —to unite us into communities of shared interpretation, loyalty, and trust.[12]

THREE SENSES OF FAITH

Within Fowler's complex definition can be found three distinct senses of faith, closely interwoven, yet clearly distinguishable in their scope and specificity.

Fowler articulates a first, fairly narrow sense of faith when he speaks of humans investing *trust* and *loyalty* in a center or centers of value and power. In chapter 2 of *Stages of Faith,* Fowler endorses Wilfred Cantwell Smith's conclusion that faith involves "an alignment of the heart or will, a commitment of loyalty or trust."[13] Faith means "*to set one's heart on. . . .* It is a mode of knowing, of *acknowledgment.* One commits oneself to that which is known or acknowledged, and lives loyally, with life and character being shaped by that commitment."[14]

In identifying faith with loyalty, trust, and commitment, Fowler seems to define the irreducible nature, the unique character of human faith activity, the core of faith. This interpretation is confirmed by Fowler's assertion that the existential issues dealt with in his faith interviews provide the best indication of the focus of faith. Issues of trust, commitment, or ultimate concern figure prominently in the interviews.[15]

A second sense of faith in Fowler's understanding has to do with forming an image of one's total or ultimate environment. Within the welter of experience, a person constructs an image of the world, an image which tries to give coherent representation to the totality of a person's environment, including one's center(s) of value and power. I would call this second sense of faith a person's *worldview.*

The third sense of faith is the broadest. Here the focus is on faith's integrational role in a person's diverse life practices. Faith is a way of leaning into life. It shapes the way humans give themselves to various relationships and causes. Faith holds together the "various interrelated dimensions of human knowing, valuing, committing, and acting that must be considered together if we want to understand the making and maintaining of human meaning."[16] Faith does this "holding together" by giving a "tone to one's entire way of understanding, reacting to and taking initiative in the world."[17] I would call this third sense of faith one's *way of life.*

When Fowler moves back and forth between these three senses of faith in his discussion, problems develop, particularly when he does not signal such shifts. It becomes difficult for Fowler's readers to hold together everything that the term "faith" designates. But this obscurity is a symptom of a deeper problem concerning the nature of faith. I have claimed that Fowler does not thoroughly deal with the core of faith. Perhaps the presence of what I have termed the first sense of Fowler's view of faith seems to contradict my claim. However, as Fowler discusses the complex dimensions of faith, its core repeatedly fades into obscurity.

Fowler never indicates unequivocally that he uses terms like trust, loyalty, and commitment (setting one's heart on) to get at the irreducible core of faith. For example, the composite definition quoted above gives no prominence to trust and loyalty, but subsumes them under "a general disposition of the self toward the ultimate environment." Trust, commitment, and loyalty are usually discussed in terms of their implications for what I have termed the second and third senses of Fowler's understanding of faith. As a result, the first sense dissolves in complex discussion and abstract definition. However, if Fowler wishes to present a theory of faith development which, among other things, meets structural-developmental criteria, he must give a consistent account of the core of faith, of what it is that develops in faith. If Fowler does not give such an account, he may have a theory of development, but not of *faith* development.

This brings us to another problem, namely, the focus and scope of Fowler's account of the nature of a faith stage (the seven aspects of a faith stage). This account is framed primarily in terms of the third sense of faith, and partially in terms of the second. Fowler is concerned to show that faith integrates various aspects of development into a whole. Thus his faith stages incorporate various areas in human development (cognitive, perspective-taking, moral), designating them all as aspects of a totality called faith. The result is that faith development appears to become synonymous with a broad process such as ego development.

This equation is qualified by Fowler's inclusion of what I have termed the second sense of faith (forming an image of an ultimate environment) in his account of the aspects of a faith stage. But the first sense of faith is absent from this account, despite the strong presence of trust and commitment issues in Fowler's interview format. Thus the complexity of Fowler's understanding of faith results in a confusing account of the nature of faith stages. While they resemble ego development stages, they are different. And yet their difference lacks focus.

These general observations locate some of the major loci of the problems with Fowler's understanding of faith. But in order to see the difficulties clearly, it is important to take a closer look at each of three key elements in Fowler's definition.

FAITH AS RELATIONAL

Fowler sees faith as irreducibly relational[18] and irreducibly a way of knowing.[19] These crucial dimensions of faith are distinguishable, but impossible to separate. As a way of knowing, faith is relational; it takes shape in one's interaction with one's total environment. And as a way of relating, it involves a knowing which grasps one's relatedness.[20] Although inseparable, these two dimensions do appear to have a certain inner/outer relationship. The relational dimension focuses on the outer structure of faith. It has to do with one's relations to other human beings and the total environment. Faith as knowing focuses on the inner structure of faith. It has to do with the structures or patterns employed by the self in faith knowing.[21] As Fowler sees it, faith or trust is a foundational quality of all human relations.[22] For human communities to be viable and lasting, human beings must "keep faith" with one another, whether it be in the use of language, the conduct of business, political activity, or in personal relationships. But such "faith keeping" is not based simply on loyalty to another person. Rather, people keep faith with one another because of shared value commitments. "Our ties to others," he says, "are mediated, formed, and deepened by our shared or common trusts in and loyalties to centers of supraordinate value."[23]

In a political community, for example, loyalty to fellow citizens is shaped by mutual acceptance of ideals of justice, peace, order, and the common good. Thus all human associations exhibit a triadic "fiduciary or covenantal" pattern, involving loyalty between persons, and mutual loyalty to a center of value relevant to the relationship.

For our present purposes, the important point is that Fowler refers to these human relationships as "triadic patterns of faith"[24] or "faith relational triangles."[25] They are instances of "the way-of-being-in-relation that is faith," and are "part of the way we give order, coherence, and meaning to the welter of forces and powers" experienced in life.[26] Understood in this way, faith is indeed a very broad concept. All interpersonal or communal relations are faith relations.

But Fowler does not conclude his discussion of faith as relational at this point. There is a fuller, richer dimension to faith as relational. "Faith as a way-of-being-in-relation has an outer boundary constituted by what we might call our *ultimate environment*."[27] This is the faith triangle that includes—when it is intact—all the others of which we are a part. This is the most inclusive triangle in which the self relates to the canvas of meaning itself."[28]

Here Fowler seems to suggest that the "ultimate environment" faith triangle differs only in scope from those previously discussed. It is the "broadest and most inclusive relationship in faith."[29] In this triangle, the person seeks a way of relating to his or her environment or life-world as a whole or a totality, in order to give meaning to the whole.

> Our tacit and explicit assumptions about the "grain" or character of the ultimate environment taken as a whole . . . provide the larger framework of meaning in which we make and sustain our interpersonal, institutional, and vocational covenants. It is our operational images—conscious or unconscious—of the character, power, and disposition of that ultimate environment toward us and our causes which give direction and reason to our daily commitments. Faith, then, is a person's or a community's way-of-being-in-relation to our neighbors and to the causes and companions of our lives.[30]

Fowler's treatment of faith as relational deals primarily with his understanding of faith as a way of organizing and integrating life's relationships. He does, of course, make a valuable point here. Human relations *do* have a fiduciary element or moment without which they could not exist. But in terms of Fowler's overall project, dealing with faith as relational in such a broad way deprives faith of specific meaning. It becomes coextensive with human life as relational. Recognizing the "faith-keeping" element in, for example, a person's relations as citizen seems to lead Fowler to characterize the citizen relation as a faith relation. But there is no reason, on the face of it, to collapse citizenship into faith. Furthermore, Fowler makes no substantive distinction between faith as a way-of-being-in-relation to an ultimate environment, and ways-of-being-in-relation in interpersonal and community contexts.

Perhaps some of his readers applaud this lack of distinction, seeing it as a way of speaking meaningfully about faith in the midst of life rather than as escape from it. Again, this is a valuable emphasis. But the point is that Fowler wishes to develop a theory of *faith* development. To do this, he must be able to give some specific focus to his understanding of faith as a way-of-being-in-relation. To achieve this focus, Fowler must discuss faith as relational in terms of what I identified as the first and second senses of his understanding of faith.

To explore what the relational character of faith means in terms of the second sense of Fowler's understanding of faith, it is necessary to deal with what he means by "ultimate environment." Thus far, we have seen that a person's ultimate environment represents the totality of one's life-world, an inclusive outer boundary of being-in-relation. It is the faith triangle that includes all others. Fowler also uses the term "ultimate environment" to refer to the integration or order in the person's many ways of being-in-relation.

In this way of speaking the *triadic* structure of the person's being-in-relation to an ultimate environment is not immediately obvious. The centers of value and power in terms of which one relates to the totality of one's world are not indicated. However, on closer examination it appears that "ultimate environment" designates a relationship *between* two points of a faith triangle: the self and a center of value and power.

The second of these two loci begins to emerge when Fowler uses "Kingdom of God" as one description of ultimate environment.[31] This metaphor for the "canvas of meaning" incorporates not only a sense of one's total environment as a kingdom, but also a sense of the king (i.e., God as the center of value and power). Fowler asserts that in constructing holistic images of the ultimate environment a person makes a "bid for relationship to a center of value and power adequate to ground, unify, and order the whole force-field of life."[32]

Ultimate environment thus refers both to the character of the "composed" totality of one's interpersonal and communal relations and also to a center of *power* that is distinct from the self and the environment the self composes. By ultimate environment, then, Fowler means not only the totality of the faith-relational triads of which one is a part, but also the ultimate center(s) of value and power in terms of which one relates. Thus an exploration of faith as worldview (what I called Fowler's second view of faith) also begins to reveal how commitment to an ultimate (his first view) enters his thinking about faith as relational.

In *Stages of Faith,* after a brief discussion of the fiduciary, triadic character of all human relations, Fowler turns to the relational character of faith understood as commitment to an ultimate center(s) of value and power. In this sense of faith, "we invest or devote ourselves because the other to which we commit has, for us, an intrinsic excellence or worth and because it promises to confer value on us."[33]

He goes on to describe faith as the "relation to that which exerts qualitatively different initiatives in our lives than those which occur in strictly human relations."[34] Fowler is here trying to deal with faith as "setting one's heart on," as an ultimate commitment to that "which seems of transcendent worth and in relation to which our lives have worth."[35]

With this treatment Fowler comes close to giving a firm core to his account of faith as relational. From this standpoint one could consider the connections between this specific sense of faith relation and the general fiduciary element present in all human relations, eliminating the confusion between specific and broad senses of faith. Then it might be possible to focus on specific developmental patterns of faith relation, rather than of being-in-relation in general.

Unfortunately, however, Fowler does not move in this direction. Instead, he takes up a discussion of "the interplay of *faith* and *identity* in the triadic pattern of faith."[36] He asserts that faith shapes a person's identity and that faith and identity must bring the many faith-relational triads in which a person participates into "an integrated, workable unity." Fowler's account of the major types of faith-identity relations is very constructive and insightful. However, the net effect is to shift his discussion of faith as relational away from that faith relation which exerts a "qualitatively different" influence in human life and back toward the very broad consideration which I identified as the third sense of his view of faith. What Fowler means by a pattern of faith-identity relation covers virtually the whole of life. It deals with faith as commitment, with the integration (or nonintegration) of identity, and with the integration (or nonintegration) of a way of life in all of a person's relational triads. Thus Fowler loses an opportunity to develop the meaning of the relational character of faith as commitment or "setting one's heart upon." Instead, he leaves the impression that his conception of faith incorporates (rather than influences) patterns of human identity, and that, consequently, his theory of faith development doubles as a treatment of ego or identity development.

Obviously, what Fowler means by ultimate environment is very complex. Unfortunately, Fowler packs so much into the term that it is difficult to be sure what he means. The three senses of faith which I have distinguished are entirely undifferentiated in Fowler's use of "ultimate environment." Perhaps this is Fowler's intention, in order to maintain a holistic and integral view of faith. However, the complexity of the term severely restricts its explanatory value in dealing with faith as relational. Considering faith as being-in-relation to an ultimate environment does little to clarify or focus the meaning of the relational character of faith.

Fowler's treatment of faith as relational is hampered by the terminological obscurity brought about by his multi-sense, undifferentiated understanding of faith. His tendency to deal with the relational character of faith primarily in terms of what I call the third, broad sense of faith indicates a lack of conceptual clarity concerning the core of faith.

FAITH AS KNOWING

For Fowler, it is unthinkable to give an account of faith without considering it as an activity of knowing. Fowler discusses faith as knowing in many of his writings. His most detailed account, however, is found in "Faith and the Structuring of Meaning," which serves as background to the material in *Stages of Faith.*

In several key respects, Fowler models his theory of faith development on the structural developmental theories of Piaget and Kohlberg. One way this link is manifested is in what Fowler acknowledges as his *"epistemological focus."*[37] Essential to structural developmental theory is a view of humans as meaning-making or knowledge-constructing beings. The construction of meaning takes place as a person interacts with his or her environment. Fowler follows Piaget and Kohlberg in asserting that all knowing

> means an acting upon and "composing" of the known. Knowing occurs when an active knower interacts with an active world of persons and objects, meeting its unshaped or unorganized stimuli with the ordering, organizing power of the knower's mind. Knowing is adequate or "true" when the mental ordering of the elements of reality correspond to their relationships as experienced and known by other reliable knowers.[38]

Fowler labels this process *constructive* knowing.

But Fowler is not entirely satisfied with this account of knowing. It does not take into consideration the fact that the self as knower may also be at stake in the interactive process. The interaction of knower and environment may lead not only to an ordering of reality, but also to a reordering of a person's understanding of his or her self in relation to the rest of reality. In this regard, Fowler finds Kegan's account of the dynamic of personality or ego development very helpful. Kegan, Fowler says, extends Piaget and Kohlberg's constructivist understanding of knowing, and asserts that ego is constituted in the totality of interactive relations in which knowing takes place.[39] Fowler uses the term *constitutive* knowing to get at this knowing "that composes or establishes both the known and the knower in relation to the known."[40]

The question now arises whether, according to Fowler, faith knowing is constructive knowing or constitutive knowing. On one occasion Fowler refers to faith as "a powerful form of constructive knowing. Here we have in view the composition (constitution) and interpretation of the *person's values, communities,* and *images of ultimate environments* to which we are related in trust (or mistrust) and loyalty (or disloyalty) in faith."[41] Otherwise, however, Fowler quite consistently refers to faith as constitutive knowing. He writes:

> The structural features of constitutive knowing disclosed to us by Piaget, Kohlberg, Selman, and now Kegan, for each of their respective domains, serve us well in understanding the constitutive knowing which is faith. Faith does involve the world of physical objects and the laws of their relatedness, movement, and change. Faith does involve the construction of the self and others, in perspective-taking, in moral analysis and judgment, and in the constitution of self as related to others which we call ego.[42]

Fowler's understanding of faith as knowing, while firmly rooted in a structural-developmental understanding of constructivist knowing, seeks to incorporate the emphasis belonging to what Fowler terms constitutive knowing.

Faith knowing thus covers all knowing that takes place in triadic trust/mistrust relations to persons, communities, and ultimate environments—in sum, all relations. It appears that Fowler is prepared to designate all knowing as faith knowing. His incorporation of the insights developed by Piaget, Kohlberg, Selman, and Kegan suggests that faith knowing refers to the totality of constructive and constitutive knowing, rather than to a specific kind of knowing within this totality. Thus, the same problem noted in our discussion of faith as relational resurfaces here: if faith knowing is understood this broadly, it becomes indistinguishable from knowing in general. The possibility of dealing with faith as a unique form of knowing is lost.

As might by now be expected, Fowler, without in any way retracting this broad emphasis, also deals with faith knowing in a more focused manner. In this context, Fowler begins to distinguish his view of faith as constitutive knowing from the views of Piaget, Kohlberg, and Kegan. Here he tries to spell out how faith knowing is a unique form of constitutive knowing.

Fowler contends that the contributions of Piaget, Kohlberg, Selman, and Kegan are useful only "up to a point" when addressing conceptually "the last relational step of faith—that of related-ness to an ultimate environment."[43] This suggests that these ac-counts of constitutive knowing may be adequate when dealing with the "prior" relational steps of faith (relations to persons or communities). But Fowler insists that "certain decisive problems arise for the effort to extend the Piagetian approach to constitu-tive knowing so as to encompass 'the domain of faith.' "[44] Appar-ently there is something so unique about the "last relational step" of faith that the notion of constitutive knowing needs to be adapt-ed.

The first "decisive problem" has to do with Piaget's and Kohl-berg's separation of cognition and affection. They favor an "ob-jectifying, technical reason" which has no room for "freedom, risk, passion, and subjectivity."[45] The second problem arises from the fact that neither Piaget nor Kohlberg intended to provide a theory of ego or personality development. As a result, they went about

> the task of identifying the forms of reason or logic characteristic of different "stages" in human thought without making a critically im-portant distinction: They have not attended to the differences be-tween constitutive-knowing in which *the identity or worth of the person is not directly at stake* and constitutive knowing in which it is.[46]

This quotation is somewhat confusing, because, according to Fowler's own definition, the person is always at stake in constitu-tive knowing. Presumably Fowler should have used the term *constructive* knowing to characterize knowing in which the iden-tity or worth of the person is not at stake. In any case, Fowler clearly finds Piaget and Kohlberg inadequate on this point. He writes,

> *in both faith knowing and the kind of moral-knowing which gives rise to choice and action, the constitution or modification of the self is always an issue.* In these kinds of constitutive-knowing not only is the known being constructed, but there is a simultaneous extension, modification, or reconstruction of the *knower in relation to the known.*[47]

Fowler's proposed solutions to these two problems vary some-what. In "Faith and the Structuring of Meaning" he deals with the first problem by appealing to Kegan, who breaks with the bifurcation of cognition and affection by recognizing that "mean-ing-making, as a constructive movement, is prior to and genera-tive of both reason and emotion. We must, Kegan asserts, see meaning-making as the self's total constitutive-knowing activity, an activity in which there is no thought without feeling and no feeling without thought."[48]

In *Stages of Faith,* Kegan's solution is not mentioned. Rather, Fowler deals with the first problem by distinguishing between a "logic" of rational certainty (affect-free) and a "logic" of convic-tion. In "Faith and the Structuring of Meaning," this discussion of "logics" is presented in detail, but as a way of addressing the second problem. Perhaps these variations indicate, not only that the noted problems are closely connected, but also that Fowler's treatment of these problems has not yet reached a definitive resolution. In any case, Fowler apparently sees his account of the two "logics" as his own answer to both problems mentioned so far. With this account he endeavors to show both how affect enters into faith knowing and how the self is at stake in it.

In faith knowing, Fowler asserts, it is necessary to examine

the relationship of what we may call a *logic of rational certainty. . .* to what we may call a logic *of conviction. . . .* This relationship between these two "logics" is not one of choice between alternatives. A logic of conviction does not negate a logic of rational certainty. But the for-mer, being more inclusive, does contextualize, qualify, and anchor the latter. Recognition of a more comprehensive "logic of conviction" does lead us to see that the logic of rational certainty is part of a larger epistemological structuring activity, and is not to be confused with the whole.[49]

This distinction between two "logics," while intriguing, does not greatly advance Fowler's attempt to spell out the nature of faith knowing. Granted, Fowler's notion of a "logic of conviction" does help to indicate that the self, a being with affections and emo-tions, fully enters into and is at stake in the activity of faith knowing. However, as Fowler has stated, there are other kinds of knowing (such as "moral knowing which gives rise to choice and action," as well as Kegan's "constitutive knowing") in which the self is at stake. Clearly, these also require "more" than a "logic of rational certainty." Does the "logic of conviction" enter into all these forms of knowing, or is it proper to faith knowing only? Fowler's account does not make this clear. Thus it remains difficult to grasp the uniqueness of faith knowing, particularly in light of the affinity Fowler sees between his own view of faith knowing and Kegan's account of knowing as the constitution of ego or personality.

Another problem with the account of the two "logics" is the lack of clarity concerning their relation. In the above quotation, Fowler says that the "logic of conviction" does not negate the "logic of rational certainty"; faith knowing is not antirational or irrational.[50] Rather, rational knowing plays the "crucial role of conceptualizing, questioning, and evaluating the products of other modes of imaginal and generative knowing."[51] Thus the "logic of rational certainty" is placed within the "logic of conviction." Fowler says that he seeks to grasp "the inner dialectic of rational logic in the dynamics of a more comprehensive logic of convictional orientation."[52] As he sees it, the "logic of conviction" contextualizes, qualifies, and anchors the "logic of rational certainty." But these three terms suggest complex and different relations which must be spelled out carefully. Does the "logic of conviction" simply provide a landscape (context) for the "logic of rational certainty"? Or, is the latter modified in some way? Fowler adds no further clarity when, in response to critics, he asserts the need to see " 'reasoning in faith' as a balanced interaction between the more limited and specialized and the more comprehensive and holistic logics."[53] It is not particularly helpful to use "interaction" to describe a relation in which one element is contextualized, qualified, and anchored by the other. The relation of the two "logics" needs to be spelled out much more specifically if the character of faith knowing is to emerge clearly.

A third problem in a structural-developmental understanding of the nature of knowing concerns Piaget and Kohlberg's "very restrictive understanding of the role of imagination in knowing."[54] Responding to this limitation, Fowler insists that since faith involves constructing images of the ultimate environment, a theory of faith knowing must deal with the powerful role of images in "imaginal knowing." It appears that imaginal knowing is at the heart of Fowler's view of faith knowing. In *Stages of Faith,* the chapter which deals with faith as knowing is entitled "Faith as Imagination."

According to Fowler, images and imaginal knowing play a role in all human knowing. We relate our knowing to deeply embedded childhood images, and the spectrum of knowing that takes place in us is always wider than our consciousness. Furthermore, new, significant learnings, in order to "register" with us, must resonate with and extend previous images, perhaps reorganizing them in the process.

In faith, the imaginal mode of knowing plays a particularly prominent part. Faith is "an active mode of knowing, or composing a felt sense or image of the condition of our lives taken as a whole. It unifies our lives' force-fields."[55]

Fowler's "logic of conviction" gets at the essence of such knowing. This "logic" involves

> coming to terms with modes of thought that employ images, symbols, and synthetic fusions of thought and feeling. It means taking account of so-called "regressive" movements in which the psyche returns to the preconceptual, prelinguistic modes and memories, and to primitive sources of energizing imagery, bringing them into consciousness with resultant reconstruals of the experience world. To deal adequately with faith and with faith's dynamic role in the total self-constitutive activity of ego means trying to give theoretical attention to the transformation in consciousness—rapid and dramatic in sudden conversion, more gradual and incremental in faith growth—which results from the *re*-cognition of self-others-world in light of knowing the self as constituted by a center of value powerful enough to require or enable recentering one's ultimate environment.[56]

Here it is helpful to return to my earlier distinction of the three senses of faith. In dealing with imaginal knowing, Fowler is no longer speaking in terms of the third, broad sense of faith. Faith knowing is not treated here as knowing that emerges in all triadic faith relations. Rather, Fowler is here speaking in more specific terms, dealing with faith understood as the activity of forming a "comprehensive image of an ultimate environment."

Thus far, however, Fowler's description of imaginal faith knowing still falls short of providing a substantive account of the unique nature of faith knowing. Fowler asserts that imagination is a powerful force underlying all knowing. Thus, to speak of faith as imaginal does not help us to distinguish it from knowing in general. From Fowler's statements, it appears that faith knowing is marked by the *prominence* it gives to imaginal knowing, as well as by the inclusive *scope* of its images (ultimate environment). But these matters of degree do not stamp faith knowing as a unique kind of constitutive knowing.

What I called the first sense of faith is present in Fowler's summary definition of faith as knowing.[57] Faith is constitutive knowing which forms images of the ultimate environment *generated by commitments to centers of power and value.* However, Fowler's analysis concentrates on the nature of constitutive knowing and of imaginal knowing—at the expense of explaining what it means that such knowing is generated by commitment. In other words, Fowler has not explored the *relation* of the first sense of faith to the second and the third in his account of faith as knowing. But more importantly, he has not dealt with the fact that commitment ("setting one's heart") can itself be described as knowing.

Certainly, in the Hebrew and New Testament scriptures, to be committed, in trust, to God is to *know* God. Such knowing is imaged in a pattern of living.[58] In my judgment, Fowler's account of faith knowing would be greatly enriched if he developed the theme that commitment to and trust in an ultimate involves a genuine mode of knowing. He could then develop an account of the developmental patterns of faith knowing without blurring his theory with general accounts of ego development, such as Kegan presents. Further, he could then say something substantive about faith knowing's contribution to the totality of knowing without enlarging faith knowing to the point that it encompasses all knowing.

Fowler moves in this direction when he describes faith as *acknowledgment,* a knowing in which one commits oneself to what is known or acknowledged, and lives loyally.[59] However, his tendency is to shift away from a specific focus on such knowing-in-commitment to a concern with the impact of the commitment on the self, the transformation of consciousness that comes in knowing the self as constituted by a powerful center of value. While it is no doubt true that faith knowing involves such a transformation, conceptually this is the second step. The first step, knowing-in-commitment, remains undeveloped in Fowler's theory.

THE OPERATIONAL ASPECTS OF A FAITH STAGE

To gain more practical insight into what Fowler means by faith, one must look at his model of a faith stage. The structural features he identifies as constituting a faith stage will reveal what it is that Fowler looks for in "faith" stages. Examining his criteria will also reveal whether the theoretical problems noted earlier have implications for Fowler's empirical stage analysis.

Fowler contends that faith's complexity makes it an "extremely complex phenomenon to try to operationalize for empirical investigation."[60] Perhaps this is why Fowler's attempts to get at the features of a faith stage have undergone considerable refinement. He used to identify five "variables," which he described as "windows or apertures into the structure of faith. Presumably, if our claim that a stage is a structural whole is correct, one will see the same essential structures, only from several different points of vantage, through these variables."[61] Later, he renamed these variable "aspects" and increased their number to seven.[62] More recently, Fowler has shifted the order of the seven aspects to focus better on the distinct operation of a faith stage.

Of the seven operational aspects that he now articulates, Aspect A, "Form of Logic," incorporates Piaget's analysis of stages of cognitive development. Fowler adds adult substages to Piaget's formal operational thought in faith stages four through six. It is important to note that "*Form* of Logic" here refers to cognitive *stage,* and not to the distinction between the "logic of rational certainty" and the "logic of conviction." By definition, Aspect A belongs to the "logic of rational certainty." For Aspect B, "Role-Taking," Fowler adopts Robert Selman's work on the person's developing ability to take the perspective of others. For faith stages four through six, Fowler modifies and extends Selman's work. Aspect C, "Form of Moral Judgment," incorporates Kohlberg's stages of moral reasoning. Aspects D, E, F, and G are ones which Fowler has defined himself. For Fowler, a faith stage is an operational system which integrates all these aspects. Stage advance involves transformation in each aspect and the attainment of a new integrational pattern.

Fowler's brief descriptions of the seven aspects have serious limitations. Each aspect is supposed to represent a structural competence with its own structural-developmental pattern across the stages, directed toward greater differentiation, comprehensiveness, and flexibility. But Fowler nowhere presents a detailed argument as to why these seven aspects should be seen as the structural features of a faith stage. Furthermore, he does not demonstrate that each individual aspect represents a "window" into the structure of faith or a unique structural competence. This is an important deficiency in his theory, particularly with respect to aspects D through G, in which Fowler does not rely on the work of others. In addressing this matter further, Fowler would need to spell out in detail, for example, how Aspect D is structurally different from (rather than a subset of) Aspect B, to which, he acknowledges, it is "in some ways" parallel.[63] As it stands now, Fowler has not yet developed an account of the aspects as "structural features" in the areas where he goes beyond Piaget, Kohlberg, and Selman.

Furthermore, Fowler's description of transformation within each aspect as presented in his chart is very brief and unspecific. The unfolding of Aspect E, for example, reads like an account of ego development and is not transparently an account of the unfolding of a structural capacity. In 1980, Fowler described his chart as "a promissory note," awaiting a "detailed and comprehensive presentation of the stage by stage transformation of these aspects and their integration in each stage" in a forthcoming book.[64] Presumably, that book was *Stages of Faith.* However, the latter leaves the promise unfulfilled; it explains the seven operational aspects with reference to a sample faith interview.[65]

While Fowler has yet to work out these dimensions of his theory, he does have a definite rationale for placing the seven aspects in a particular order. This rationale must be understood against the background of his discussion of faith as knowing and of the two "logics." Fowler's "logic of rational certainty" has to do with Aspect A (Piaget's cognitive stages). Aspect B and C (Role-Taking and Form of Moral Judgment) are seen as derivatives of the "logic of rational certainty."[66] These three are "contextualized by and integrated with aspects of a logic of conviction (D,E,F, and

G)."[67] In other words, the aspects of Bounds of Social Awareness, Locus of Authority, Form of World Coherence, and Symbolic Functioning together represent the "logic of conviction." And these aspects, too, appear in a definite order. Fowler's description of the "logic of conviction," noted earlier, places special stress on an imaginal mode of knowing, dealing with the composing of a holistic image of the ultimate environment. Fowler's operational Aspects F and G try to account for this dimension of faith, and thus represent the "purest" expression of the "logic of conviction." In Aspect G, says Fowler, the "logic of conviction" must be seen as "operative with powerful transforming potential for the orientation and functioning of the total psyche."[68] The seven operational aspects, then, appear in a definite sequence, moving from "pure" logic of rational certainty to "pure" logic of conviction. This arrangement suggests that an ordered consideration of the seven aspects brings us closer and closer to that which belongs uniquely to faith. In this regard it is notable that Fowler feels the least settled about his articulation of Aspect G, Symbolic Functioning. He writes that this aspect is not yet well-defined, requiring much additional work. There is, of course, nothing wrong with acknowledging that his theory is still in process. However, the aspect which approaches the key structural feature of faith is the one in question. Fowler's uncertainty here tends to confirm my contention that his view of faith lacks a solid core.

Significantly, the first sense of faith is absent in Fowler's description of the seven operational aspects. Aspects F and G express the second sense (composing an image of the ultimate environment). While this image is generated by a person's ultimate commitment, the latter element is not an explicit part of the description of a faith stage. In an earlier essay, Fowler defended this omission.

> It may seem that the dynamic which lies at the heart of faith—namely a centering affection, an organizing love, a central object of loyalty and trust—is missing. And this is true. To note this is to be reminded again of the formal and structural focus of this stage theory.[69]

This lack of focus, says Fowler, allows the theory to be applied to a variety of religious contents.

But it appears that at this crucial point Fowler fails to make a basic distinction between the universal human capacity for trust and commitment and the content-full variation in the object(s) of that trust. If faith, understood as trust or commitment (setting one's heart), is a universal part of what it means to be human, then it must have structural features that can be "operationalized" in a faith stages description. If what Fowler calls the "heart of faith" (see quote above) has no such features, then he lacks grounds for calling his theory a treatment of *faith* stages.

Because Fowler's seven aspects fail to get at the commitment core of faith, the third or broad sense of his view of faith comes to dominate the characterization of faith stages. The question arises: Why should a person's cognitive stage be considered an aspect of a *faith* stage, rather than, for example, a developmental concern which is related to faith but not absorbed by it? The answer: A faith stage virtually becomes a description of a person's overall development. Faith stages are said to model "a sequence of certain holistic patterns of feeling, valuing, thinking, and committing."[70] They describe not just "spiritual or religious experience," but a "person's mode of orienting himself or herself more generally."[71] Faith is said to be a "core process in the total self-constitutive activity that is ego."[72] Fowler asserts that his theory of stage progression presumes and describes a simultaneous process of centering (individuation) and decentering of the self.[73]

The point of my criticism is not to deny that faith development involves centering and decentering of the self. Rather, the point is that this is not unique to faith development. Kohlberg's theory of moral development presumes and describes this centering and decentering as well, from a different angle. Nor do I wish to deny that faith development is a core process in ego development. Rather, the problem is that when Fowler makes such a claim in the context of his all-encompassing description of a faith stage while failing to deal with the core of faith, it then becomes impossible to distinguish between faith development and a general theory of development.

CONCLUSION

My argument has been that the complexity of Fowler's view of faith makes his concept of faith amorphous and unwieldy. In dealing with faith as relational, faith as knowing, and with the seven operational aspects of a faith stage, I have repeatedly pointed to ways in which, in my judgment, Fowler could sharpen his concept of faith and strengthen his theory. These suggestions all elaborate on my contention that Fowler has not integrated the core of faith (faith as commitment) into his entire theory. I have maintained that Fowler's theory dwells on what I called the second and third senses of faith. Fowler's theory would be greatly enhanced, I believe, if he devoted concentrated attention to the first sense. In proposing this, I am not suggesting that Fowler dispose of the second and third senses. Rather, I am suggesting that faith's role in integrating life and in shaping an image of the ultimate environment be dealt with *from the vantage point* of the first sense (trust and commitment). This would allow Fowler to continue making the point, for example, that faith is *for life* without tending to let faith become a totality word.

A focus on the first sense of faith would make it possible to explore whether there are identifiable patterns of *commitment,* and whether they can be correlated with patterns of integration in life. This would break through the amorphous character of Fowler's stage descriptions and greatly strengthen his case for the viability of a theory of faith development. Further, such a focus would, I believe, allow Fowler to provide a much sharper account of the distinguishing features of faith knowing. If it is possible to develop a case for knowing-in-commitment as a unique form of knowing, then the whole discussion of the relation of the two "logics" could be advanced considerably. Similarly, a focus on the first sense of faith could clarify and enhance Fowler's consideration of faith as relational.

This critique of Fowler's understanding of faith provides the beginnings of a proposed agenda for the further development of his theory. The first order of business on that agenda is to get a firm grasp on the core of the faith cube. Without such a grasp, the many valuable elements in Fowler's theory will tend to dissipate.

NOTES

1. James W. Fowler, "Faith and the Structuring of Meaning," in *Toward Moral and Religious Maturity,* ed. J. Fowler and A. Vergote (Morristown, N.J.: Silver Burdett, 1980), p. 53.

2. See James W. Fowler, *Stages of Faith* (San Francisco: Harper & Row, 1981), p. 32.

3. Ibid., p. 92.

4. Lawrence Kohlberg, *The Philosophy of Moral Development,* Essays on Moral Development, Vol. I (San Francisco: Harper & Row, 1981), p. 335.

5. See *Stages of Faith,* p. 24; also James W. Fowler, "Faith Development and the Aims of Religious Socialization," in *Emerging Issues in Religious Education,* ed. G. Durka and J. Smith (New York: Paulist Press, 1976), p. 204.

6. James W. Fowler, "Moral Stages and the Development of Faith," in *Moral Development, Moral Education, and Kohlberg,* ed. B. Munsey (Birmingham, Ala.: Religious Education Press, 1980), p. 135.

7. Fowler, *Stages of Faith,* p. 33.

8. Fowler, "Moral Stages and the Development of Faith," p. 134.

9. Ibid., p. 135.

10. Ibid., p. 134.

11. Ibid., p. 136.

12. Ibid., p. 137.

13. Fowler, *Stages of Faith,* p. 11.

14. Ibid.

15. For a list of these issues, see "Stages in Faith: The Structural Developmental Approach," in *Values and Moral Development,* ed. T. Hennessey (New York: Paulist Press, 1976), p. 181; and *Stages of Faith,* pp. 3, 309-12.

16. Fowler, *Stages of Faith,* p. 92.

17. Fowler, "Stages in Faith," p. 175.

18. Jim Fowler and Sam Keen, *Life Maps* (Waco, Texas: Word Books, 1978), p. 18.

19. Fowler, "Stages in Faith," p. 175.

20. Fowler, "Faith and the Structuring of Meaning," p. 54.

21. See Fowler, "Stages in Faith," pp. 175-79.

22. Fowler, "Faith and the Structuring of Meaning," p. 54.

23. Ibid., p. 55.

24. Fowler and Keen, *Life Maps,* p. 21.

25. Fowler, "Faith and the Structuring of Meaning," p. 55.

26. Fowler and Keen, *Life Maps,* pp. 20, 21.

27. Ibid., p. 21.

28. Fowler, "Faith and the Structuring of Meaning," p. 56.

29. Ibid.

30. Fowler and Keen, *Life Maps,* p. 21.

31. Fowler, "Faith and the Structuring of Meaning," p. 56.

32. Ibid.

33. Fowler, *Stages of Faith,* p. 18.

34. Ibid., p. 33.

35. Ibid., p. 18.

36. Ibid.

37. Ibid., p. 98.

38. Fowler, "Faith and the Structuring of Meaning," p. 57.

39. Ibid., p. 58.

40. Ibid., p. 59.

41. Ibid.

42. Ibid.

43. Ibid.
44. Ibid., p. 60.
45. Ibid., p. 61.
46. Ibid., p. 60.
47. Ibid., p. 61.
48. Ibid., p. 60.
49. Ibid., pp. 61-62.
50. See Fowler, *Stages of Faith,* p. 103.
51. Fowler, "Faith and the Structuring of Meaning," p. 64.
52. Ibid.
53. Fowler, *Stages of Faith,* p. 103.
54. Ibid.
55. Ibid., p. 25.
56. Fowler, "Faith and the Structuring of Meaning," p. 63.
57. Ibid., pp. 64-65.
58. See Thomas Groome, *Christian Religious Education* (San Francisco: Harper & Row, 1980), pp. 141ff.
59. Fowler, *Stages of Faith,* p. 11.
60. Fowler, "Faith and the Structuring of Meaning," p. 53.
61. Fowler, "Stages in Faith," p. 186.
62. Fowler and Keen, *Life Maps,* pp. 39-41.
63. Fowler, "Faith and the Structuring of Meaning," p. 77.
64. Ibid., p. 79.,
65. See Fowler, *Stages of Faith,* ch. 22.
66. Fowler, "Faith and the Structuring of Meaning," p. 76.
67. Ibid.
68. Ibid., p. 78.
69. Fowler, "Faith Development and the Aims of Religious Socialization," p. 199.
70. Fowler, "Stages in Faith," p. 191.
71. Ibid., p. 205.
72. Fowler "Faith and the Structuring of Meaning," p. 64.
73. See Fowler, "Faith Development and the Aims of Religious Socialization," p. 200.

Chapter 4

The Political Psychology of Faith Development Theory

JOHN M. BROUGHTON

It seems, as one grows older,
That the past has another pattern,
    and ceases to be a mere sequence—
Or even development; the latter a partial fallacy
Encouraged by superficial notions of evolution,
Which becomes, in the popular mind,
    a means of disowning the past.
            —T. S. Eliot, *The Four Quartets*

In order to understand both the power and the problems of
Fowler's theory of faith development, it is important to be aware
of the intellectual tradition in which it stands—and to which it
contributes as it works toward the development of a new psychology of religion. The power and the problems of faith development
theory participate in the power and problems of this larger heritage, which, I shall argue, contains within it a political ideology
which should not be left implicit and unexamined.

Faith development theory has its intellectual origins in the
American functionalist, pragmatist, and symbolic interactionist
traditions. Distally, James Fowler's ideas owe much to the turn-of-
the-century introduction of genetic psychology into theology
brought about by Mark Baldwin, Josiah Royce, and George Herbert Mead.[1] Proximally, he draws on the evolutionary and developmental concepts transmitted by the modern descendents of the
University of Chicago and Harvard postwar social science: Tal-
cott Parsons, Robert Bellah, Erik Erikson, Lawrence Kohlberg,
and H. Richard Niebuhr.[2]

Fowler resurrects the psycho-theology of his distal forebears. "Faith," in this tradition, is conceived as the process and product of psychological development—and psychological development originates and culminates in faith. "Faith" gives the psyche its self-consciousness, its unity, and its possibility of stage by stage transcendence. It relates the psyche to "a center of value and power,"[3] an "ultimate environment, an environment of environments, in relation to which we make sense of the force field of our lives."[4] It is a safety net that prevents us from disappearing into "the abyss of mystery that surrounds us."[5]

Faith, defined by Fowler in terms of personal responsiveness to divine creation and action, is indispensible to human life and inherent in human nature. Faith transcends cultural and historical differences—*and* religious differences. It is an innate potential for social interactivity and self-consciousness that is manifested equally, although differently, by proponents of different religions and even by those who are not religious. Here, faith development theory departs sharply from the views of its distal ancestors for whom, traditionally, the concept of faith has served to demarcate the sphere of religious phenomena from other realities. Faith development theory holds that faith is "prior to our being religious or irreligious,"[6] and is "at once deeper and more personal than religion."[7] Only by a specific conversion does faith become qualified as specifically religious faith or further qualified in terms of a particular denomination.

By defining faith in this way, Fowler allows the development of cognition in general to be the basis of faith development. Faith is a form of "knowing"[8] in which the ego's concepts and "images"[9] are central. Faith cultivates itself through the search for cognitive understanding. Consequently, faith development theory is a form of cognitive-developmental ego psychology. Appropriated through a conceptual merger of Kohlberg's work with Erikson's,[10] ego psychology becomes Fowler's theoretical "center of power and value." Much of the appeal of faith development theory derives from its ability to capitalize upon the considerable power, scope, and empirical fruitfulness of the secular cognitive-developmental tradition.

Cognitive-developmental theory is philosophically attractive because it is able to order types of faith orientation as more or less "adequate"[11] according to the different degrees of developmental differentiation, coherence, and adaptation they exhibit. The epistemological appeal of such an approach lies in the fact that the prescribed sequence of improvement in faith is not dependent upon nonrational biological maturation, socialization, or learning.[12] The ethical and political appeal is that the stage sequence is therefore "natural," increasing the legitimacy of encouraging individuals to move through it. The educational appeal is that the theory specifies the mechanism (equilibration) whereby movement occurs.

EMPIRICAL AND METHODOLOGICAL PROBLEMS

The research on which faith development theory claims to rest has a variety of problematic aspects to it. For example, Fowler reports that out of 359 individuals studied, only one case of "stage 6" was found. He also reports an apparent superiority of the scores of male subjects over those of female subjects,[13] a finding that he fails to account for. There are also many problems of design and method; for example, the marked ethnic and religious bias of the sample, the use of cross-sectional rather than longitudinal design, the lack of rationale for the repertoire of interview questions, the circular, self-fulfilling nature of the coding and scoring procedures, and the failure to demonstrate intraindividual structural consistency either within the faith domain or between faith and other domains of cognitive development. It would seem that some of these desiderata may be remediable.

Perhaps the most serious methodological difficulty is one that is intrinsic to the Rogerian style of interviewing that the research employed. It allows autobiography to eclipse the interviewer's potential attempts at biography.[14] Since neither clinical symbolic interpretation nor cognitive structural probing were used, the derivation of the stages and the coding of interviews in terms of them are incapable of distinguishing between factual reports and fabrications, actual beliefs and verbally espoused beliefs, reality and phantasy, conscious and unconscious, real self and false self, or insight and defense mechanism. The theory thus rests on three assumptions: (1) that we know ourselves objectively, (2) that the actual self is identical with the self-image and self-presentation, and (3) that the interview situation itself is one without systematic constraint. Unfortunately, these are assumptions that the research of clinical and social psychologists has shown to be largely unwarranted.

It is a sad consequence of the idealism in cognitive-developmental theory that it has ceased to be interested in actual experiences, actions, beliefs, or existence. It has, in reality, subordinated "accommodation" to "assimilation."[15] Real world events, concrete materiality, sensuous apprehension, and authentic subjectivity all pale in the dominant luminosity of cognitive structure. "Worldview" replaces the world itself, "sense of self" and "self-image" replace the actuality of self, and "sense of community" supplants actual community.[16] Even the ultimate environment has been replaced with "the ultimate environment as faith has imaged it."[17]

IS FAITH UNIVERSAL?

Fowler defines faith both broadly and narrowly. On the one hand, the scope of "faith" is such that all worldviews—theistic, nontheistic, and even atheistic—are included. Even the youngest child or most ignorant adult has faith. Only nihilists do not. On the other hand, like Niebuhr, Fowler is informed by anthropology and comparative religion which lead him to distinguish genuine or "radical monotheistic" faith from spurious "polytheistic" and idolatrous "henotheistic" faiths. (The criteria that he uses are enumerated in Table 1.) Stage 6, the ultimate form of genuine faith, is "universalizing" in character. It transcends particularistic ("henotheistic") commitments to specific churches, political movements, philosophies, or ideologies.

However, when we look at what faith development theory does rather than what it says, we find some peculiar departures from its own ideals. When Fowler lists kinds of faith, he tends to exclude anything other than formal religions, particularly theistic ones.[18] Among the religions, he ignores oriental ones almost entirely. In fact, he gives short shrift to anything outside the Judeo-Christian tradition. The central image that he chooses in his definition to stage 6 is the biblical "kingdom of God."[19] More-

Table 1: The ten criteria used by Fowler to distinguish genuine or "radical monotheistic" faith from other kinds of faith

Intensity	Faith must involve a deep conviction.
Ultimacy	The object of concern must be of "ultimate" or "absolute" worth, not relative worth.
Genuineness	The center of value must be real, not "false" or "inappropriate."
Centrality	The ultimate concern must be a major one, not a "minor center of value and power."
Unity	Faith must be a unified "orientation of the total person."
Objectivity	The conviction of faith cannot be self-oriented or just a "focal unity of personality and outlook."
Singularity	Faith must be singular rather than multiple; totality and intensity are insufficient.
Permanence	Faith must have a constancy and "loyalty" and not be "transient" or "shifting."
Transcendence	The center of value and power that is the ultimate concern must surpass particular, "finite," or "parochial" commitments.
Universality	Faith must take a form fit for all human beings, everywhere, at all times, capable of being definitive of human life itself.

over, the "Judeo-" tends to drop away, leaving Christianity as the major focus.[20] In this regard, it should be noted that over 80 percent of the sample for his empirical study were Christians. This suggests that Fowler, his colleagues, and their audience are subject to a pressing interest in the development of *Christians,* an interest at cross-purposes with their espoused concern about faith development in general.[21]

Although faith development theory formulates its task as charting the discovery of "the absoluteness of particularity,"[22] it never seriously attempts to show how this discovery of the universal might take place. Somehow, stage-by-stage cognitive equilibration is presumed to eventuate in such a discovery. But the "still-shots" of the stages do not a movie make. Rather, their discreteness and structural character tend to obscure the very process by which "faith cultivates itself."[23]

Furthermore there is a kind of possessive individualism to faith development theory. The exclusively psychological approach leaves the impression that "inter-faith differences"[24] can be resolved by multiple individual development alone, without differing groups ever having to understand each other or learn how to coexist. But if the complex difficulties of communication and rational persuasion between different faith groups are preempted, it is hard to see how, in practice, faith would ever be universalized.

THE PROBLEMATIC NATURE OF "STAGE 6"

The failure of faith development theory to account explicitly and clearly for either the universality or the universalizability of faith is related to a certain incoherence in the way that the final stage of faith development is conceptualized. The aura of mystery surrounding stage 6 is heightened by the fact that Fowler fails to tell us about the one man out of 359 studied who managed to meet the stringent criteria specified for the attainment of this level. When Fowler gives examples of stage 6, he ignores the exceptional individual located by his own study and refers instead to well-known figures (e.g., King, Hammarskjold, and Gandhi). These figures could be said to possess, not only public visibility, but also a certain world-historical importance. Although they were "religious" men, their historical significance was more a matter of their political power and effectiveness. However, they have not been studied by Fowler and his colleagues, nor could they ever be interviewed since they are deceased. Thus, in these exemplary cases, the appropriateness of the theoretical interpretation of the "data" of their lives is beyond validation. In the only instance where Fowler presents such data and shows how the theory interprets them, the deceased political-historical figure— Malcolm X—comes out at stage 5, not stage 6.[25]

Fowler's claims concerning the attainment of ultimate faith by King, Hammarskjold, Gandhi, and others are based, not on available data, but on appeal to our intuitions and general level of admiration.[26] Our respect is certainly great for the heroism of these men whose dissent against the illegitimate authority of dominant race, state, nationalism, or empire entailed their risking their lives. However, our opinion tends to be more a reflection of their moral and political significance than the salience of their religious or even nonreligious faith.

The empirical rarity of stage 6 and the particular kinds of individuals who exhibit such a structure suggest that there may be a discontinuity between the highest level of faith and the previous levels. This observation is reinforced by the fact that the stage 6 individuals whom Fowler discusses have been assessed by him through a different method than that which he prescribes for the study of subjects in his empirical research. The stage 6 accolade seems to be ascribed only on the basis of retrospective biography,[27] while the other stages are ascribed on the basis of retrospective autobiography.

The discontinuity is further underlined by the rather intellectual quality of Fowler's prototypical examples. The paragons of faith tend to be individuals who were able not only to act, but also to formulate their vision in a theoretical, sometimes theological fashion. They communicated with considerable rhetorical skill through speeches and/or written tracts. The very definition of stage 6 seems to presuppose such reflective, theoretical, and rhetorical capacities.[28] The famous men held up as examples were, on the whole, rather highly educated, and their education was at established Western institutions. This brings "development" closer to "learning" and so threatens the apparent naturalness of the stage sequence that is crucial to the appeal of cognitive developmental theory. The claims of cognitive developmental theory that only *content* can be learned, while formal structure can only develop, would appear to be unexamined assumptions.[29] Once the matter is looked into, it turns out that they are incorrect assumptions: sociologists have documented empirically that modern education is designed precisely to inculcate a structural *form* of consciousness.[30]

By introducing into the "developmental" attainment of mature faith the form or structure of educational acquisitions, faith development theory further undermines the potential universality and universalizability of faith. It slides from fact to value, from "is" to "ought." Moreover, since educational privileges are tied to the way in which societies are segmented and stratified by class,[31] developmental stage, like I.Q., becomes confounded with existing social hierarchy.[32] The way that the current constitution of the meritocratic structure *is* turns almost imperceptibly into the only rational way that it *ought to be*. Insofar as the policy implications of faith development theory are pursued, this established structural form of inequitable advancement thereby becomes the only rational way that development *can be*. By such a series of tacit elisions, what we happen to be is transformed into what we must be.[33]

When we see this, we see one dimension of the subtle politics of cognitive-developmental psychology. As Piaget demonstrated, cognitive development constructs the *a priori* logical form of true knowledge and is therefore a matter of the production of *necessity* itself. The necessary is the medium of power and power is always political. But it is very subtle, since no one can be accused of coercion for encouraging or facilitating someone's doing what is necessary and unavoidable. Still, knowledge implies power. The fact of voluntary choice does not cancel that implication. Knowledge is still a form of power when someone is so convinced of its necessity that it serves to elicit his or her voluntary submission to the assumptions that it embodies. This is the preemptive power that constitutes the political dimension of knowledge: its faculty for convincing us of a single course of action on the grounds of an implicit presupposition that no other is possible.

DOES GOD EXIST?

The discontinuity between stage 6 and the previous stages is apparent also in the relation posited between the stage 6 individual and "the Transcendent." At stage 6, there is supposed to be a direct relation of the self to the Transcendent. However, development through the stages up to that point certainly could not be attributed to such a relationship. According to the cognitive developmental theory that is the basis of faith development theory, movement through the stages must derive from the natural cognitive process of progressive equilibration through social interaction. It is through cognitive organization and adaptation that faith cultivates itself. Appeal to some supernatural object is entirely superfluous in accounting for developmental progress of this kind. When a progressivist conception of rationality is adopted, faith itself ceases to serve as a motive force in cognitive evolution. Faith becomes more like a content within the self-organizing form of the evolving structures. Thus the idea that the prime mover is some supernatural object seems to be grafted awkwardly onto the top end of an otherwise naturalistic sequence. Insofar as Fowler is able to convince us to share in his commitment to the cognitive developmental approach, then, the existence of a relationship to the Transcendent appears difficult to justify. His failure to give any serious consideration to the relationship of faith to reason makes the theistic commitment at the top end of the scale of rational development appear to be a parochial preference, particularistic rather than universalistic in nature.[34] Consequently, the claims for the natural superiority of the final stage take on a quality of arbitrariness.

A second reason for uncertainty about the existence of the Transcendent arises from Fowler's subjectivism. As we saw above, the interview method employed by Fowler and colleagues confounds objective reality with the subjective sense that we have of it. Fowler tends to speak of our "*image* of the ultimate environment,"[35] not that ultimate environment itself. He speaks about the content of faith as "*human relatedness* to the Transcendent,"[36] not the Transcendent itself. In describing stage 6, he focuses on subjectively apprehended qualities of the ultimate object, such as its "attractiveness."[37] One's *sense* of it is more salient than its objective presence. One lives with a "*felt* participation in a power."[38] Even those terrestrial sons of God, the rare stage 6 individuals, are characterized by the way they appear to us: they "*seem* more lucid, more simple, and yet somehow more fully human than the rest of us."[39] They are "contagious."[40] They "are often experienced as subversive."[41]

There is a third major reason that faith development theory communicates uncertainty about the existence of the Transcendent: its equivocality concerning the form that the Transcendent is supposed to take. The theory defines faith in terms of a "center of value and power,"[42] "worthy to give our lives unity and meaning,"[43] thus permitting an "orientation of the total person."[44] The vague, abstract spatiality of the geometric term "center" gives the phrase "center of value and power" a distinctly noncommittal quality. It certainly avoids the question of whether or not the Transcendent has personal qualities of the kind that have come to be associated with the term "God."[45] In fact, Fowler describes the "center" in vague and subjective terms, as though it referred to nothing more than the organizational capacity of mind or the centripetal feeling of "getting it together" which that capacity gives rise to.

Furthermore, when Fowler deals with the "power" of the Transcendent, he tends to do so by referring negatively to it as "not subject to personal control."[46] He fails to speak positively about its actual activity or efficacy, for example, in its capacity to direct individual lives. Here, once again, one suspects divided loyalties, since cognitive developmental psychology would suggest that the motive force in development derives from equilibration and adaptation immanent to the life process, not from the Transcendent.

However, if the "center" is not granted agency, any reference to it as a substantial reality—an existence beyond the subject's personal mental world—would appear to constitute a *reification*. At best, it would possess transcendence only in a metaphorical sense. The sacred would collapse into the profane; devotion, worship, petitioning, indeed all the religious sentiments and practices, would appear as idolatrous and necessarily "henotheistic." Faith in general would be interpretable as a mere projection of ego or ideal self. The object of ultimate concern would be hard to distinguish from an unresolved parental introject, just as Freud's skeptical account suggested some time ago.

THE STATE AS A CENTER OF VALUE AND POWER

We have seen how faith development theory tends to present part as whole, particularity as universality, and how the special concerns and commitments of stage 6 faith do not emerge as the natural outcome of psychological development. We have also seen that the theory tends to confound allegiance to mechanisms of equilibration with allegiance to the deity, how the given form of the developmental process may be mistaken for the ideal goal of all human aspiration and the fitting object of its admiration. Finally, we have discovered a variety of possible ways in which the objective existence of a Transcendent being may be indistinguishable from errors of projection, reification, or the literal interpretation of metaphor.

Much as we found that a particular psychological approach may provide a costume in which the structure of power can masquerade, we can draw connections between these various confusions inherent in faith development theory and the complex contradictions endemic to the structure of society. Thus the confusions that we have just been discussing—between self and other, centrality and agency, personal and impersonal, control and dependence, internal and external, reality and phantasy—are precisely those that characterize the relation of the individual to the state. We think of the state as external to us, yet rationally we know that we are an intrinsic part of it and have participated to some degree in making it what it is. It appears to operate in a sphere beyond our control, even though we know (from the examples of King, Gandhi, and Hammarskjold, for instance) that it actually is possible to fight City Hall. We confront its "agencies" and their apparent omnipotence, but, *a la* Kafka, find them powerless to help us. The agents of the state appear in human form, but are implacably impersonal. Bureaucracy is composed of and by people—among which we may sometimes number ourselves—but its "mechanisms" make us feel depersonalized. We experience fear and awe in the face of the authority of state agencies or officials and despite our antipathies feel genuine dependence upon them. We relate to them as real-life instantiations of our parental phantasies, often accepting and even stimulating their "paternalism." We take their regulatory mechanisms into ourselves, losing our sense of the distinctness of self and other, or of internal and external. We suffer repeatedly, but continue to have faith.

Is it possible that faith development theory has confounded these sentiments of the administrated, these subjective apprehensions of bureaucratized authority, with genuine religious experience? Is it possible that the "stages of faith" actually serve to mystify our sensitivity to the personal contradictions of life within modernized social structures? Has the separation of church and state made it possible for the latter to become heir to the affections that used to be directed to the former? Is this another example of what Marx and Engels called the "ideological" function of science and religion?[47] Is "faith development" a way of disguising subjection as salvation?

It certainly would appear to be the case that the criteria for genuine faith specify that intense and exclusive commitment must be made to a transcendent ideal but are incapable of excluding devotion to *malignant* centers of value and power. The pervasive subjectivism in the theory—apparent from the stress on "*felt* participation in a power" and encouraging us to admire those who "*seem* more lucid"—does not assist in the differentiation of good from bad or authoritative from authoritarian objects of ultimate concern. In fact, such stress on subjective potency and rhetorical force might well play into the malignant dynamics of what Wilhelm Reich called the "mass psychology of fascism" and Max Weber described as obeisance to "charismatic authority."

Fowler's remarks about autonomy and submission are particularly telling in this regard. He disparages "environments which place a premium on rational discourse . . . (and) encourage self-reliance and independence of perception, interpretation and action," classifying them at stage 4. Instead, he recommends "a post-critical theistic commitment," the central requirement for which is that one *"subordinate the self to something beyond the self."*[48] The autonomy of reason must be overruled by the surrender that faith is intent on making.

What is frightening about such deference to "sources of power and value which impinge on life in a manner not subject to personal control"[49] and which "exceed our grasp"[50] is that it would appear to be quite compatible with the abdication of reason and subjection of self required by totalitarian or even fascist regimes. It is precisely the feeling that the prevailing political power is beyond one's control that underwrites fanatical allegiance to malignant administrations, as writers from Marx to Adorno and Arendt have documented.[51] It is hard to find anything in faith development theory that offers resistance to such illegitimate allegiances. Rather, appeal to the utopian vision of a "kingdom" in which there is a "ruler" is suggestive of Machiavellian nostalgia for the feudal era of the deceased imperial patriarch. Fowler's unfortunate suggestion that concern for the "liberation and empowerment of minorities" typically represents a nonuniversalizing, henotheistic kind of faith[52] engenders the suspicion that the subordination of self in mature faith requires a subordination of movements aimed at emancipation from autocratic, monarchic, and colonial forces. In its haste to secure religious and quasi-religious experience from the voracious jaws of twentieth-century secularism, faith development theory appears to have run the serious risk of condoning oppressive ideals and of serving an ideological mystification of illegitimate authority by making blind obeisance to power appear like a natural development.

THE UNITY OF SELF AND THE
AUTHORITARIAN PERSONALITY

In tune with its interactionist commitment, faith development theory posits a unity of self corresponding to the putative unity of the Transcendent. This unity of self is conceived as an integrated and internally self-consistent organization of the individual person. This ordered state is brought about by faith.[53] Faith is the self's guidance system, an agency of control that regulates "the setting of our goals . . . the ways we respond to emergencies and crises . . . the ways we make plans."[54] The organizing capacities of faith are held to comprise the moral virtue of "ego integrity which is the ego's accrued assurance of its investment in order and meaning."[55] In short, it is the master program for organizing instrumental action and maintaining internal stability. Fowler has allowed "faith" to be assimilated to the concept of "the ego" as formulated by ego psychologists such as Erik Erikson, H. S. Sullivan, and Carl Rogers.[56] It is these theorists who reshaped the traditional European concept of the "self" in terms of American functionalist psychology, with its exclusive focus on instrumental action and the preservation of system equilibrium.[57]

Unfortunately, as writers such as T. W. Adorno, Paul Ricoeur, and J. Lacan have pointed out,[58] this systems approach has serious problems. It entails a constant tendency toward homogenization within the psyche, a continuous centripetal synthesizing of antinomies. "Development" then becomes synonymous with integrative organization. This makes it difficult to account for the considerable body of evidence that psychic life is not governed by a predominant tendency toward self-consistency.[59] Systems theory collapses existing tensions, particularly the dialectic between rational and irrational. Thus, in faith development theory, as in ego psychology, the relationship between the conscious and the unconscious is progressively eliminated.[60] The creative irrationality of dream, phantasy, and desire is homogenized with the ordered organization of conscious rationality. Even the concept of rationality is impoverished as reflective judgment is replaced by instrumental self-management.[61]

The fundamental problem with "unity" and "consistency" as criteria of development is that, like "complexity," they are utterly relativistic concepts.[62] Irrationality can be as unified or self-consistent as rationality.[63] Defense mechanisms use their monolithic consistency to create a "false self" and maintain self-deception.[64] The psychotic world system possesses a particularly complex and seamless unity of structure.[65]

What is omitted or disguised by the ego-psychological dilution of clinical discourse is the centrality and conflictedness of *authority* in the development of personality. Thus, when Fowler presents his interesting case study of "Mary,"[66] he downplays the rather obvious unconscious dynamic conflicts of authority that are at the root of her recurring life problems. When her concerns are parsed into scoring categories, authority issues are classified under the cognitive category "Locus of Authority." Authority itself is reduced to the *knowing* or *image* of authority. Within this mental domain called "Locus of Authority," progressive stage-by-stage development abstracts only formal relations and erases the significance of the specific relationship to the parents along with all other concrete life experiences. Like everyone else in the narrative of faith development, Mary learns the natural necessity of replacing concrete authorities with abstract ones, and of relocating in the internal world authority that was once invested in external objects. Here faith development theory simply repeats the standard social psychologists' concept of internalizing the "locus of control."[67]

From a clinical point of view, this type of blind, wholesale internalization of unresolved conflictual relations with authority represents a temporary pacification of the individual. It comprises an emergency defensive measure that contributes to the development of psychopathology.[68]

From a sociological or political point of view, it represents an example of the psychologization of prevailing conditions of authority that prevents any critical examination of their legitimacy.[69] Faith development theory is promoting a notion of maturation which requires that one develop more and more internal locus of control whether or not one actually has effective control over the political context of one's life. What is important is that one *have the sense of* being a self-determining individual.[70] One gains this feeling by privately managing one's own mind and body through a single internal control system that combines legislative and executive functions. Sequential structural revampings erase memories of loss and suffering and eliminate the possibility of conflict, leaving a general sense of well-being.

A thoroughly privatized self, organized hierarchically in this manner, possesses "ego integrity." It can write its own history, not from remembered experience, but from its insight into the rule-governed processes of structuration. It rewrites its life history as a spiral of systematic structural differentiation, integration, and upgrading (see Figure 1). The progressive formalization of sensuous social being—represented in Fowler's diagram by the replacement of identifiable persons with stick figures and then finally abstract geometric shapes—produces the sense of self-possession and inevitability:

Ego-integrity is . . . the experience of post-narcissistic love of the human ego—not of the self—as part of a world order. . . . It is an acceptance of one's own and only life cycle as something that had to be and that, by necessity, permitted of no substitutions. . . . The possessor of integrity is ready to defend the dignity of his or her own lifestyle against all physical and economic threats. For this person knows that all human integrity is at stake in the one style of integrity of which he or she partakes.[71]

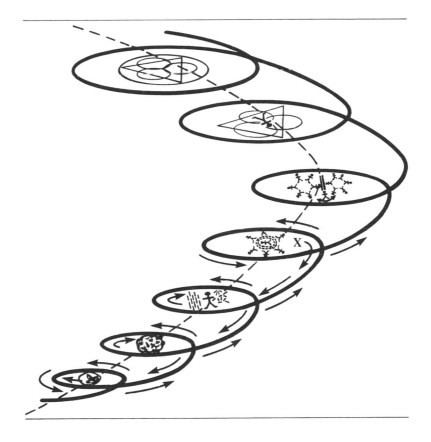

Figure 1: The spiral system of progressive abstraction in James Fowler's stages of faith. From *Stages of Faith,* James W. Fowler, published by Harper & Row, San Francisco, © 1981 James Fowler, reprinted by permission.

In this telling quotation we see how biography is transmuted into the predictable regularities of system growth. The end-point of structural development is reached when the individual appreciates fully that development is regulated, not by what you do, but by the way that you do it; life is life-"style." It is to this style of life that everyone gradually becomes accustomed. Once the self gains a complete grasp of the universality of this single growth principle that it obeys, it is able to identify the world with its own ego. The ego becomes a world unto itself. Its wholeness gives it the moral value of integrity. This value attached to the ego is its "accrued assurance of its investment in order."[72] The absolute conviction of its own integrity, which surpasses all narcissism, gives it the right of self-preservation and corrective action against any threat to this order. Thus private unification and wholeness are not as quiescent as they sound. We are reminded that liberal individualism is fiercely possessive, defending itself aggressively, and requiring that difference and disunity be opposed with force if necessary.[73]

The tragic quality of this vision, with its almost social Darwinist implications, is somehow not appreciated in faith development theory. Rather, the theory seems to aspire to an ideal world of unbridled assertiveness, of *hubris* free from *nemesis*.

THE RATIONALIZATION OF RELIGION

Faith development theory's failure to differentiate the life of faith from that of a politically submissive citizen corresponds to its failure to distinguish subjectivity from internal control. As the extensive researches of Adorno and others demonstrated, these are the concomitant social and psychological aspects, respectively, of the authoritarian relationship between state and individual.[74] Capitulation to the individualist imperatives of functional system organization and maintenance in the internal psychic world produces an individual who willingly cooperates in unquestioned conformity to the system imperatives of the bureaucratized political structure. It is this voluntary endorsement that the modern state requires in order to preserve its authority and protect it from criticism, while still maintaining the semblance of decentralization and participation necessary in democratic society.[75]

The submissive authoritarian personality is produced and promoted in the modern, privatized family through child-rearing techniques that foster arbitrary internalization and the rational management of desire.[76] Ironically, then, it is precisely the dissidents—the Gandhis, the Kings—that faith development theory cannot account for. Threatening to undermine social order and dying for a cause do not quite fit into the model of system equilibrium and survival at either the individual or societal levels.

Faith development theory has attempted to identify faith with the general integration and purposeful directedness of the self. The intention behind this formulation is ecumenical and cross-cultural in nature. However, in trying to transcend cultures and their specific traditions, the theory has succeeded only in dispensing with them. It has failed to recognize the socio-historical constitution of those traditions and has failed to appreciate the significance to the individual of appropriating interpretively a specific tradition of special meaning in relation to his or her special biography. The theorist's desire for universality has eventuated in an intolerance of specificity. Since the vital significance of tradition for an embodied life inheres in the meaning of a concretely experienced symbolic form,[77] "development" in Fowler's sense unwittingly requires detachment from the heritage of a specific culture. Thus "faith development" is not so much trans-traditional as *post*-traditional in nature. It requires a giving up of past and present in the hope of a utopian future, the future of democratic individualism or modernity, especially as conceived within the American sphere of influence.

This is why "faith" is presented in such a general way. In faith development theory, the universal is arrived at merely by disengaging from the national, ethnic, cultural, and religious specificities rather than by undertaking the difficult task of "introducing" them to each other. In traditional idealist fashion, integration is achieved through the supercession, denial, and dissolution of differentiation. In the quest for a principle of unification, pure generality is preferred to the political *action* of engaging differences in an attempt at mutual understanding that could flow into consensual social reconstruction. But the only thing of such generality that the various world inhabitants actually share is the context of the contemporary world-historical process. Currently, this is dominated by modernization.[78]

Like all "politically neutral" science, faith development theory cannot offer a challenge to, or even an interpretation of, modernization. As a consequence, it necessarily describes and prescribes an individual development that systematically converges with and unintentionally promotes the production of modernity. The imperatives of the world system[79] are imported into the individual person in the form of a quiescent, functional ego, intent only upon its own efficient rationalization and self-management. Since organization is the very air that this ego breathes, the individual is systematically incapable of discerning the structures of power and authority implicit in the form of organization itself. Resistance to such structures becomes simply irrelevant, and the production of alternative social orders totally inconceivable. Thus the need for direct political socialization is avoided. The requisite program for civilizing the individual is built into the precepts of "development" itself, as an invisible self-pedagogy.[80]

CONCLUSION

In failing to recognize the validity of cultural histories, faith development theory disowns its own past, in which were formed the specificity of its own socially located interests and the particular political goals implicit in its own practices. As a result it falls victim to its own history. This is why, despite Fowler's attempts to construct and maintain a seamlessly disinterested perspective, the same partiality keeps seeping through the cracks. The "faith development" endeavor, as theory and practice, is currently involved in the single-minded pursuit of a future whose reality conflicts in every respect with that endeavor's declared intentions. We can only hope that eventually, in the process of objectifying itself in its products, it will come to a salutary self-recognition. In reinterpreting its mission in the light of its own historical contribution, it would then deepen its own faith in a way that would truly deserve the name of "development." Under the conditions of such development, we would be in a better position to grapple with the question of what "the Transcendent" means, and to discover what kinds of relationship to it we conceivably might have. "We" would then be people, not systems, that develop. Our development might then be an action in which we engaged more or less freely and voluntarily.

NOTES

1. See, for example, J. M. Baldwin, *Social and Ethical Interpretations in Mental Development* (New York and London: Macmillan, 1897); J. Royce, *The World and the Individual* (New York and London: Macmillan, 1899); and G. H. Mead, *Mind, Self and Society* (Chicago: University of Chicago Press, 1934).

2. See, for example, T. Parsons, *Essays in Sociological Theory* (Glencoe, Ill.: Free Press, 1944) and *Toward a General Theory of Action* (Cambridge, Mass.: Harvard University Press, 1951); R. N. Bellah, "Religious Evolution," *American Sociological Review* 29 (1964), pp. 358-374; E. Erikson, *Insight and Responsibility* (New York: Norton, 1964); L. Kohlberg, "Stage and Sequence," in *Handbook of Socialization Theory and Research,* ed. D. Goslin (Chicago: Rand McNally, 1969); H. R. Niebuhr, *Radical Monotheism and Western Culture* (New York: Harper & Row, 1960).

3. J. Fowler, *Stages of Faith: The Psychology of Human Development and the Quest for Meaning* (New York: Harper & Row, 1981), p. 17.

4. Ibid., p. 28; cf. P. Tillich, *The Courage to Be* (New Haven, Conn.: Yale University Press, 1952), pp. 171-176.

5. Fowler, *Stages of Faith,* p. xii.

6. Ibid., p. 5.

7. Ibid., p. 9.

8. Ibid., p. 25.

9. Ibid.

10. See, for example, L. Kohlberg, "Continuities and Discontinuities in Moral Development Revisited," in *Lifespan Developmental Psychology,* Vol. III, ed. P. B. Baltes and K. W. Schaie (New York: Academic Press, 1973); G. G. Noam, L. Kohlberg, and J. Snarey, "Steps Toward a Model of the Self," in *Developmental Approaches to the Self,* ed. B. Lee and G. G. Noam (New York: Plenum Publishing Co., 1983).

11. J. Fowler, "Toward a Developmental Perspective on Faith," *Religious Education* 69 (1974), p. 218.

12. See Kohlberg, "Stage and Sequence."

13. These references to Fowler's empirical findings are all based on his most complete summary, presented in *Stages of Faith,* pp. 313-23. It should be noted that when Fowler gives examples of stage 6, the individuals that he chooses tend to be predominantly male. The one case of stage 6 that he was able to identify through his interview research was also a man.

14. See, for example, Fowler's interesting case study of "Mary" in *Stages of Faith,* pp. 217-268.

15. See R. H. Wozniak, "Dialecticism and Structuralism," in *Structure and Transformation,* ed. K. F. Riegel and G. C. Rosenwald (New York: Wiley, 1975); J. Glick's comments in J. M. Broughton, B. Leadbeater, and E. Amsel, eds., "Reflections on Piaget," *Teachers College Record* 83 (1981) 2, pp. 158-161; and J. M. Broughton, "Piaget's Structural Developmental Psychology," parts 3 and 4, *Human Development* 24 (1981), pp. 257-285 and 325-350.

16. See J. M. Broughton, "The Genetic Psychology of James Mark Baldwin," *American Psychologist,* 36 (1981) 4, pp. 396-407, and J. M. Broughton and K. F. Riegel, "Developmental Psychology and the Self," *Annals of the New York Academy of the Sciences* 291 (1977), pp. 149-167.

17. Fowler, *Stages of Faith,* p. 27.

18. See, for example, ibid., pp. 4 and 29.

19. See ibid., p. 29, and "Future Christians and Church Education," in *Hope for the Church: Moltmann in Dialogue with Practical Theology,* ed. T. Runyan (Nashville: Abingdon, 1979), p. 111.

20. Fowler, "Future Christians," p. 109. See also reference to Fowler's Christian critics in Fowler, *Stages of Faith,* p. 91.

21. See, for example, "James Fowler Talks with Lisa Kuhmerker About Faith Development," *Moral Education Forum* 3 (1978) 3, pp. 1-8, where Protestant concerns appear to dominate over other Christian orientations, suggesting an even greater difficulty in maintaining the ecumenical promise of the theory.

22. Fowler, *Stages of Faith,* p. 209.

23. This Anselmian notion, as mediated by the Niebuhrs (see, for example, R. R. Niebuhr, "Preface," to H. R. Niebuhr, *The Responsible Self* (New York: Harper & Row, 1963), p. 4, is central to Fowler's conception of the way in which faith develops.

24. On "inter-faith differences" and proposals for their resolution, see Fowler, *Stages of Faith,* p. 209.

25. J. Fowler and R. W. Lovin, *Trajectories in Faith* (Nashville: Abingdon, 1980).

26. It should also be noted that this aspect of faith development theory appears to encourage "The Great Man" approach to history. In addition, the exclusive modernity of the representative individuals chosen would appear to encourage the "Whig" interpretation of history that treats the past egocentrically only as a sequence leading up to the accomplishments of the present.

27. Biographical and autobiographical methods each possess their own advantages. From the point of view of validity, however, one important potential advantage of the biographical approach, as exhibited perhaps in Fowler's interesting study of Malcolm X in *Trajectories of Faith,* is that it does not necessarily equate self with self-report.

28. It is my impression that in the early phases of his work Fowler strove to represent heroic activist theists like Nate Shaw, the black sharecropper unionist (see T. Rosengarten, *All God's Dangers* [New York: Knopf, 1974]), as exhibiting advanced faith development despite illiteracy or other socio-cultural handicaps. Oppression itself was viewed as a major catalyst for faith development. However, the criteria for universalizing faith have since become more intellectual (cf. S. Keen, "Body/Faith: Trust, Dissolution, and Grace," in *Life Maps: Conversations on the Journey of Faith,* ed. J. Berryman [Waco: Word Books, 1978]), so much so that the current version of the theory is predisposed to view individuals like Shaw as "stage 4" at best (see Fowler, *Stages of Faith,* pp. 282-285).

29. See Kohlberg, "Stage and Sequence."

30. See, for example, B. Bernstein, *Class, Codes and Control,* Vols. 1-3 (London: Routledge & Kegan Paul, 1971-75); R. M. Kanter, "Experience Management in a Nursery School," *Sociology of Education* 45 (1972) 2, pp. 186-212; P. Bourdieu and J. C. Passeron. *Reproduction in Education, Society, and Culture*

(London: Sage Publications, 1977); M. Apple, *Ideology and Curriculum* (Boston: Routledge & Kegan Paul, 1979); and H. Giroux, *Theory and Resistance in Education* (South Hadley, Mass.: Bergin & Garvey, 1983).

31. See C. Jencks, *Inequality: A Reassessment of the Effect of Family and Schooling in America* (New York: Basic Books, 1972); S. Bowles and H. Gintis, *Schooling in Capitalist America* (New York: Basic Books, 1976); H. Entwhistle, *Class, Culture, and Education* (London: Methuen & Co., 1978); and P. Willis, *Learning to Labor* (New York: Columbia University Press, 1982).

32. Some remarks on this confounding are contained in A. Blasi, "Issues in Defining Stages and Types," in *Ego Development,* ed. J. Loevinger (San Francisco: Jossey-Bass, 1976); and in J. M. Broughton and M. K. Zahaykevich, "From Authoritarian Personality to Ego Development: Ideological Dimensions in Loevinger's Theory," in *Development Criticized,* ed. J. M. Broughton (submitted for publication).

33. See M. Foucault, *Power/Knowledge* (New York: Pantheon, 1980). Note that the homogenization of Piagetian scientific thinking (the "is") and Kohlbergian moral judgment (the "ought") within the structure of the faith stages serves to facilitate such elisions of fact, value, and power. The way in which apparently "neutral" social science theories conceal their "policy" dimensions is well explicated by B. Fay in his book *Social Theory and Political Practice* (London and Boston: Allen & Unwin, 1975). See also J. M. Broughton, "The Surrender of Control: Computer Literacy as Political Socialization of the Child," in *Computers in Education: Critical Perspectives,* ed. D. Sloan (New York: Teachers College Press, 1985).

34. E. Wallwork, "Morality, Religion, and Kohlberg's Theory," in *Moral Development, Moral Education, and Kohlberg,* ed. B. Munsey (Birmingham, Ala.: Religious Education Press, 1980).

35. Fowler, *Stages of Faith,* p. 28 (emphasis added). This infelicitous phrasing reflects that of H. Richard Niebuhr, for example, when he refers to faith cognitively as "the *reinterpretation* of existence" in *The Responsible Self,* p. 144 (emphasis added).

36. Fowler, "Toward a Developmental Perspective on Faith," p. 218 (emphasis added).

37. Ibid.

38. J. Fowler, "Moral Stages and the Development of Faith," in *Moral Development, Moral Education, and Kohlberg,* ed. B. Munsey (Birmingham, Ala.: Religious Education Press 1980), p. 149 (emphasis added).

39. Fowler, "Toward a Developmental Perspective," p. 127 (emphasis added).

40. Fowler, "Moral Stages," p. 149.

41. Ibid. (emphasis added). It should be noted that faith development theory tends to equate faith with the intuitive and arbitrary commitments commonly associated with the assumptions underlying rationality. (See J. Fowler, "Stages in Faith: The Structural-developmental Approach," in *Values and Moral Development,* ed. T. Hennessy [New York: Paulist Press, 1976], p. 209.) The incoherence of such a position on the relationship between faith and reason was originally spelled out in R. G. Collingwood, *Faith and Reason: Essays in the Philosophy of Religion* (Chicago: Quadrangle Books, 1968) and is demonstrated in the case of faith development theory by E. Wallwork, "Morality, Religion, and Kohlberg's Theory."

42. Fowler, *Stages of Faith,* p. 17.
43. Ibid.
44. Ibid., p. 14.
45. The typicality of associating personal qualities with "God" is documented by both Baldwin, *Social and Ethical Interpretations,* and E. Wallwork, "Religious Development," in *The Cognitive Developmental Psychology of James Mark Baldwin,* ed. J. M. Broughton and D. J. Freeman-Moir (Norwood, N.J.: Ablex Publishing Co., 1982). Both these authors argue persuasively that the meaning of "God" is lost when the deity is divested of personal qualities.
46. Fowler, "Stages in Faith," p. 175.
47. See K. Marx and F. Engels, *On Religion* (New York: Schocken Books, 1964). The Introduction to this volume is written by none other than Reinhold Niebuhr.
48. Fowler, "James Fowler Talks with Lisa Kuhmerker," p. 3 (emphasis added).
49. Fowler, "Stages in Faith," p. 175.
50. Fowler, *Stages of Faith,* p. 204.
51. See Marx and Engels, *On Religion;* T. W. Adorno, E. Frenkel-Brunswik, D. J. Levinson, and R. N. Sanford, *The Authoritarian Personality* (New York: Norton, 1950); and H. Arendt, *The Origins of Totalitarianism* (New York: Harcourt, Brace & World, 1951).
52. Fowler, *Stages of Faith,* p. 21. It should be noted that Fowler equivocates on this issue. He points to a "more noble form of henotheistic faith (in which) identity is found in losing the self in the service of a transcendingly important, if finite, cause" (ibid.). Again, it is the psychological attitude of surrender that qualifies this relationship for approbation. However, Fowler points out the instrumental nature of such henotheism: for good causes to have impact "they have to be loved by a few people for far more than they are worth" (ibid.). The "few" suggests the relative rarity of this noble henotheism. The "more than they are worth" underlines the still spurious quality of its attempted universalization. "The transcending center of value and power . . . is inappropriate, false, not something of ultimate concern" (ibid., p. 20). It is, in fact, exactly that "noble lie" that Plato recommends for its social utility in the *Republic.*
53. See, for example, J. Fowler, "Faith and the Structuring of Meaning," in *Toward Moral and Religious Maturity,* ed. J. Fowler and A. Vergote (Morristown, N.J.: Silver Burdett Co., 1980), p. 65; Fowler, *Stages of Faith,* pp. 14 and 86; and Fowler, *Life Maps,* p. 1.
54. Fowler, *Stages of Faith,* p. 97.
55. Ibid., p. 86.
56. Perhaps the first to note that faith development theory is a theory of ego development was J. Snarey, "Review of *Toward Moral and Religious Maturity,*" *Journal of Moral Education* 12 (1983) 2, p. 137. On the ideological problems of ego psychology and its relationshp to G. H. Mead's symbolic interactionism (so influential in H. R. Niebuhr's thinking), see J. M. Broughton, "The History, Psychology and Ideology of the Self," in *Psychology and Ideology,* ed. K. Larsen (Norwood, N.J.: Ablex Publishing Co., 1986).
57. See J. M. Broughton, "From Substance to Function: Psychology and the History of the Self," in *Psychology: Theoretical-Historical Perspectives,* ed. R. W. Rieber and K. W. Salzinger (New York: Academic Press, 1980). See

also, R. Jacoby, *Social Amnesia* (Boston: Beacon Press, 1975), who describes in some detail the way in which Freud's concept of the "ego" was appropriated by American functionalist psychology as the agent of rationality for the purpose of the bureaucratic administration of the self.

58. See T. W. Adorno, "Sociology and Psychology," parts 1 and 2, *New Left Review* 46 (1967), pp. 67-80, and 47 (1968), pp. 79-97; P. Ricoeur, *Freud and Philosophy* (New Haven, Conn.: Yale University Press, 1970); and J. Lacan, *Ecrits* (New York: Norton, 1977).

59. See J. Voneche, "Commentary," *Toward a Theory of Psychological Development,* eds. S. Modgil and C. Modgil (Slough, Eng.: NFER Publishing Co., 1980); and E. Wallwork, "Religious Development," p. 383.

60. See, for example, the way in which faith development theory proposes that at the advanced levels of faith development there is an "integration" of unconscious processes with conscious ones (Fowler, *Stages of Faith,* p. 186).

61. On the instrumentalisation of rationality in cognitive developmental theory, see Broughton, "Piaget's Structural Developmental Psychology."

62. See Broughton and Zahaykevich, "From Authoritarian Personality to Ego Development."

63. See D. J. Bem, *Beliefs, Attitudes and Human Affairs* (Belmont, Calif.: Brooks-Cole Publishing Co., 1970), pp. 13ff.

64. See D. W. Winnicott, *The Maturational Processes and the Facilitating Environment* (New York: International Universities Press, 1965); and R. D. Laing, *The Divided Self* (London: Tavistock Publications, 1960).

65. See J. Gabel, *False Consciousness* (Oxford: Blackwell, 1975). Gabel documents the ways in which the self-deceptive psychotic world meshes with societal ideology, a view that is reflected in Laing's work.

66. Fowler, *Stages of Faith,* pp. 217-268.

67. See R. deCharms, *Personal Causation* (New York: Academic Press, 1968). On this topic of control, see Broughton, "The Surrender of Control."

68. See W. R. Fairbairn, *Psychoanalytic Studies of the Personality* (London: Routledge & Kegan Paul, 1952); and J. Benjamin, "The Decline of the Oedipus Complex," in *Toward a Critical Developmental Psychology,* ed. J. M. Broughton (New York: Plenum Publishing Co., 1986).

69. See Adorno, "Sociology and Psychology"; Adorno et al., *The Authoritarian Personality;* and Jacoby, *Social Amnesia.*

70. See Broughton, "The History, Psychology, and Ideology of the Self." See also the excellent critique of "locus of control" theory by L. Furby, "Individualistic Bias in Studies of Locus of Control," in *Psychology in Social Context,* ed. A. Buss (New York: Irvington, 1979).

71. Fowler, *Stages of Faith,* p. 86.

72. Ibid.

73. See C. B. MacPherson, *The Political Theory of Possessive Individualism* (Oxford: Oxford University Press, 1962).

74. See Adorno et al., *The Authoritarian Personality.*

75. See H. Marcuse, *One Dimensional Man* (Boston: Beacon Press, 1964).

76. See J. Kovel, "Rationalization and the Family," *Telos* 37 (1978), pp. 5-21; D. Dinnerstein, *The Mermaid and the Minotaur* (New York: Harper & Row, 1977); and Benjamin, "The Decline of the Oedipus Complex."

77. See E. Cassirer, *The Philosophy of Symbolic Forms* (New Haven, Conn.:

Yale University Press, 1953); and P. Ricoeur, *Conflict of Interpretations* (Evanston, Ill.: Northwestern University Press, 1974).

78. See P. Berger, B. Berger, and H. Kellner, *The Homeless Mind* (New York: Random House, 1973).

79. See I. Wallerstein, *The Modern World System* (New York: Academic Press, 1974).

80. See B. Bernstein, "Class and Pedagogies: Visible and Invisible," in *Class, Codes and Control,* Vol. 3, ed. B. Bernstein (London: Routledge & Kegan Paul, 1975).

Chapter 5

Completion and Faith Development

MARIA HARRIS

In *Images of Faith,* William Lynch writes, "I have always thought that the best way to write a book for Everyone . . . is to grasp hold of a question that has long been meaningful and important for yourself, then to objectify it, externalize it into public and human terms, so that (one hopes) it does not remain private . . . but becomes a public question in which a good number of the tribe will be interested."[1] As a religious educator, teacher, and designer of curriculum, I have been grasping hold of three such questions for some time, and our discussion on faith development provides a singular occasion to raise them with the tribe.

My first question concerns *knowing* and the emphasis on one form of knowing in education, an emphasis which can be filled out and completed by art. My second concerns *experience* and the emphasis on the experience of one segment of humanity in education, an emphasis which can be filled out and completed through sisterhood. My third concerns *time* and the emphasis on activity and individuality in time, an emphasis which can be filled out and completed through Sabbath. In this essay, my intention is to write of the three questions of knowledge, experience, and time through the "companions" of art, sisterhood, and Sabbath, drawing from each implications for faith development theory. My underlying metaphor is *completion.* I am eager for religious education to have and to be what this metaphor connotes: in possession of all necessary parts: fullness, entirety, wholeness. However, I would ask the reader not to understand me too quickly. I am not asserting conclusions about faith development theory. Rather, I am saying: let us begin here, in the context of completion in religious education, and after reflection on the fullness offered by art, sisterhood, and Sabbath together consider the implications, if any, for faith development theory.

ART AND THE COMPLETION OF KNOWING

A prevailing understanding of knowing exists in curriculum and teaching today, whether in the setting of a seminary ("theological education") or of the schools of our nation, or of church schools, or of textbooks, or, indeed, of a society which teaches us the meaning of mature, educated adults. It is an understanding which equates knowledge with what is definite, objective, publicly verifiable; as what enables control of the physical world. Knowledge, in many sectors, is equivalent to information, facts, concepts, technical skill ("know-how"). Knowledge is the same as the possession of categories which enable us to organize reality. The word "cognitive," itself an abstraction, is assumed to be at its "highest" when one attains the capacity for abstract, "formal" mental operations, a limitation alluded to several times in *Stages of Faith.*[2] The assumed division of educational objectives into cognitive and affective offers a separation and a split too readily acceded to, without examining whether the division itself is false. One of the most impressive aspects of faith development theory is the awareness, expressed in *Stages of Faith,* of a need to enlarge, enrich, and complete knowing. Indeed, artistic knowing is exemplified throughout, from the *Ordinary People*[3] citation at the beginning to the continuing emphasis on and return to imagination. The work is obviously aware of and attentive to a perfection of knowing, although at the same time characterized ineluctably by the scientific emphasis on knowing so prevalent in this century.

We trace the emphasis on this one form of knowing back, of course, to Descartes: "I think, therefore I am"; not "I love, therefore I am," "I care, therefore I am," or even, "I am *imago Dei,* therefore I am." This is a method and a metaphor leading to a vision of ourselves as "decorpitated"—as disembodied minds.

William Blake once commented on the result and loss created by such a truncated view of knowing:

> Entering into the Reasoning Power
> forsaking Imagination, they became Spectres.
> —from *Albion*

The knowing I describe, nevertheless, *is* knowing. Further, such rational, scientific, conceptual knowledge is of inestimable value. I do not wish to be understood as lamenting, disparaging, or belittling a form of knowing which makes arid land fertile, unlocks the secrets of obscure texts, or repairs damaged hearts. What is lamentable and discouraging is the equation of *all* knowing with this one form of knowing, and even more lamentable, because so limiting of us humanly, the separation, the split, the divorce in our ways of knowing. To speak of desiring completion is appropriate here. That desire is that knowing have all its necessary parts—in order that we human beings, in our knowing may be full, fulfilled, entire, whole. So that we may be complete. I know of no companion more suited to empowering such completion than art. It may be the companion in knowing that faith development theory seeks.

Philosopher Susanne Langer suggests an interpretation of artistic knowing in *Philosophy in a New Key*.[4] She writes of our ordinary form of knowing, discourse or *discursive form,* as one which has a vocabulary and a syntax, definable, translatable meanings, and the capacity of general reference. Discourse implies words strung out in linear fashion and the intent to communicate ideas, concepts, thought.[5] If this is the only form for knowing we possess, everything we know can, of course, be said—and what cannot be said cannot be known, a position taken by some contemporary linguistic philosophers. But, Langer continues, this is not so. We *do* possess other forms of knowing which are particularly appropriate for "unspeakable things," where our sense of receiving knowledge comes from encountering being "all of a piece." These are forms of knowing where, although the medium of words is used, but not discursively, other media are also appropriate: sound, as in music; silence, as in prayer; stone and wood, as in sculpture; color, shape, line, the human body itself. Such forms, rather than offering understanding discursively or conversationally, project experience metaphorically and symbolically. These forms preserve multiple interpretation and enable us to know what is not amenable to discourse—to know, in contrast to discourse, unspeakable things. Art is this kind of form, a *presentational* form. Langer's definition of art as "the creation of perceptible form expressive of human feeling"[6] suggests the kind of knowledge art is: knowledge which enlarges and widens intelligence and rationality, knowledge available in no other way. Such knowledge, paradoxically, is the sort where

> Knowing slows for a moment
> And not-knowing enters, silent,
> Bearing being itself.[7]

One begins, I should hope, to see the appropriateness of such knowing to faith, to religious education, and to theology. Indeed, "God's knowledge of us, and our knowledge of God and of ourselves and the world in and under God is the subject matter of theology."[8] Religious knowledge is characterized, from Exodus to Apocalypse, by the "Negative Capability" Keats ascribed to Shakespeare: the capability of being in uncertainty, mystery, and doubt without any irritable reaching, straining, grasping after fact and reason. Such knowing is appropriate in education as well. Indeed, perhaps the most valuable mental attitude of the educator, whether parent, pastor, preacher, or pedagogue, is closer to the poetic, artistic intelligence than to discursive intelligence. For the subject matter of education is, as is the subject matter of theology, knowledge profoundly entered, knowledge in which one dwells. Guilt, forgiveness, death, reconciliation, resurrection, love, and faith are not primarily concepts. They are primarily human realities, best understood in immediacy and involvement.[9]

Art offers unique (in the sense of peculiar and proper to itself) material and processes for entrance into such realities. I wish to name two which are especially pertinent to our conversation here. First is the material of the *word*. Artists, in using words, search for the richest, most textured word, starting from the perception that *how* we think is determined by the material with which we think, and that how we think determines what we think we are.[10] One form of thought moves from data to hypothesis to conclusions, with reason in control, and concentrates on the idea, the concept.[11] The other form concentrates on the vehicle chosen for the perception and/or idea and on the power of that vehicle to shape the material itself, the form being the shape of the content.[12]

"Consider Johannes Kepler," writes Norwood Hansen,

> imagine him on a hill watching the dawn. With him is Tycho Brahe. Kepler regarded the sun as fixed, it was the earth that moved. But Tycho followed Ptolemy and Aristotle in this much at least: the earth was fixed and all other celestial bodies moved around it.
>
> Question: Do Kepler and Tycho see the same thing in the east at dawn?[13]

Or, consider this: It is 1953. In the Western world, the headlines are: "Hilary conquers Everest." In the Eastern world, they read, "Everest has been befriended." Question: Do we know the event in the same way? Or, consider this: One of my students reported to me a part of a conversation she had with her field education supervisor.

> SHE: I feel like a phoenix which has risen from the ashes.
> HE: Why don't you just say you had a hard time, but now things are better?
>
> Question: Would it be the same?

The point of recording these "shapings," these formings, is that our thinking, our knowing, is determined by the metaphorical material we employ. It matters which words we choose, and it matters what forms arrange those words. Further, the metaphors and forms we use can paralyze the capacity to perceive what is there—no matter how plain or abundant the evidence. It is not that we willfully refuse to look. It is that, if we do not have the fitting metaphor, we are not able to see. But words can not only paralyze. They can also redeem. The point is critical. People, Paul Ricoeur assures us, are not motivated by direct appeals to the will. People are redeemed by imagination. They are moved by someone or something that excites them into hoping and acting.[14]

Second, art offers us concrete, sensible, material reality as that through which we may know. In artistic knowing, thought and reason and intelligence are diffuscd over the whole frame. Joyce Cary, in *The Horse's Mouth,* suggests the way to look at a painting: "Feel it with your eye."[15] Paul Klee's notebooks are entitled *The Thinking Eye.*[16] Phyllis Froelich stuns an audience into knowing through her signing, a dramatic form of expression in *Children of a Lesser God.* Art is the primordial form of knowing through our bodiliness. Through and with our bodies, a knowing emerges which is the basis and ground for knowing other concrete being and not just concepts and thought. A person speculating, thinking, knowing in the artistic mode does not think *about* objects: trees, rivers, clay, tone. A person knows *them,* thinks through *them,* in actual sensible, concrete engagement.[17] In religious terms, this knowing is the source of the sacramental imagination, the "persistently central assumption that certain objects or actions or words or places belonging to the ordinary spheres of life may convey a unique knowledge of the whole mystery of existence, because in these realities something numinous resides, something holy and gracious."[18]

Perhaps the knowing, the construing imaged and symbolized in faith development theory implicitly includes or might include such artistic knowing. I am not ready to make that determination. Rather, I take the issue as at least one possible focus for further consideration. I would speculate, however, that the foregoing provides enough basis to illuminate some points of departure toward making such a determination. Others will be able to identify additional concerns, but here let me articulate five.

1. Is the theory as developed thus far limited or incomplete because it draws exclusively on verbal, discursive responses in its research? What dimensions of religious knowing are automatically excluded by the process and questions of interview? If some interviews could be designed and conducted along an artistic model, what might emerge?[19] Are there, in other words, any ways to incorporate other forms of knowing, especially the sacramental knowing which is less focused on the psyche, the self, the individual?

2. Are the forms of knowing so basic to this work, implicit in the schemes of Piaget and Kohlberg, ones which force hierarchical and/or linear imaging of faith to dominate to the extent other possibilities are eliminated? The return to this issue in *Stages of Faith* several times[20] demonstrates how deep a concern reliance on Piaget and Kohlberg continues to be, and yet how essential they are to the theory. My question here is whether the theory *can* be widened or completed by incorporating "right-brain, left brain" as suggested,[21] or convictional knowing as posited.[22] Or do even these latter still imply a too limited base. Is it true that the process we use "constructs the mind at the same time it constructs the constructions of the mind"?[23] If so, does faith development theory implicitly teach that human faith is, in the last analysis and despite description of convictional knowing, an overwhelmingly rational reality?

3. In artistic process the outcome, the endpoint, is not known. The movement is *through* the material toward revelation, disclosure, discovery of a form within. In T. S. Eliot's poetic language,

> There is, it seems to us
> At best, only a limited value
> In the knowledge derived from experience.
> The knowledge imposes a pattern and falsifies,
> For the pattern is new in every moment
> And every moment is a new and shocking
> Valuation of all we have been.
>
> —*from East Coker*

Is faith development theory, positing as it does an ordered and expected set of stages, in danger of missing the shock of the new? Could it be enhanced, enriched, and completed, on these grounds, toward constant renewal of the pattern?[24]

4. Artistic knowing assumes the "multiplicity of the mental"— multiple, manifold interpretation of any given object or event. Does positing a final stage which is describable as, for example, "the Kingdom of God"—indeed, does positing any final stage— prejudice not only alternate interpretations but the notion of interpretations-always-capable-of-being-reinterpreted, even the notion there *is* no final interpretation?

5. Finally, how crucial are the chronological assignments of the six stages at certain ages? Is it possible to present large portions of each stage description "all-at-once" in the manner of presentational form, completing the more familiar rendering of them as sequential? Can the boundaries and limits of the descriptions be more fluid so that elements in several stages form new constellations? What might this mean for such persons as the retarded, the very young, the nonliterate?

SISTERHOOD AND THE COMPLETION
OF EXPERIENCE

The second question I bring to this discussion centers on experience. I am using the word "experience" in the Deweyan sense of interaction of organism and environment, the relational matrix in which we are always involved.[25] We are never not engaged in experience, though we can, of course, distinguish that broad matrix from the more specific moment plucked from it called "an experience."

When we shape and design both theories of human development and educational curricula, we draw on a limited interpretation and/or assessment of experience. If we examine them, we become aware, with only a little probing, that the experience on which we draw is, largely if not exclusively, the experience of a very small segment of the human community. This is not an opinion; the data is overwhelming.[26] But let me be direct: Experience, as we usually write, teach, study about, and conceptualize it, is that of white men. More specifically, powerful white men. More specifically, powerful white men with access to the organs and instruments which transmit information, skills, and knowledge. In Christian religious circles, these men tend to be clergymen, and, more often than not, theologians and/or biblical scholars.

Once again, I would not want to be understood too quickly. Do not read this as the position that such an emphasis on the experience of some, as interpreted by the most articulate of white men, is wrong or in error. But do consider the position: Such an emphasis is narrow, limited, limiting, and incomplete. Given such emphasis, any theory of faith development and any curriculum of religious education characterized as full, whole, integral, and "having all necessary parts" would need to be extended and, where necessary, revised and reformed. I will attempt to specify how, in the following pages, by describing and commenting on three curricula that all institutions (and all theories) teach, and then posit as complement the fullness offered by sisterhood. I will then suggest implications this might raise for faith development.

All institutions teach three curricula: the *explicit,* the *implicit,* and the *null.*[27] Explicit curriculum refers to the actual field of study, courses, lessons, units, ideas, activities, skills presented or consciously engaged in. Explicit refers, too, to what point of view or discipline is normative and on whom one draws for an authoritative argument or comprehensive view of humanity. One of the most revealing sources of the explicit curriculum in a book or article is its bibliography, naming the "experts." But dominant images, symbols, and metaphors also comprise it.

The implicit curriculum, in contrast, is taught indirectly. It is the organizational structure, the rules for participating. This includes not only who does and does not speak, who does and does not contribute, but, more subtly, whose ideas are built on, who is taken seriously, who gets heard in what Gloria Steinem calls the "politics of talking."[28] The implicit curriculum deals with patterns of authority, criteria for decision making, selection and arrangement of questions in interviews, including such "hidden" elements as who is praised, who has power, and who really "is boss."[29] Chinese painter Li-li Weng illuminates the distinction between explicit and implicit curricula when he says, "First you see the hills in the painting; then you see the painting in the hills."

The null curriculum is third: what is taught by what is *not* taught. An obvious paradox, this is a curriculum which does not exist. The point of including it is that ignorance, not being educated to or in something, is not neutral. Ignorance affects the options we consider, the alternatives we examine, the perspectives we choose.[30] The absence of a set of considerations biases and skews the evidence we are able to take into account. The null curriculum has two major elements: the *areas* left out, and the *processes* left out.

When examining these curricula, my own experience and that

of innumerable women in church and world is similar to many women and men throughout the globe. We find ourselves in the culture of silence.[31] Indeed, silence is the starting point. The explicit curriculum is characterized by a silence of women, by women, about women. Adrienne Rich, in an essay called "Taking Women Students Seriously,"[32] writes of the assumption that because women and men, or girls and boys, are sitting in the same classroom or the same church, hearing the same lectures and reading the same books, women are receiving an equal education. Women are not, she writes, "because the content of education itself validates men even as it invalidates women. Its very message is that males have been the shapers and thinkers of the world and that is only natural."[33] More subtly, the implicit curriculum teaches with extraordinary force (precisely because it is subtle) that for an authoritative voice, for the determination of an important issue, including that it *is* important, and even for illustration from art and literature, one far more naturally turns to male experience. With reference to the null curriculum, what is not taught, the conclusion is the same. In this connection, Valerie Saiving's 1960 essay, asking whether the notion of sin as equivalent to pride or will to power (she was studying Reinhold Niebuhr and Anders Nygren, as well as Margaret Mead and her own experience) did not come out of male experience, is apt. She wondered whether *our* sinfulness was not better described by items such as triviality, distractibility, and dependence on others for self-definition, rather than "pride," "will to power," and "self love."[34] My concern here is not only this substantive question but the historical datum that theology and theologies have been, until recently, largely created by men who lived amid the tensions, competition, and contest of a masculine culture.

As women as a whole, and many men, have become aware of such silences, additional moments follow. After silence comes political awareness—that sense that "I am silent, and therefore *we* exist."[35] The aphorism so familiar to feminists, "the personal is political," attests to this realization of corporateness which awareness of silence immediately creates. Political awareness leads to action, even if it is only the action of acknowledgment. But the movement from silence to political awareness also includes two other dimensions. One moves into mourning—into a dying and grieving based on a commitment to completeness. For if the reality under consideration is to be completed and widened not only to *include* women and men, but also *formed* and *shaped* from a base which incorporates the experience of both, present concentration and practice calls for a tremendous and painful shift, a "sea change." The shift is asked especially from those who have the power to make such change. Thus the mourning metaphor seems apt: letting go of what is no longer viable, and, in Keats' phrase, "dying into life." In most religious education, the concepts, the ideas, the doctrines of mourning and dying are taught. But this is, literally, a moment of putting off the old "man" and recognizing that mourning is not just a topic of learning. It is the content and process and stuff of the education itself.

Should mourning occur, another dimension emerges, one of mutuality and capacity for partnered, human relationship. Here I offer the interpretive power of sisterhood because of its relational component, its feminist undersong, its reconciling and completing energy. Sisterhood calls attention not just to human relating but to the *oikumene* as well. For humans exist not only in a *polis* with one another as sisters and brothers, but in relation with earth, too, and with sun and moon and stars and ground. And if that interpretation should or could be included in curriculum as a whole, what might it suggest as issues for what is taught in faith development theory? What questions might it raise?

1. What does the authoritative and normative selection of Kohlberg, Piaget, Erikson, and Selman as sources of the data for structural wholes say to women and men about experience? How much does *their* (the theorists') social location determine their conclusions? Certainly the source of Kohlberg's original data is not a peripheral point here. (I've often wondered, too: "What if Heinz were the one who was dying? Would the answers be the same?") Selman's work with reference to perspective taking might be in need of further examination around this issue: being seen as a girl, a female, is different from being seen as a boy, as a male. I do not just see you seeing me. Then, too, perhaps in the future Erikson could be complemented by work similar to that done by Penelope Washbourne.[36] In sum, however, an underlying question for the theory might not only be bringing women's perspective into the theory as a way of "picking up dropped

stitches"[37] in the academic fabric but as a way to study how one's approach to and interpretation of experience is shaped by one's social location.

2. As we continue to work on and teach faith development theory, would it be possible to work toward equalizing citations and sources for positions taken? The initial balance might be toward drawing on authors, writers, and thinkers who are women as well as men. But if sisterhood is fruitful as completion metaphor, it would also lead to drawing far more on persons from other cultures than our own, people who have written and reflected on issues of faith and not just on interviewing such persons. This might even cause us to ask such questions as those raised by Saiving, but in this case applied to faith. That is, is our understanding of faith, as well as our understanding of sin, drawn exclusively from male experience?

3. The null curriculum thus far is evident in Fowler's use of Levinson's work without explicit attention to its being done exclusively with men and the passing on of that work without such notation.[38] It is also evident, in my view, in the minimal reference to Carol Gilligan, although her work has already had enormous impact on women and men who have studied it.[39] Her work, as completion of the more limited perspective offered as normative, has implications for renewed insight, especially when linked to novels and artistic renderings. In addition to studying main characters such as Conrad Jarrett and Sol Nazerman (I acknowledge Guest and O'Connor), we need to cite such works as Margaret Atwood's *Surfacing* and Mary Gordon's *Final Payments,* where the protagonists appear to embody the Gilligan pattern so definitively.[40] Finally, as a long-range goal, we need studies by and of women's experience relative to religious issues, along lines similar to Gilligan's.[41] Universality as a characteristic of faith stages may be a long way away.

4. Emphasis on sisterhood and the sisterhood of humans with the planet, again, calls attention (as art does) to the imagery offered by faith development theory. Two examples: (1) "Kingdom of God," both *Kingdom* as monarchical and male, and *God* as anthropomorphically masculine, may not be as universally Jewish-Christian as posited. Perhaps in retrospect, as Sonya Quitslund has suggested, the "Death of God" in the sixties was a

more significant symbolizing than many of us suspected. A more complete, inclusive theology might, she writes, enrich our experience of the holy as far more mysterious, enigmatic, and unnameable than often imagined.[42] (2) The *imagery* of cognition as developing upward to the abstract, or moral reasoning as toward a higher universal principle, may be more consonant with male than with female experience. Women's bodiliness in the past has had the impact of "involving us in" as the deeper sign of humanity, in contrast to "abstracting us from." In any case, the comparison of these images could prove fruitful.

5. Finally, a position which asserts the personal as political cannot, even as psychology, be one of exclusive concentration on one's own construing, structuring, forming. Could future interviews, in this connection, be designed to focus more on relational, corporate, and political construing and forming, and less on the individual than is the case thus far? I do not know if this is possible, but it may be important to try.

SABBATH AND THE COMPLETION OF TIME

A final question I bring from the perspective of religious education concerns the issue of time. Three impulses lead me to the conviction of its importance here, not just as an "interesting" inclusion, but as essential. The first impulse is the rediscovery of spirituality, especially in the West. Contemporary persons are conscious of a "wild prayer of longing" (Auden) where descent beckons. A second impulse is the nagging question, "Where is the *religious* in religious education?" Are we not in danger of drowning in techniques and behavioral objectives, in methods and procedures? And the third question is a recapitulation of a theme introduced in the section on art: the certain "guess" that what moves us most profoundly is metaphor, image, and symbol. I am persuaded that we need fresh ways of seeing, new ways of imagining and addressing reality, which, while they transcend the here and now, anchor us in the here and now. The question is one of relocating transcendence in the here and now, in the present. The discovery of Sabbath—it was there all the time—is a response to this concern. How do we dwell in time in a way that allows us to be truly present to one another, so that we balance our extraordinary emphasis on activity, even on activism, so that we balance our typically individualistic and product-oriented biases in dwelling together? My response is the ancient religious command, which is both a historical lived reality and a religious ground, telling us what we are and do as religious educators. My response is to lift up the gift of Shabbat, of Sabbath. Biblically, in both Jewish and Christian scriptures, and throughout four millenia of both Jewish and Christian religious history, Sabbath is a central affirmation *of* and completion *in* time. I will comment briefly on the dominant Sabbath motifs, and then, as previously, attempt to draw implications for faith development theory.

To begin, Sabbath is essentially a word about *time* and dwelling in time, whether one speaks of the seventh-day Sabbath, twenty-four hours long, of Exodus 20:10; the Sabbath of the Exile, seventy years long, of 2 Chronicles 36:21; or the quality of temporal existence attributed to Yahweh after the work recorded in Genesis. Sabbath is both quantitative, linear time, measurable by hours and days and years, and qualitative, describing attribute and attitude. As such, it symbolizes completion. The first, the quantitative image of time is, of course, dominant in our society. We generally conceive, perceive, and speak of time as sequential, a series of points moving from past through present to future.[43] If this is our only image, I would assert, our sense of time remains incomplete. But we do have a fuller, more developed understanding of time, where the meaning is not to be at a point somewhere along a continuum, or even in a physical space. This is the sense of time as presence, the revelatory way-of-being proper both to humans and to divinity.[44] Religiously, Sabbath is an invitation in the direction of depth, rather than distance. For Rabbi Abraham Heschel, it is "like a palace in time. . . . The meaning of Sabbath is to celebrate time rather than space. . . . In Sabbath we try to become attuned to holiness in time."[45]

Sabbath is, in addition, a law demanding from human beings a withdrawal from activity or, to continue with the metaphor central to this paper, a law concerned with completion.[46] For it asserts that humans become complete, not only by doing, but by not-doing, by *rest*. One translation in Heschel's work on Sabbath suggests that the meaning of the verb *shavat* is not *to rest* but *to be complete*.[47] Normally, however, the command is to rest: to cease, to desist from work, to let go. Paradoxically, the command is almost immediately ethical. In Deuteronomy it moves from being an imitation of the rest of the Creator God to being a statement about human relationships. It intrinsically involves a concern with humane provision of rest for family, strangers, servants, animals, land. Sabbath is an early attempt to equalize human beings, regardless of diverse social positions, and to favor mutuality in and beyond human relationships. "Hallow the Sabbath" means hallow one another; but also, hallow the cattle, hallow the earth. You may not use others. This mutuality of rest and ethical movement is beautifully captured by the Scandinavian poet, Par Lagervist:

> May my heart's disquiet never vanish;
> May I never be at peace;
> May I never be reconciled to life nor to death either;
> May my path be unending.[48]

The irony to which Lagervist points is that in quiet, we learn disquiet; in peace, never to be at peace; in the completion known as reconciliation, to hear the pain of the world. If I read correctly, this is at least a collegial imagining to conjunctive faith.

Finally, in addition to activity in time we have learned very well, especially in the Western world, to be in time as individuals. Sabbath is a reminder of the other side of individuality. For, as metaphor, it is embodied and enfleshed ceremonially in corporate and community ritual. By law, celebration of Sabbath occurs in a *polis,* as part of a people. As vehicle for celebration, Sabbath depends on recreation in both senses: as play and festivity and as renewal and resurrection. And that depends on the communal. Sabbath is a reminder not so much of our uniqueness before Yahweh, but of our communality. "They shall be my *people.*" Furthermore, the reality the community celebrates, primarily, is the biblical datum of God-with-us in time, of the divinity as Presence. Covenant, according to Samuel Terrien, is only possible because God is first present. Only a present god can make a compact with a people.[49] And so, Sabbath is the imaging of an essential in both divine and human being: to be is to-be-with. *"Esse est co-esse"* (Marcel).

What might such understanding of time offer to faith development? I name four in conclusion.

1. The motif of Presence, proper to biblical religion and to human time, offers completion to the emphasis in the Kingdom image on "the futurity of God and to the coming Kingdom as the universal shared future of all being."[50] As such, it situates (relativizes?) the too exclusively eschatological and ameliorates the danger of removing persons to some place outside of time.

2. The image of a Divinity of Presence assists those of us working in a developmental framework to clarify the underlying religious images guiding us as we work and to examine whether these images are only sequential, only images of motion and movement-toward. Sabbath affirms the more complete view of time as here as well as there, now as well as then, already as well as not yet. Sabbath is presence, not absence. In this connection, Fowler's spiral image is crucial. Perhaps it could be emphasized earlier and more centrally in the future.

3. Sabbath, as a physical, concrete, corporal, bodily, earthly reality completes the emphasis on the abstract, mental, overly removed already alluded to. It also fleshes out a view of spirituality, religiousness, and faith which could be in danger of being too cerebral. Sabbath brings body and blood.

4. Sabbath is but one reminder of the plethora of images welling up from other than Christian traditions, images alive not only in theory and theology but in the living experience of human beings throughout the world. As a shared way of worship and adoration, of command and ceremony, or ethical disposition and mystical absorption, it is claimed both by Jews in all their Jewishness and by Christians in all our resurrection trust. As such, Sabbath recalls us to the emerging possibility that despite our incompleteness, we already participate in a universal oneness as sisters and brothers to one another, and to the world.

NOTES

1. William Lynch, *Images of Faith* (Notre Dame, Ind.: University of Notre Dame Press, 1973), p. vii.

2. James W. Fowler, *Stages of Faith* (San Francisco: Harper & Row, 1981).

3. See ibid., pp. 5-8.

4. Susanne K. Langer, *Philosophy in a New Key* (Cambridge, Mass.: Harvard University Press, 1969). First printed 1942.

5. Ibid., pp. 94-97.

6. Susanne K. Langer, *Problems of Art* (New York: Charles Scribner's Sons, 1957), p. 80.

7. Theodore Roethke, "How Can I Dream Except Beyond This Life," from "The Abyss," *Collected Poems* (London: Faber, 1968), p. 187. Quoted in Brenda Lealman and Edward Robinson, *Knowing and Unknowing* (London: Christian Education Movement, 1981), p. 18. Lealman and Robinson have collaborated to produce three books concerned with the exploration of art and education.

8. James B. Nelson, *Embodiment* (Minneapolis: Augsburg, 1978), p. 35.

9. See Sharon Parks, *Faith Development and Imagination in the Context of Higher Education* (Cambridge, Mass.: Harvard Divinity School, 1980; Ph.D. dissertation). I am indebted to the section on p. 404 where Parks illustrates this principle by describing an experience of Rosemary Ruether recorded in "Beginning: An Intellectual Autobiography," in *Journeys,* ed. Gregory Baum (New York: Paulist, 1975), pp. 40-41.

10. See Elizabeth Sewell, *The Human Metaphor* (Notre Dame, Ind.: University of Notre Dame Press, 1964).

11. See Fowler, *Stages of Faith,* pp. 70-71.

12. See Ben Shahn, *The Shape of Content* (New York: Vintage, 1957), pp. 62ff.

13. Norwood Hansen, *Patterns of Discovery* (Cambridge, Mass.: Cambridge University Press, 1958), p. 5.

14. See Paul Ricoeur, *History and Truth,* trans. C. A. Kelbley (Evanston, Ill.: Northwestern University Press, 1965), p. 127.

15. Joyce Cary, *The Horse's Mouth* (New York: Harper & Row, 1944), p. 98.

16. Jurg Spiller, ed., *The Thinking Eye: Paul Klee's Notebooks* (New York: George Wittenborn, 1960).

17. See John Dewey, *Art As Experience* (New York: Capricorn. 1934), pp. 73-74.

18. Nathan Scott, *The Wild Prayer of Longing* (New Haven, Conn.: Yale University Press, 1971), p. 49.

19. With reference to artistic process as model, see Gibson Winter, *Liberating Creation* (New York: Crossroads, 1982). In this work, Winter suggests artistic process as root metaphor in today's society for the forming of social, political, and economic life.

20. See Fowler, *Stages of Faith,* pp. 273-274.

21. See ibid., p. 104.

22. Ibid., p. 297.

23. Sewell, *The Human Metaphor,* p. 34.

24. The interview procedures of the Religious Experience Research Unit at Manchester College, Oxford, could be a fruitful source of alternative form here. See especially Edward Robinson, *The Original Vision* (Oxford: Manchester College, RERU, 1977) and Edward Robinson, ed., *Living the Questions* (Oxford: Manchester College, RERU, 1978).

25. See Dewey, *Art As Experience,* esp. chs. 1-3. See also Gabriel Moran, *Design for Religion* (New York: Herder, 1970), pp. 63ff., for application to religious education.

26. The "we" in these sentences is literal; I refer to my own work. In one chapter of *Portrait of Youth Ministry* (New York: Paulist 1981), for example (chapter 7), two of the thirty-five citations are of other women. And in this paper, where I am self-conscious about the issue, I still count twelve more citations of males as authoritative than females.

27. The formulation is Elliot Eisner's. See his *The Educational Imagination* (New York: Macmillan, 1979), pp. 74-92.

28. See Gloria Steinem, "The Politics of Talking in Groups," *Ms.* (May, 1981), pp. 43-49.

29. See Philip Jackson, *Life in Classrooms* (New York: Holt, Rinehart & Winston, 1968).

30. Eisner, *The Educational Imagination,* p. 83.

31. See Tillie Olsen, *Silences* (New York: Delacorte, 1978), for a profound poetic analysis of the silence of artists in general, especially, but not exclusively, of women. The phrase "culture of silence" is Paulo Friere's.

32. Adrienne Rich, *On Lies, Secrets and Silence* (New York: Norton, 1979), pp. 237-245.

33. Ibid., p. 241.

34. See Valerie Saiving, "The Human Situation: A Feminine View," in *Womanspirit Rising,* ed. Carol Christ and Judith Plaskow (New York: Harper & Row, 1979), pp. 29-42.

35. A further development of Albert Camus', "I rebel, therefore we exist." See *The Rebel* (New York: Vintage, 1956), p. 22.

36. See Penelope Washbourne, *Becoming Woman* (New York: Harper & Row, 1977), where serious attention is given to female life changes such as menstruation, pregnancy and birth, and change of life.

37. See Barbara Wheeler, "Accountability to Women in Theological Seminaries," *Religious Education* 76 (July-August, 1981) 4, p. 390.

38. Fowler, *Stages of Faith,* pp. 110-114.

39. See Carol Gilligan, "In a Different Voice: Women's Conception of the Self and of Morality," *Harvard Educational Review* 47 (November, 1977) 4, pp. 481-517; "Woman's Place in Man's Life Cycle," *Harvard Educational Review* 49 (November, 1979) 4, pp. 431-446; and *In A Different Voice* (Cambridge, Mass.: Harvard University Press, 1982). The last includes revised versions of the two articles here cited.

40. This comparison, suggested to me by Gabriel Moran, is one I have used with female and male students in course work on religious adulthood.

41. The journal *Anima* has been naming some of the issues involved here for some time. See also Charlene Spretnak, ed., *The Politics of Women's Spirituality* (Garden City, N.Y.: Doubleday, 1982).

42. Sonya Quitslund, "Review of Joan Chamberlain Engelsman's *The Feminine Dimension of the Divine,*" *Horizons* 8 (Spring, 1981) 1, pp. 143-144.

43. See Gabriel Moran, *The Present Revelation* (New York: Herder and Herder, 1972), pp. 118-135, for a developed understanding of temporality as I am using it here.

44. See Samuel Terrien, *The Elusive Presence* (New York: Harper & Row, 1978).

45. Abraham Heschel, *The Sabbath: Its Meaning for Modern Man* (New York: Noonday Press, 1959), p. 18.

46. For application of this theme to religious education, see Mary Margaret

Funk, "The Sabbath, or Don't We Have Time?" *PACE 11* (Winona, Minn.: St. Mary's Press, n.d), n.p.

47. Heschel, *The Sabbath,* p. 122.

48. Margaret Woodward, who works with Filipino political prisoners in northern Australia, shared these lines with me. I do not have the exact citation.

49. Terrien, *The Elusive Presence,* p. 3. Terrien refers to the Sabbath as, for the Jews, "the Sacrament of Presence," p. 393.

50. Fowler, *Stages of Faith,* p. 210.

PART III

Enhancing Faith Development Theory

Chapter 6

Imagination and Spirit in Faith Development: A Way Past the Structure-Content Dichotomy

SHARON PARKS

Faith development theory as pioneered by James Fowler and as exemplified in his central book *Stages of Faith* is contributing to contemporary religious thought in two primary ways. It helps to expand our understanding of the character of faith (offering a place to stand from which religion and belief may be freshly and critically examined), and it serves as another prod toward the recognition of the dynamic character of all knowing and being— even knowing and being in faith. This theory, therefore, has the power to assist the task of theology in a pluralistic and changing culture which is increasingly aware of the dynamic character of the whole cosmos. But if the power of this theory is to be fully realized, the interrelationship of faith, development, imagination, and Spirit must be more profoundly articulated.

Building on the thought of Paul Tillich, H. Richard Niebuhr, and Wilfred Cantwell Smith, Fowler understands faith to be a generic human activity, meaning that the relationship of self and other is conditioned by a shared center (or centers) of power and value transcending and ordering that relationship.

This description of faith assists in enlarging the notion of faith beyond a too facile equation with either religion or belief narrowly conceived, as faith is recognized as a prior capacity or activity—the activity of knowing, valuing, and trusting—which undergirds the whole of human life.

Fowler has then forged the essential linkage between faith and the dynamics of human development by joining this generic understanding of faith with the insights of developmental psychology (particularly Piagetian or constructive-developmental psychology). In so doing, he has compelled attention to the dynamic character of faith by empirically demonstrating that faith is not static across the life span. It is conditioned by the development (through stages) of the underlying structures, operations, or capacities for knowing and being. He has rendered a significant service by bringing into the realm of theological discourse and religious educational practice Jean Piaget's careful mapping of the development of the power of cognition, Lawrence Kohlberg's understanding of moral development, and Robert Selman's insights into the development of our capacity for role taking. To these aspects of structure he has added structural descriptions of the power and evolution of the bounds of social awareness, the locus of authority, and the form of world coherence—aspects essential to an adequate structural description of the phenomenon of faith.

Faith development theory, however, like all constructive-developmental theories has had a tendency to focus on structures and stages rather than on the process that gives rise to the stages and to shear structure (stages) from content (image-symbols). This focus on stages has two distorting consequences. First, it obscures the dynamic motion which developmental theory potentially discloses (in this instance reinforcing the assumption of the static character of faith). Second, within structural developmental psychology, the imaginal is made secondary to the formal operational dimensions of intelligence.

Fowler has endeavored to incorporate the imaginal by recognizing that our centers of power and value are expressed by means of symbols or "master images," and that the "role of symbols" undergoes development and is therefore different at each stage. Nevertheless, as a participant in the constructive-developmental tradition, faith development theory is vulnerable to being perceived as attending to the underlying structure of faith in disproportionate measure to the power of image and symbol. This is to say that when faith development theory focuses on stages it may be perceived as attentive to the generic, universal character of faith and as inattentive to questions of the adequacy of faith as determined by the particularity of the images and symbols by which it is expressed. As a result, faith development theory has sometimes been too easily appropriated by those who are uncritically attracted to its resonance with natural theology and to its universalizing and/or defining power. On the other hand, it has been dismissed by those who perceive faith as divine revelation occurring independently of human processes and, ironically, also by those who focus their concern upon the social-historical conditions of faith formation—the particular in contrast to the universal.

The potential of faith development theory to embrace these several perspectives and to serve both the descriptive and normative tasks of theologians, pastors, counselors, and other educators will not be realized until the linkages have been more profoundly made between the *processes* of faith, development, and imagination. Further, these processes must be considered in relationship to the activity of Spirit. This essay attempts to suggest how we may begin to forge these linkages with a strength that will enable faith development theory to make a yet more profound address to the theological and educational tasks.

FAITH AND THE COMPOSING OF MEANING

Robert Kegan addresses some dimensions of this task by identifying several "neglects" within the Piagetian paradigm. He asserts that "Piagetians ('neo-' or otherwise) must still be characterized as about *cognition,* to the neglect of *emotion;* the *individual,* to the neglect of the *social;* the *epistemological,* to the neglect of the *ontological* (or *concept,* to the neglect of *being); stages . . .* to the neglect of *process;* and . . . what is *new and changed* about a person, to the neglect of *the person who persists through time* [the *discontinuity* of the self to the neglect of the *continuity* of the self]."[1]

Kegan seeks to demonstrate that these several "neglects" are one. He perceives that they stem from a single truncation in the attention of the paradigm. The dynamic interaction between self and other which Piaget described as giving rise to the structures of cognition, Kegan perceives as no merely cognitive activity. Rather, according to Kegan, the "deep structure" in all constructive-developmental stage theories is the means by which the differentiation and relation of self and other is composed. Piaget's insight into the process of cognition thus becomes enlarged so as to enhance our understanding of the activity of ego and the formation of personality. In this enlargement, cognition and affect, the personal and the social, knowing and being, process and stages, and the continuity and loss of the self are all gathered up in a larger conception. This "larger conception" Kegan names "meaning-constitutive evolutionary activity."[2]

This is to say that Kegan perceives the process of meaning-making as the central human activity. Indeed, at the core of human life is a demand to find or be found by meaning. To have meaning is to have a sense of fitting and trustworthy relation, connection, and pattern in the disparate elements within the force field of life. Engagement in meaning-making involves the whole person and his or her environment. This seeking and composing activity of meaning-making is integral to the human being and is the larger conception (beyond children, stages, cognition, and the individual) toward which Kegan invites the primary attention of constructive-developmental theory.

When Fowler speaks of faith as the composing of an "ultimate environment" it is the making of meaning toward which he also points. But his notion of an *ultimate* environment distinguishes the activity of faith from more mundane forms of meaning-making. For while human beings must compose a sense of the fitting relationships within a particular hour or day or room or group or neighborhood, etc., ultimately human beings must also compose a sense of life intuited as a whole.[3] In this way of seeing, faith is, at least in part, the activity of participating in a dynamic interaction constitutive of a convictional sense of what is ultimately powerful, of value, and trustworthy.

When Fowler and Kegan are placed in dialogue, the activity of faith may be perceived, at least in part, as the activity of composing meaning at the level of ultimacy. And the central insight of faith development theory is that the composing of meaning at the level of ultimacy undergoes predictable patterns of development in the direction of an enlarged capacity to embrace and discern complexity—and thus to compose a more adequate faith (a more adequate and trustworthy perception of a fitting composition of self, world, and "God").

KANT AND PIAGET

This recognition of the composing character of faith is dependent not only upon the insight of Piaget, but also upon Piaget's indebtedness to Immanuel Kant (1724-1804). In the Enlightenment, Western philosophical and theological thought became freshly aware of the powers and limits of its own knowing. Philosophers began anew to critique and purify their understanding of the activity of the human mind. Religious thought was compelled to recognize that the human mind does not passively receive its world, but acts upon it to compose it. The consequence of this recognition was an awareness of the finite character of all knowing and the relativized nature of all "truth." Kant particularly distinguished the powers of human reason in relation to the knowing of the sensible and supersensible. The power of the mind to know the sensible or empirical world (pure reason) was differentiated from the necessity of human reason to deduce—though it cannot know—eternal truth (practical reason). These distinctions enabled us to become aware of the nature and limits of our knowledge—particularly in the realm of the supersensible, in the realm of faith.

Those who appropriate and/or critique faith development theory frequently fail to recognize adequately that behind Fowler stands Piaget, behind Piaget stands Kant, and that matters much more fundamental than "stages" are being addressed. We are still living into the implications of Kant's insight. We still find it difficult to take as seriously as Kant did the fact of the composing, finite mind. Faith educators (theological professors, preachers, Sunday School teachers, and pastoral counselors) too frequently do not practice the radical implications of the awareness that each person, community, and culture composes their ultimacy—meaning, truth, and "God"—in a particular fashion distinguishable from the knowing-composing of any other. It is easier to assume that others should easily "see it our way" than it is to act consistent with the recognition that we do not have undistorted access to transcendent truth, that all truth is mediated by particular finite experience, and, further, that, when people listen to religious teaching, they do not "receive the teaching whole" but to at least some degree recompose the teaching—each according to his or her own capacity and experience.

When we do recognize that this is so we are more able to respect the opposing points of view and "confusion" of colleagues, children, graduate students, laity, and clients/patients as differing constructions of reality (differing forms of meaning-making), which may represent an integrity deserving of our respect if not our affirmation. Further, we are opened to the certain awareness that a dialogue between persons holding differing and finite compositions of truth is not merely collegial or a fashionable educational trend, but is essential to both teacher and learner—is essential to the discernment of truth.

Jean Piaget met children in such a manner. He recognized what Kant saw—the power and limits of the knowing mind—and he extended Kant's insight. He observed the power of the child to compose its world and discerned the strength and limits of that power by observing how that power develops slowly over time. He observed that the infant, the child, and the adolescent know their world in different ways. He discovered that knowing is dependent upon the development of increasingly complex operations of the mind. The infant can see the world, but cannot remember it; the child can remember what she or he sees, but cannot reflect on its meaning; the adult can reflect on what things mean and even ask whether there is any meaning at all. Piaget described such development in terms of an increasingly complex series of underlying structures or operations of thought. Each transformation of the underlying structure of thought constitutes a new integrated set of operations, a new capacity, a new stage. When with the help of Piaget we once recognize this, it follows that being a good educator involves taking these structural developmental differences seriously.

Faith development theory assists us in doing so. For example, we are enabled to understand that the school-age child is not able to grasp the complexity toward which the doctrine of the Trinity points because of the literal, concrete character of the child's knowing—the child's inability to think in formal or abstract terms (stage 2). Or we may see that paradox as a mode of religious knowing (a comfortable mode of knowing in stage 5) is resisted by an adult who is developing the capacity to reflect critically upon competing claims and to formulate an explicit, formally expressed faith from which to adjudicate such claims (the task of stage 4).

STRUCTURE AND CONTENT

The contribution of Piaget as mediated by faith development theory tends to focus, however, upon the structures with which the learner handles images and symbols (precisely what Fowler means by "role of symbols"). It does not give the same measure of attention to the significance of the character of the symbols themselves, their adequacy, or the process that gives rise to them. Faith development theory has linked faith and structural development, but our understanding of the dynamic character of development and the relationship of both faith and development to normative issues would be enhanced by a more profound linkage between faith, development, and the *process* of imagination. When the process of imagination is not linked to the process of development, the descriptive and normative tasks are artificially divided.

It is not the case, however, that Fowler has attended to one to the exclusion of the other. Fowler is first a theologian and ethicist and then a psychologist and social scientist. He has explicitly stated that faith development theory is both descriptive and normative.[4] Indeed, the descriptive work expressed in Fowler's stages potentially reorders the normative task, and Fowler has consistently been particularly concerned with the moral capacity of persons at each stage of faith and its implications for normative issues. But an awkward division between the descriptive and the normative is manifest in the distinctions between Fowler's first five stages and his stage 6. The descriptive contribution of the theory is most dominant in stages 1 through 5; these stages are grounded in empirical method and descriptive of generic faith knowing. The first five stage descriptions focus on the elements of structure—structures which may hold a variety of contents, each having differing consequences for the shaping of behavior. In contrast, the normative character of Fowler's work has been most vivid in his description of stage 6. Stage 6 is formed by a particular "content"—a particular image. This image is Fowler's concept as a Christian theologian of the Jewish-Christian vision of the Kingdom of God as the fulfillment of faith. And this image determines a particular behavior—the capacity for "radical commitment to justice and love and . . . selfless passion for a transformed world."[5]

Stage 6 further departs in its formulation from the earlier stages in terms of method. Fowler has not interviewed the persons he identifies as exemplars of stage 6. Thus, stage 6 functions less as empirical description and somewhat more as a theological construct logically consistent with the empirical work of the earlier stages and with Fowler's theological convictions. Further, it is only within his discussion of stage 6 that Fowler addresses the issue of "the absoluteness of the particular."[6] (This discussion does not necessarily exclude the other stages since by this phrase he means simply the capacity of the particular to "bear the quality of ultimacy"; but he does not elaborate the theological implications of this dynamic for other stages.) Within this same discussion he also speaks of the "scandal of the particular," recognizing the tension between accountability to the universal and the integrity of discrete symbols and traditions. He suggests that traditions are to affirm the integrity of their particularity while recognizing the claims of the universal, but within this discussion he does not directly address in relation to the other stages the fact that to do so is both a developmental and imaginal achievement.

I suggest that this disjuncture between the descriptive and the normative in Fowler's work is not of his making *per se*. Rather, this disjuncture is embedded in the Piagetian paradigm itself. Accordingly, I wish to point toward another "neglect" in the attention of the Piagetian paradigm which is not addressed by the "neglects" Kegan has identified, nor is it adequately embraced by his description of meaning-making activity.

Piagetians (including Kegan) have focused on structure or stage to the neglect of content or image-symbol. Piagetians have "forgotten" that the significance of stages-structures is their capacity to receive, to hold, and to manipulate images. An understanding of the composing of "meaning" is insufficient without the recognition that meaning is composed by means of images which are inevitably particular and as such contribute their own particular strength and weakness, adequacy and inadequacy, to the dynamics of knowing.

It is here that descriptive and normative power are linked. We can see this exemplified in Piaget's recognition of the significance of the development of concrete operations for the development of the power of conscience. He saw that only when a person can hold an image of alternative behavior in hierarchical sequence (value one impulse or behavior more highly than another—something the infant and very young child cannot do) that a person can move from impulse to choice.[7] The point here, however, is that we must add that the adequacy of choice will be equally dependent, not only upon the capacity to hold an image of alternative behavior in hierarchical sequence, but also upon the particular character of that image.

The fact that we who are concerned with the appropriation of the Piagetian paradigm in relation to faith must now refocus attention upon the power of the image itself is conditioned not simply by Piaget's emphasis upon formal stage structures to the "neglect" of the symbols they hold. Rather, just as the antecedents of the power of faith development theory are rooted in Enlightenment thought, even so are the antecedents of its limitations. In Kant's thought we can perceive not only a profound recognition of the composing mind but also the source of the split between structure and content which plagues constructive-developmental theory.

IMAGINATION: KANT AND COLERIDGE

Along with recognizing the fact of the composing mind and distinguishing between the knowing of the sensible and the super-sensible, Kant also identified imagination as the active, creative, constructive power of the knowing mind. He described imagination as the power that both acts upon the senses and unifies, organizes, and creates the categories of understanding. For Kant, imagination is the free composing activity of the mind, essential to all perception of the sensible world and to speculative reason (or the power of the mind to hypothesize).[8] But having drawn a firm boundary between sensible and supersensible knowing, Kant then confined this crucial role of imagination to the activity of "pure reason"—the knowing of the sensible world. Kant did not allow imagination a central role in "practical reason"—the composing that is faith.[9] It was given to Coleridge to extend Kant's recognition of imagination as the composing power of the knowing mind into the composing that is faith, and faith development theory takes a wrong turn if it moves directly from Kant to Piaget without passing through the reflection and insight of Coleridge.

Samuel Taylor Coleridge (1772-1834) followed Kant in recognizing imagination as the mind's composing, creative activity. But he made the boundary between the knowing of the sensible and the supersensible more permeable. Coleridge was particularly intrigued with Kant's German word for imagination, *Einbildungskraft*, "the power of shaping into one." He remarked in a notebook entry: "How excellently the German *Einbildungskraft* expresses this prime and loftiest faculty, the power of coadunation, the faculty that forms the many into one—*in-eins-bildung!* "[10] This "shaping into one" is integral to the activity of intuiting life as a whole, the activity of composing meaning at the level of faith. Indeed, in Coleridge's view, the composing of pattern and coherence in the most comprehensive dimensions of being and knowing, the composing of ultimacy, occurs by the power of imagination.

Coleridge made a clear distinction between imagination and fantasy. In contemporary usage, the distinction between fantasy and imagination is frequently blurred. Coleridge identified fantasy as having a merely associative power: "memory emancipated from the order of time and space."[11] In fantasy, everything is possible. In a fantasyland, animals and human speech may be so associated as to entertain us. But fantasy, in this sense, does not engage the real. Imagination, however, is, for Coleridge, a "distinct and widely different" faculty.[12] The task of the imagination is to imagine the real. Imagination is the power of realization.

Coleridge saw that while the physical world can be interpreted by signs appropriated as direct correspondences, this is not the case when we wish to express our intuitions and convictions concerning things we cannot point to in the physical world. When we want to express feelings and concepts, we must say, "It is like. . . ." We must appropriate an object or act from the sensible world, an image, to serve as metaphor or transport for the knowing of the supersensible. We give form to our experience of life, our experience of acting and being acted upon, by appropriating images through which we grasp and name and comprehend. We meet reality, participate in that reality, and express our experience of reality by embracing it in metaphor. We know and articulate our experience of the real and fitting relation between self and world—we compose our sense of ultimate reality, our faith—by means of images functioning as metaphors: it is like a father, a mother, a judge, one who makes covenant, or like a force acting within us or upon us or abandoning us. Horace Bushnell, informed by the thought of Coleridge, describes this dynamic as follows: "The soul that is struggling to utter itself flies to whatever signs and instruments it can find in the visible world, calling them in to act as interpreters, naming them at the same time, to stand ever after, as interpreters of the soul, when they themselves are out of sight."[13]

Coleridge's conception of reason and imagination confirms both Kant's distinction between the knowing of the sensible and the supersensible and his recognition of imagination as the highest activity of the knowing mind. But it contradicts Kant's firm boundary between pure and practical reason and thereby emancipates the imagination from its bondage to the sensible or empirical world. Coleridge recognized a boundary between the sensible and supersensible but perceived this boundary as a threshold, porous enough to make it possible to know (though only partially) the Divine.

When Fowler speaks of faith knowing as "a relatedness to the ultimate conditions of existence which simultaneously informs and qualifies our relations and interactions with the mundane everyday world of other persons and things,"[14] he stands in the tradition of Coleridge in which all knowing is ultimately one. This perspective stands in contrast to Fowler's suggestion in another instance of a more Kantian formulation where he draws a sharper distinction between "a logic of rational certainty" (corresponding to Kant's pure reason) and faith as a "logic of conviction" (corresponding to Kant's practical reason).[15] But Coleridge's assertion that the activity of imagination is one with the whole of knowing and that there can be no final barrier between the sensible and supersensible world is, I believe, critical to our understanding of faith as integral to the entire fabric of life and most consistent with the whole of Fowler's work.

IMAGINATION: THE POWER AND MOTION OF SPIRIT

Key to Coleridge's understanding of imagination is his conception of reason as the power to grasp the whole of knowledge including the apprehension of spiritual truth. "Reason is the power by which we become possessed of principle (eternal verities) and of ideas . . . as the ideas of a point, circle, Justice, Holiness, Free Will in Morals."[16] For Coleridge, reason (not to be confused with mere cognition) is the highest and most complete power of the human mind. Coleridge perceived reason as including all of the powers of the mind—sense, fancy, understanding, judgment, and imagination. But the completing, transcending, unifying power of reason is wrought by the imagination; and imagination is the power by which the transcendent, unseen ideal is apprehended.

Above all, reason is "the integral *spirit* of the regenerated person, reason substantiated and vital, 'one only, yet manifold, overseeing all, and going through all understanding; the breath of the power of God, and a pure influence from the glory of the Almighty, which remaining in itself regenerateth all other powers, and in all ages entering in Holy Soul maketh them friends of God and prophets' (Wisdom of Solomon, cviii)."[17] Reason knows transcendent truth by means of the imagination. Thus, imagination is the activity of Spirit and "the breath of the power of God." For Coleridge, imagination is not a merely human activity independent of Spirit; rather the human imagination participates in or is permeated by the activity of Spirit. Imagination is the activity of Spirit. The boundary between the knowing of the sensible and the supersensible is porous enough to accommodate the motion of Spirit. Spirit is both transcendent and immanent.

The notion of Spirit is itself, of course, composed by the imagination and can serve to illustrate how image grasps a truth beyond itself. The word *spirit* is rooted in the images of breath or
wind connoting a power moving unseen. Human beings have
harbored the conviction that there is an animating motion, energy, and power that moves within us, among us, and beyond us;
and we speak of such power as Spirit. We cannot see it; it is
apprehended by faith—it is composed by the power of the imagination. Coleridge, reflecting on this power in relation to the powers of the mind, perceived that the composing that is faith is an
act of the imagination and the activity of Spirit.

Interestingly, Kegan, reflecting on the religious dimensions of
"meaning-constitutive evolutionary activity" as the central activity of ego, also suggests that this activity is not simply the activity
of ego but is the "creative motion of life itself."[18] He invites us to
recognize that meaning-constitutive evolutionary activity gives
rise to the stages and hence shifts our attention from stages as the
ground of our concern to a figure upon the ground. The motion
or process becomes the ground, and stages become reference
points to periods of dynamic stability in that process. Then,
referring to this process as an underlying motion, he writes that
"the *same* reality said to be philosophically real, biologically real,
psychologically real, and socially real, is also 'religiously' real,
that it partakes of the numinous . . . , the graceful . . . , the holy, the
transcendent, and the oneness of all life. This underlying motion,
especially as it is seen in its spiritual reality, is, I believe, what
James Fowler refers to when he speaks . . . of an 'ultimate
environment.' "[19]

It seems to me that Kegan is being generous here, because
Fowler's use of "ultimate environment" has tended to connote
"ultimate construct" in the sense of structure rather than connoting the dynamic motion toward which Kegan points. But Kegan
is quite right that Fowler's metaphor is capable of embracing
Kegan's insight. Indeed, as the physical sciences compel the modern mind to recognize the dynamic motion of all life, we are now
perhaps drawn toward more adequate metaphors by which to
name the ultimate character of reality.[20] This suggests that the
linkage between faith development and an ultimate construct

may be appropriately superseded by a more profound linkage between faith development and an ultimate motion, between development and Spirit.

DEVELOPMENT, PROCESS, AND IMAGINATION

Now we are ready to return to the work of Piaget and reconsider the relationship of structural development and imagination. The central motion Piaget describes is that of equilibration. Piaget perceives an ongoing interaction between the organism and its environment; this interaction seeks equilibrium. Equilibrium is the balancing of assimilation and accommodation. The human being is constantly assimilating the world as she or he encounters it so as to fit the structures of the knowing mind. At the same time, the human being is having to accommodate, to modify previously composed structures so as to take in the world, constructing it in a more fitting way. When we only assimilate our world we are probably distorting it—and we probably also feel bored and/or stuck. When, on the other hand, we must do too much accommodating, we become stressed. Either over-assimilation or over-accommodation creates a condition of disequilibrium.

This concept of equilibration is useful to our understanding of the development of the underlying structures of thought, and it informs our educational and therapeutic practice. Particularly, it helps us to respect the time and process involved in any change of mind and heart which requires the development of new structures by which we may more adequately handle a more complex understanding of reality. However, both our respect and our practice become significantly better informed when we integrate this understanding of the development of structures through the process of equilibration with an understanding of the transformation of thought through the process of imagination.

Again, we want to remember that the significance of Piaget's underlying structures or operations of thought is the strength and limits of their capacity to handle images. But now we can add the recognition that these structures develop as a consequence of interaction with their environment (images) which must be more adequately accommodated. This accommodation requires the

more adequate fit between inner structure and the images constituting their experience. This moves the process of symbolization
in the imitative sense Piaget described into the more profound
activity of imagination which Coleridge described—into a process of transformation which involves the whole of knowing and
being.

IMAGINATION: A PARADIGM

Another theologian, psychologist, and theorist of religious education, James Loder, has described the creative activity of imagination and its relationship to the transformation of knowing at
the level of faith. His work is helpful to us because the paradigm
he offers serves to organize the insights of Coleridge (which are
much less systematically available, being richly but randomly dis-
tributed through his many essays and notebooks). In Loder's
description of the process of creativity we do not find a contradiction of the motion Piaget and Kegan describe (equilibration and
meaning-making). Rather, we find a more robust attention to
imagination which corrects Piaget's almost exclusive focus on the
formal aspects of intelligence to which imaginative understanding
has been made subservient. The resulting complementarity serves
to point the way toward an understanding of the relationship of
structure and content in the composing that is faith.

Loder offers a paradigm of creativity which involves five
steps.[21] The first he names "conflict," signifying that a rupture
occurs in the knowing context. From the perspective of the activity of meaning-making at the level of faith, we might say that
there is a sense that something is not fitting, right, or appropriate.
From a Piagetian perspective, we might say that the structures of
knowing are confounded by a new experience, or by an experience now occurring in a new juxtaposition, experienced in a new
light. As a consequence equilibrium gives way to disequilibrium.

The second step he terms "interlude for scanning" signifying
the receptive searching for a resolution, a form of holding in a
new way what has become a conflicted puzzle. This step involves
an activity which is experienced as passive, as pause. Here the
mind is asleep but the soul is awake.[22] This is a dimension of the
knowing process which is provided for in every spiritual practice

of meditation—a relaxed attention to the conflict. The essential nature of this interlude for scanning to the knowing process is not suggested by the Piagetian paradigm. Coleridge, however, used the images of both the snake and the waterbug to try to capture this relationship of passive and active motion within the act of imagination.

The third step is the "constructive act of the imagination." An "insight, intuition, or vision appears on the border between the conscious and unconscious, usually with convincing force, and conveys, in a form readily available to consciousness, the essence of the resolution."[23] Coleridge and Bushnell would say that the "form readily available to consciousness" is first an "image." The constructive act of the imagination that occurs in this step is the appropriation of an image which serves to provide a more fitting form for the conflicted situation, thereby enabling its resolution. The consequence is that the dissonant elements of experience are now transformed into a new whole, and a new composition of reality has taken form.

The fourth step is "release" and "opening." The energy which previously was engaged in the conflict is now released and the consciousness of the knower is opened to embrace a larger awareness of his or her context. From the perspective of faith there is now a new knowing, a new trust, and a larger pattern of meaning. The earlier equilibrium and then disequilibrium has been transcended and the person now lives into a new equilibrium.

The fifth step is "interpretation." The imaginative solution operative at the level of faith must find behavioral and public form. It must make congruent connections with the original conditions that gave rise to the disequilibrium, and it must also correspond to a public, consensual view of reality. The image which gives form to a new equilibrium, a new knowing, a new faith must be fitting to a *shared* understanding of reality. This is so for two reasons. The first is that we do not seem to have an inner sense of the completion of the knowing-learning-reconciling process, or a sense of equilibration, until we have anchored our new knowing in a public, behavioral world. But second, this process is vulnerable. We may choose an image that is not adequately fitting.

THE SEARCH FOR RIGHT IMAGES

H. Richard Niebuhr, influenced by both Coleridge and Bushnell, recognized that "the heart must reason; the participating self cannot escape the necessity of looking for pattern and meaning in its life and relations. It cannot make a choice between reason and imagination but only between reasoning on the basis of adequate images and thinking with the aid of evil imaginations."[24] "And anyone who affirms the irrationality of the moral and religious life simply abandons the effort to discipline this life, to find right images by means of which to understand one's self, one's sorrows and joys."[25]

The distortions of inadequate images arising from the finitude of all images and the vulnerability inherent in our subjectivity cannot be transcended by some escape from our dependence upon images into the illusions of the power of formal operational intelligence. Rather, our subjectivity must self-consciously and repeatedly be brought to the forum of shared experience. Even as "evil imaginations are shown to be evil by their consequences to selves and communities,"[26] right imagination can only take form in the test of "repeated, critical, and common" experience.[27] Our meaning-making, even and especially at the level of ultimacy, must be brought into public life and tested for its fittingness to historical, shared experience.

But, on the other hand, faith development theory and its Piagetian insight in turn modifies Niebuhr's statement and the understanding of the theological task it implies. Theology must serve the finding of right images; but theology must also consider the adequacy of images relative to their interaction with each of the psycho-social structures that hold them across the lifetime of persons and communities. In this way of seeing, one test of a religious image is its adequacy within differing stages of faith development and its capacity to serve on-going faith development. The image which is fitting to ongoing lived faith experience must be able to meet us where we are—to be assimilated, to comfort. But it must also confound. It must educate us; it must lead us out; it must require our accommodation, our development, our transformation.

For example, the image of the Kingdom of God has served the Christian faith community in precisely this way. This image has given form and access to spiritual comfort, and it has also continually awakened persons and communities from the comfort of equilibrium into disequilibrium. This image has led Christians from faith to faith; and Christians have expressed their experience as one of being led or called out by Spirit. The same image, however, has also served the interests of exclusiveness and domination. In the context of an increasingly self-conscious religious pluralism, the capacity of this image to serve the demands of faith is being freshly challenged. An understanding of the vulnerability of this image as well as its strengths in relation to Fowler's descriptions of conventional and individuating faith knowing (stages 3 and 4) is as essential to testing the adequacy of this image in the present cultural context as is its appropriation as a stage 6 content.[28]

SUMMARY

What we have done here is to suggest the character of the linkages between faith, development, imagination, and Spirit—linkages which require further exploration in other places and in many voices. Here we have recognized the power of the notion of the structures of the composing mind as illuminated by Kant, Piaget, Kegan, and Fowler. We have invited attention to the shearing of structure from content which occurs in all constructive-developmental theory. And we have suggested that the aligning of the processes of development and imagination, assisted by insights of Coleridge, Bushnell, and Loder, can help to heal this split and its consequent distortions. Further, we have been so bold as to suggest that when we integrate a constructive-developmental understanding with a robust understanding of the imagination, the study of faith development may be seen as a study of the activity of Spirit.

A theory of faith development inclusive of an understanding of imagination and spirit may serve to give access to an understanding of faith formation and the theological task adequate to the need of the human community which now must—in light of a shrinking planet and an enlarging cosmos—imagine a new faith.

NOTES

1. Robert Kegan, "There the Dance Is: Religious Dimensions of Developmental Theory," in *Toward Moral and Religious Maturity,* ed. J. W. Fowler and A. Vergote (Morristown, N.J.: Silver Burdett, 1980), p. 406. See also, Robert Kegan, *The Evolving Self: Problem and Process in Human Development* (Cambridge, Mass.: Harvard University Press, 1982).

2. Kegan, "There the Dance Is," p. 407.

3. See James W. Fowler, *Stages of Faith: The Psychology of Human Development and the Quest for Meaning* (San Francisco: Harper & Row, 1981), esp. chap. 5.

4. Ibid., pp. 197, 296-302.

5. Ibid., p. 201.

6. Ibid., p. 207.

7. Jean Piaget, *Six Psychological Studies,* trans. Anita Tenzer (New York: Random House, 1967), pp. 58-60.

8. A. D. Lindsay, *Kant* (London: Ernest Benn, 1934), pp. 95, 275.

9. Lindsay suggests that Kant did not extend the role of imagination because he never saw that freedom and necessity had somehow to be reconciled within reason itself. Ibid., pp. 247-251 and 288.

10. Quoted in Ray L. Hart, *Unfinished Man and the Imagination: Toward an Ontology and Rhetoric of Revelation* (New York: Herder and Herder, 1968), p. 338. See also Samuel Taylor Coleridge, *Biographia Literaria,* ed. J. Shawcross, 2 vols. (Oxford: Oxford University Press, 1907), I, 107.

11. Ibid., I, 202.

12. Ibid., I, 60.

13. Horace Bushnell, "Dissertation on Language," *God in Christ* (Hartford, Conn.: Brown and Parsons, 1876), p. 23.

14. James W. Fowler, "Stages in Faith: The Structural-Developmental Approach," in *Values and Moral Development,* ed. T. Hennessy (New York: Paulist Press, 1976), p. 175.

15. James W. Fowler, "Faith and the Structuring of Meaning," in *Toward Moral and Religious Maturity,* ed. J. Fowler and A. Vergote (Morristown, N.J.: Silver Burdett Publishing, 1980), pp. 61-62.

16. Samuel Taylor Coleridge, *The Friend,* ed. B. Rooke, 2 vols. The Collected Works of Samuel Taylor Coleridge, gen. ed. K. Coburn, Vol. 4 (Princeton, N.J.: Princeton University Press, 1969), I, 177.

17. Samuel Taylor Coleridge, "The Statesman's Manual," *Lay Sermons,* ed. R. White. The Collected Works of Samuel Taylor Coleridge, gen. ed. K. Coburn, Vol. 6 (Princeton, N.J.: Princeton University Press, 1969), p. 69.

18. Kegan, "There the Dance Is," p. 407.

19. Ibid., pp. 409-410.

20. Coleridge wrote, "The material universe . . . is but one vast MYTHOS (i.e., symbolical representation): and mythology the apex and complement of all genuine physiology." *The Friend,* I, 524.

21. James E. Loder, *The Transforming Moment: Understanding Convictional Experiences* (San Francisco: Harper & Row, 1981), p. 29-53.

22. See Gaston Bachelard, *The Poetics of Space,* trans. M. Jolas (Boston: Beacon Press, 1969), p. xviii.

23. Loder, *The Transforming Moment,* p. 32.

24. H. Richard Niebuhr, *The Meaning of Revelation* (New York: Macmillan, 1941), p. 111.

25. Ibid., p. 107. (Language has been modified to be inclusive.)

26. Ibid., p. 99.

27. Ibid., p. 96.

28. It should also be noted that an examination of the metaphors central to the theory itself may also be called under similar review. This discussion is intended to invite a reexamination of the images of *stages* (in contrast to process, motion, and balance), *knowing* (in contrast to meaning), *linear journey* (in contrast to expansion of consciousness and complexity), and perhaps most importantly the image of *development* itself. In naming the theory, the word *faith* has been chosen with self-conscious theological discipline in preference to *religion* or *belief.* The word *development* has been less reflectively appropriated from the discipline of developmental psychology. Dwayne Huebner has deftly suggested that the potential that the theory may most fundamentally serve—a larger compassion and a more faithful truth—may be cut at its root by the appropriation of the metaphor of development. Development is an image rooted in the process of biological maturation, but it also participates in a cultural-economic ethos in which developmentalism has served as disguised imperialism. The consequent resonance of the metaphor of development may significantly distort an adequate understanding of the dynamics of faith that serve the maturity of faith that Fowler describes in his stage 6. (Dwayne Huebner, in his "Response to Fowler," given at the Consultation on Faith Development, Auburn Theological Seminary, March, 1982 [unpublished].) See Dwayne Huebner, "Toward a Political Economy of Curriculum and Human Development," in *Curriculum and Instruction,* ed. Henry A. Giroux (Berkeley: McCutchan, 1981); also, John Broughton's chapter in this volume.

Theorists of faith development concerned with the normative as well as the descriptive task may consider the metaphor of transformation in addition to or as preferable to the metaphor of development. The story of "faith development and transformation" may more adequately embrace both the developing structural power of the underlying operations of thought and the formative power of the images they hold, while simultaneously opening up a more faithful and critical distance between faith educators and pastoral care providers and inadequately examined cultural assumptions.

Chapter 7

Basic Sources and New Possibilities: H. Richard Niebuhr's Influence on Faith Development Theory

STUART D. McLEAN

James Fowler makes quite clear in his various writings his fundamental indebtedness to H. Richard Niebuhr. Although Fowler's theory also reflects the influences of Paul Tillich and Wilfred Cantwell Smith—as well as of such psychological theorists as Jean Piaget, Lawrence Kohlberg, and Erik Erikson—the influence of them all is dwarfed by that of Niebuhr, who was the subject of Fowler's first major book.[1]

Many readers of Fowler's theory of faith development do not know Niebuhr's work firsthand. Because it is of such importance to Fowler, it is crucial that the basic themes which Fowler picks up from him be isolated and described. The first half of this essay identifies four of them: (1) the dialectical relationship between theology and the social sciences, (2) the relationship of faith to its object, (3) the understanding of the human self as fundamentally relational and communal, and (4) the nature of transformation/conversion. These themes are central to the work of both Fowler and Niebuhr and constitute the axes around which their work is most deeply related.

There are two other themes in Niebuhr, however, which Fowler does not fully explore. These are the themes of "reference groups" (or multiple communities of faith) and "root metaphors." I believe that exploration of these dimensions of Niebuhr's work would further enrich Fowler's theory of faith development and help him to buttress his theory at points where it may be weak or, at least, lack adequate clarity.

THEOLOGY AND SOCIAL SCIENCES

Fowler wears two hats and speaks to two audiences. He commutes between the theological and the social scientific modes of understanding. In doing this he follows Niebuhr who also worked both as a social scientist and a theologian. Niebuhr, for example, submitted the life and theology of the church to sociological analysis—particularly in relation to the issues of race and class—in *The Social Sources of Denominationalism.* But he also developed a theological analysis of American culture in *The Kingdom of God in America.* In *The Meaning of Revelation,* Niebuhr explored the transforming nature of existential relationship with Jesus Christ as the particular, significant revelation of a dynamic and loving God. The heart of *Radical Monotheism in Western Culture,* on the other hand, sets forth a generic theory of faith as a human universal.

The same interplay between the social scientific and the theological is found in Fowler. On the one hand, the general theory of faith development is an attempt to explicate, analyze, and describe what is involved in faith from the human side, explicitly bracketing the content and character of the center of value and power (God or idol) and reducing the rich and particular life of specific believers and religions in order to ferret out the formal structure that may be applicable across the particularities. On the other hand, Fowler is avowedly a Christian theologian—more specifically, a Methodist—who expresses the particular, concrete, involved, existential, and convictional dimension of his faith, not only in his personal commitment and in his preaching, but also in his scholarship as evidenced in his new book, *Becoming Adult, Becoming Christian.*[2] Although each pole creatively and intentionally influences the other, Fowler attempts to "play by the rules" of the audience he is addressing.

Faith development analysis is an attempt to theorize, not only across religious lines, but also about secular centers which function as gods among believers and nonbelievers alike. It is a formal theory; that is, it focuses on the forms and structures of the faith relationship, and, consequently, should not be expected to pick up on the contents of particular religious traditions or on the particularity of a believer's faith. Religious faith is lived out in particular communities by particular persons whose inner religious life and meaning cannot be reduced to formal categories. Faith development theorists do not attempt fully to describe this specificity, believing that these aspects can best be witnessed to in different terms when writing to a different audience. Fowler, however, contends (like Niebuhr) that the formal description of faith in relationship to a center of value and power is clarifying in regard to certain essential aspects of *all* particular expressions of faith—religious and secular.

FAITH AND CENTERS OF VALUE AND POWER

Niebuhr understands faith as relationship to a center or centers of value and power. The passive or receptive side of faith is *trust;* the active side is expressed as *loyalty* and *commitment*.[3] In this understanding, too, Fowler follows Niebuhr—and both are developing an insight of Josiah Royce. Royce argued that faith always has some object and that all human beings relate, both consciously and unconsciously, to some center or centers of value which, in turn, influence their lives and behavior. Martin Luther made the same point when he asked: "What does it mean to have a god?" His answer was that "trust and faith of the heart alone make both God and idol. . . . Whatever then thy heart clings to . . . and relies upon, that is properly thy god."[4]

Niebuhr provided a set of categories by which he described what functions as god in a person's life. These are analytical tools for discerning not only what a person considers holy, sacred, or god, but also the idols—finite aspects of life lifted up for worship (such as the nation, family, science, sports, business). They become *de facto* centers, often with a full array of beliefs and symbols attached to them which virtually govern a person's behavior. Often the least acknowledged, the taken-for-granted realities of common life, have the greatest influence on day-to-day existence, while formal religious commitments and trusts may be quite separate from it. Erikson illustrates the point when he says that "industrial man's attempt to identify with the machine as if it were a *new totem animal* leads him into a self-perpetuating race for robot-like efficiency."[5] The machine has become god, the industrial reveals the pattern of ultimate reality, and we ourselves behave like robots. The distinctions between transcendence and immanence, sacred and profane, holy and secular are not important in this phenomenological description. For the purposes of this kind of analysis, that certain centers *function* as gods for human beings and communities is all that is essential.

These ideas, which Fowler adopts, seem to me to be relatively self-evident. They have, in one form or another, played a significant role in religious discussion of false gods or idol worship for centuries. Jesus' warning, in Matthew 6:19-21, is an example of their use in the New Testament: "Do not lay up for yourselves treasures on earth. . . . For where your treasure is, there will your heart be also." *Treasure* points to one's center of value and power; and *heart* refers to the manner of relating to it, through trust and loyalty. This language implies no particular content in the object trusted. It indicates only that faith is relational and has an "object." The character of the "object" may be personal or impersonal, dynamic or inert, loving or indifferent. From the perspective of particular theological traditions, the character of God is crucial. But it is not the task of social science to describe or evaluate the content of the particular, living, existential, involvement. Fowler's definition is broad and inclusive enough to recognize the fact that virtually anything can function as a center of value. But it focuses only on that which is lifted up, explicitly or implicitly, into a supraordinate position and which thereby order all other aspects of life. According to his definition, centers of value and power are found in any of an innumerable variety of mythic, symbolic, ritual, narrative, and often institutional complexes.

A particular virtue of this related pair—faith *and* center of value and power—is its ability to expose what life is like when trust and loyalty are invested in *multiple* centers. This, by Niebuhr's and Fowler's definition, is what polytheism is. And, according to their analysis, it is the source of the alienation and fragmentation that many people experience under the centrifugal pulls of proliferating centers.[6] Some way of naming these centers and their dynamics in our lives must be made available. This formal, structural, and relational approach to the condition of polytheism meets this need. There is descriptive and analytical power here, whatever the content and character of the centers under scrutiny.

This formal, structural description effectively poses a central question, however: How, if at all, can gods (centers of value and power), competing for our loyalties, be subordinated to one God? Donning their Christian hats, Niebuhr and Fowler both fill in the blanks theologically with a radically monotheistic God—one who is transcendent but who works through all the subordinate centers, a God who is revealed to persons in history in the concrete particular, ultimately through the incarnation of Jesus Christ. This Center does not negate other centers, but only relativizes them, robbing them of their idolatrous pretensions.

SELF AND COMMUNITY

Fowler has a fundamentally relational view of the human self. In this, too, he has been influencd by Niebuhr. Niebuhr's critique of two images of the human being as moral agent, together with the development of his own constructive alternative—all presented in *The Responsible Self*[7]—has particularly provided the basis for Fowler's own view. The first image Niebuhr critiques is "man-the-maker." Here the person is seen primarily as a producer who makes things (and life) after a pattern already given. It is a teleological understanding of the self. The primary focus is on goal-oriented human agency, nondialogically understood. The second image—"man-the-citizen"—is one in which understanding of and alignment with the regulative structures of reality defines the core of human being. Kant and Kohlberg are major representatives of this deontological view. Here the focus is on obedience to universal law, nondialogically understood. Niebuhr finds both of these images inadequate. They are only partial, and neither provides an adequate, over-arching image for what our actual life as moral agents is really like.[8] Thus Niebuhr goes on to articulate a third option, the image of "man-the-answerer" who responds to the actions of others as a responsive or responsible self. Niebuhr's analysis of this third image reveals his understanding of the human self—one that is at the heart of Fowler's understanding as well.

According to Niebuhr, human beings are constituted by dialogue in relationship. This implies a psychology of interaction and interrelationship. Niebuhr found such a psychology in the work of George Herbert Mead as well as in Martin Buber. As Niebuhr articulated the matter, there are four elements. First, human beings act in *response* to action upon them. Second, the response always involves *interpretation.* That is, our responses are governed by a meaning system which relates the action to a larger framework of interpretation—of what is going on and of what is being done to persons. This meaning system is conveyed through the operative symbols, myths, and narratives brought to bear by the person participating in communities of interpretation. One of the important contributions of faith development theory is that, whatever the content of this meaning framework, it is accessed or interpreted by people in different ways at different stages of development. Third, through accountability, responses are made in anticipation of answers-to-our-answer. A person's action is like a statement in a dialogue. Responsibility lies with the agent who stays with his or her action, accepts the consequences, and looks forward to continued interaction. In other words, the dialogical exchange is understood as one aspect of an ongoing interchange. Finally, continuity builds social solidarity. "Our action is responsible . . . when it is response to action upon us in a continuing discourse or interaction among beings forming a continuing society." This implies "the continuity of a self with a relatively consistent scheme of interpretations," and by the same token "continuity in the community of agents to which response is being made."9

The definition of self and community outlined above is implied, I contend, wherever Fowler discusses either of these concepts. Although the particular focus of *Stages of Faith* is on the development of individual persons, the self is always seen as developing in community. This is an essential aspect of Fowler's anthropology. Development occurs in communities, whether in the primary community of the family, among close friends in face-to-face groups, or within larger public entities. Any participation of the self with others, near or far, is through symbols, images, and stories which contribute to the interpretation of those spheres. Fowler pays particular attention to this when he studies people's "Bounds of Social Awareness" and "Perspective-Taking."

Further, Fowler, utilizing Niebuhr's concepts, has more than a dyadic understanding of the self: "Niebuhr wants us to see the *triadic* structure of the tacit covenant that makes possible and sustains community and selfhood."[10] Persons come to selfhood by commitment to a cause through which they find themselves associated with other loyalties. Thus loyalty is a double bond—to the companion and to the cause. There is something personal and interpersonal *and* something that transcends both persons and community. The triadic structure assumes the dialogical interaction of persons with each other and also with a supraordinate cause or center of value and power. Faith development theory suggests that at different stages the person will understand this triadic form in changing ways.

It can also be demonstrated that aspects of Paul Tillich's theology are evident in Fowler's understanding of self and community. In Tillich's *Systematic Theology* one of the self-world polarities essential to Tillich's theology is "individualization and participation," an expression of which is person and community.[11] Tillich contends that only a dialectical relation of these two poles overcomes alienation. Any theoretical or practical focus on the person to the exclusion of the community leads to errors of atomistic individualism; any excessive focus on the community without concern for the individual person leads to collectivism and loss of the self. Reading Fowler's work with these eyes, one is aware of his attempt to maintain the Tillichean dialectic.

Several critics claim that Fowler has an inadequate understanding of the self. Robert Wuthnow says that "the theory, finally, is individualistic." John Broughton argues that the self, in Fowlers' interpretation, has no agency, is possessively individualistic, and just a unit in bureaucratic society.[12] It is difficult for me to understand the sources of these criticisms. It seems that much of the criticism of Fowler's work as excessively individualistic has chosen to read into him a mechanistic interpretation of Kohlberg rather than the dyadic and triadic definitions of selfhood which he utilizes from H. Richard Niebuhr.

These critics, in my opinion, are mistaken on two counts. First, they misunderstand Kohlberg, not acknowledging the social constructionist (John Dewey) and symbolic interactionist (G. H. Mead) components of his theory. And, second, they do not understand the contrasting uses Kohlberg and Fowler make of these common sources. Kohlberg, while seeing the importance of inter-action between the self and others, seems to leave behind this relational and interactional insight as he describes the latter stages of moral development (especially stages 4, 5, and 6). At this point the self becomes increasingly cognitive for Kohlberg, and rationality takes the place of relationality. By contrast, Fowler seeks ultimately to hold together "cognition and affection,"[13] "ra-tionality and passionality,"[14] in a relational and dialogical under-standing of the self.

TRANSFORMATION/CONVERSION

Fowler is obviously interested in the theme of human transfor-mation. His theory is a theory of development. The theme of transformation is also very important to Niebuhr. Most of the emphasis in Fowler's work is on transformation through stage change, however. In Niebuhr's work the primary transformation-al theme comes under the rubric of conversion and appears in writings where he is speaking as a Christian theologian. The question arises: Are the language and categories of faith develop-ment theory open enough to include Niebuhr's understanding of conversion?

In *Stages of Faith* Fowler describes faith as a "dynamic existen-tial stance, a way of leaning into and finding or giving meaning to the conditions of our lives."[15] But it is more than that. First, he incorporates the affective, valuational, imaginal, and relational modes of knowing that Piaget and Kohlberg have not highlight-ed. Reading Fowler as a simple extension to faith development of Piaget's and Kohlberg's modes of knowing misreads him and does not take into account the influence of Niebuhr and Tillich on his thought.[16]

Second, Fowler distinguishes the *logic of rational certainty* (Pia-get and Kohlberg) from the *logic of conviction*. The former aims at objectivity, understood as a knowing free from all particular and subjective investigation. Its truths need to be impersonal, propositional, demonstrable, and replicable.[17] On the other hand, the latter more comprehensive form of knowing, the logic of conviction, "gives rise to choice and action [and] the constitution or modification of the self is always an issue. . . . [T]here is also a simultaneous extension, modification, or reconstitution of *the knower in relation to the known.*"[18] Thus the logic of conviction implies freedom, risk, passion, and subjectivity. The logic of conviction within the phenomenological framework of faith development theory significantly breaks with Piaget and Kohlberg and gives "space" for concepts of transformation and conversion.

Third, Fowler argues that Piaget does not take another form of knowledge—the imagination—seriously, but relegates it to fantasy and adult play in later stages.[19] Faith recognizes

> the modes of knowing we call ecstatic and imaginative. . . . The mind employs the more aesthetically oriented right hemisphere of the brain in these kinds of knowing. . . . To move in this direction requires coming to terms with modes of thought that employ images, symbols, and synesthesial fusions of sense and feeling. . . . To deal adequately with faith and with faith's dynamic role in the total self-constitutive activity of ego means trying to give theoretical attention to the transformation of consciousness—rapid and dramatic in sudden conversion, more gradual and incremental in faith growth—which results from the re-cognition of self-others-world in light of knowing the self as constituted by a center of value powerful enough to require or enable recentering one's ultimate environment.[20]

Finally, his own discussion of conversion seems to allow for and affirm much of the dynamic of conversion affirmed by some Christian perspectives. "Conversion is *a significant recentering of one's previous conscious or unconscious images of value and power and the conscious adoption of a new set of master stories in the commitment to reshape one's life in a new community of interpretation and action.*"[21]

Although Fowler says conversion can occur in any of the faith stages or in any of the transitions between them,[22] I would like to propose that the stage 2-3 transition, in particular, be correlated with the basic notion of religious conversion. The stage 2 formulation is, in effect, a description of the classical understanding of the law as an external, legalistic, *quid pro quo* interaction. Although there is interaction between persons (or between persons and God) at this stage, it is conditional: "I'll scratch your back, *if* you'll scratch mine" (Kohlberg). Persons are understood externally as "its" in relationship both to the ultimate environment (the "vertical") and to the interpersonal environment (the "horizontal"). Transformation or conversion occurs when one discovers that these "horizontal" and "vertical" relationships can be understood in personal categories (stage 3), entered into by persons who have stories and rich-textured internal lives, and who are "thous" rather than objects or "its." One discovers one is loved "in spite of," not "because of"; therefore, one can love in a similar manner. This is the time when "the miracle of forgiveness," in an interpersonal sense, comes to be appreciated and where retribution (stage 2) is recognized as destructive. This transition can occur in "vertical" and/or "horizontal" dimensions; or the "vertical" can occur through the "horizontal." The discovery that life is interpersonal and dialogical releases energy and joy, and leads to a new way of being. The interpersonal dimensions of community, of small groups, of friendship, of God as personal, all acquire new meaning. Although there is an argument that each stage transition, and content change within a stage, can be the occasion for a religious conversion, the conversion point that is central to much religious life and literature is, in my opinion, this law-grace, stage-2-to-stage-3 transition. Although this conversion is limited (the broader and deeper vision and reality of God as ruler of the universe, and of all persons as brothers and sisters, is reserved for stages 4, 5, and 6), nevertheless, the transition from law, death, and egocentrism to grace, life, and relationship—with others, and to a God who is gracious—fits the most familiar, traditional understanding of religious conversion.

In summary one can say that Fowler's understanding of transformation/conversion incorporates faith as a "dynamic existential stance," which involves affective, valuational, imaginal, and relational modes of knowing, as well as the ecstatic and imaginative. The "logic of conviction" and "the recentering of one's previous conscious and unconscious images of power and value" not only point to the critical role of stage change but also to transformation within stages.

It is evident that much of what Fowler says here about transformation and conversion is influenced by the relational and holistic theology of Niebuhr. But there are also significant differences between them that must be pointed out. First, Niebuhr indicates no awareness of stages of faith development. The relationship of transformation/conversion and stages is not on his horizon. Second, Fowler's understanding of conversion does not focus on reinterpreting personal and communal history (sin) through the love and forgiveness of God through Jesus Christ. For Niebuhr, however, it is not just the heart (and all that entails) that is important but the specific character of the revelation through Jesus Christ.

> The revelatory event resurrects [the] buried past. It demands and permits that we bring into the light . . . our betrayals and denials. . . . In the personal inner life revelation requires the heart to recall the sins of the self and to confess fully what it shuddered to remember.[23]
> Revelation does not accomplish the work of conversion; the reasoning heart must search out memory and bring to light forgotten deeds. But without the revelatory image this work does not seem possible.[24]

Niebuhr is concerned here, beyond the categories of faith development, with the specific character of the center of value and its role in transformation. Take, for example, his discussion of forgiveness:

> [Psychologists] have found that if present relations of selves to others are to be reorganized, if the responses of selves to others and to themselves in interaction with others are to be made constructive rather than destructive, if they are to fit better into the total process of interpersonal life, then the past must not be forgotten but remembered, accepted, and reinterpreted. What such analysis calls again to our attention is related . . . to the understanding of themselves which Christians have had when they looked for newness of life not by way of forgetting the past but by the forgiveness of sins, the remembrance of their guilt, and the acceptance of their acceptance by those against whom they had offended.[25]

This reinterpretation also affects the future.

> The reinterpretation of the actions of others upon us . . . which gives us the possibility of new response in the present, results also from reinterpretation of our future, since we react in the present predictively as well as in recollection.[26]

The question is whether Niebuhr's view of conversion, which entails the "timeful self" and the reinterpretation of the past and future through forgiveness, fits into the categories of faith development? Another way of raising the question is to ask whether the theory of faith development is so significantly governed by an organic metaphor, which involves unfolding stages as well as a relational, affectional, and convictional mode of knowing, that it obscures both the past and future modes of time, and the radical character of forgiveness?

REFERENCE GROUPS

I have argued that it is impossible to understand and appreciate Fowler's theory of faith development without understanding his relationship to his theological mentor, H. Richard Niebuhr. In this section and the next, I want to lift up two themes that Niebuhr included in his theological ethics but which Fowler has for the most part ignored. I believe that work with the two themes of "reference group theory" and "root metaphor analysis" would increase the analytic, descriptive, and constructive power of Fowler's developmental theory.

Niebuhr, explicitly in *The Responsible Self* but implicitly in much of his other writing, began to use the phrase "reference group" to describe the variety of communities in which he found persons to be embedded and to which they empirically and "trans-empirically" relate.[27] The symbolic interactionist school, in which George Herbert Mead was a principal figure, initially developed and refined the notion of reference group.[28] This school had a profound influence on Niebuhr. He found in the concept "reference group" a logical extension of his ideas about polytheism—that persons have many centers of value, each of which implies a community of discourse—and of his affirmation of persons as symbolic and dialogical beings.

A good example of his use of the term "reference group" is found in his discussion of the *triadic* form of the moral life.

In other analyses of human self-conduct the third may appear as that reference group to which the self relates himself as he reacts to present challenges. He plays his various roles . . . in meeting the challenges and expectations of his immediate fellowmen by referring always to some prestige persons or societies with whom he identifies himself and of whom he asks—in interior dialogue at least—not only how they would act in his situation but how they would approve, disapprove, or correct his conduct and reaction to his companions.[29]

This third reality has a double character.

On the one hand it is something personal; on the other it contains within itself again a reference to something that transcends it or to which it refers. The generalized other or the impartial spectator . . . is a knower and evaluator, representing the community but also the community's cause. . . . In the situation of the patriot, the third to whom he is related besides his co-patriots is a nation or country, but that country is not only a community of persons living and dead—hcroes of the past and the future, founding fathers and historical posterity to whom appeal is made; it is always such a community plus that to which these representatives make their reference. . . . They represent not the community only but what the community stands for. Ultimately we arrive in the case of democracy at a community which refers beyond itself to humanity and which in doing so seems to envisage not only representatives of the human community as such but a universal society and a universal generalized other, Nature and Nature's God.[30]

Here Niebuhr represents reference groups, not only as those empirical groups with which persons interact face-to-face, but also as larger communities which themselves have centers of value beyond themselves to which they point—in some cases to a yet more inclusive community and its center, God. These are "transcendent reference groups" which, from Niebuhr's perspective, form an essential aspect of human, social, and symbolic consciousness.[31]

Notice also that reference groups extend to the future and to the past. He asks:

What is the time span in which our responsive actions take place? Into what history do we make these actions of ours fit? For the most part it seems that responsive man has short spans of time in view. He acts in the light of brief pasts and brief futures; and yet these short periods . . . are surrounded by his sense of his lifetime, of his social and human history. Hence his interpretations of present events are always modified by larger contexts in which they are placed.[32]

The spatial, communal, and temporal contexts are crucial for Niebuhr's understanding of reference groups and the role they play in interpretation of the religious and moral life.[33]

It is not possible further to refine this concept here, except to emphasize three aspects of reference groups in Niebuhr's work.[34] First, persons exist, not just in one reference group, but in several. The usual litany of groups includes family, school, work, politics, friends, church, avocation, etc., but the repertoire is much larger, especially in a mass-media culture. Second, participation in a reference group implies participation also in a community that has a past (made present in memory) and a future (made present in expectations, anticipations, and promises). Third, all reference groups in which we participate are ambiguous, reflecting their heritage of sin, explicit and buried, as well as of goodness and grace.

Several critics fault Fowler for individualism and for not taking the social context seriously. I have indicated where, in my opinion, this critique has missed the mark. Nevertheless, faith development in its present form is to a significant degree a theory of the development of the self, albeit in a relational context to centers of value and to others. The social, in the larger sense of class, community, and institutions, is not given its due. Fowler does acknowledge that we are persons-in-community and, in a number of writings, suggests that stage analysis can also be applied to communities. He begins to develop his thought in this direction with the category "bounds of social awareness." He also maintains that communities may take on a dominant mode of development and that persons whose faith development goes beyond that of the community may feel uncomfortable or marginalized. Nevertheless, his view of the stage development of the primary faith community is not yet integrated into the overall theory.

In addition, too often persons using faith development theory, and even at times Fowler himself, assume that persons live in only one reference community, usually envisioned as church-family-friends. Thus the issue of growth and pilgrimage is confined to that one reference group. However, reference-group theory (and faith development itself) suggests to us that persons soon after school age, if not before, gradually add groups to their reference group repertoire, and, at adolescence, through experience and reflection made possible by formal thinking, become self-conscious of their context. That a person is a member of *several* reference groups, each of which has a future and a past as well as a present, has significant implications for faith development theory.

To begin with, the "given situation" of persons in modern heterogeneous culture is one in which we are selves in *many* communities. Each community has more or less articulated centers of value and power, which are expressed in symbolic and narrative ways to which ritual and ethical behavior is related. Some such centers are hidden, and their *de facto* power to function as idols is not understood. If this is so, and if persons are participants in multiple reference groups, each with its explicit or implicit center or centers of value and power, then the religious situation which the church confronts is more complex than is usually appreciated. That is, the situation is one of *de facto* polytheism. For example, a parishioner may be not only a member of First Church with its central loyalty but also an administrator in a multinational corporation doing business with South Africa and thus be subject to the tensions and conflicts which such a combination of loyalties implies. A resultant imperative is the need to describe the actual reference group complexes in which persons find themselves. Or, as Niebuhr said, "the first step of ethics is to discover what is going on."

Second, for the Christian, one of these reference groups, and its center in Jesus Christ,[35] serves as the key interpreting community. Consequently, while most of life is lived in numerous reference communities, the Christian community, the church, evokes special loyalty and therefore incurs special responsibility for providing a liturgical, communal, and educational context in which the process of interpreting can be acquired and growth in faith affirmed.

As the key to interpretation, the Christian community functions not only for the private dimensions of personal life but also for the public reference groups—with their centers of value—relating and ordering one to another through its supraordinate center of value. Thus the key faith community facilitates an ordering or subordinating of the gods of the polytheistic world.

Third, let us assume that the unit of faith development is the reference group (or Christian community) as well as the individual. In 1 Corinthians 12, we read:

> Now there are a variety of gifts, but the same Spirit; and there are varieties of service, but the same Lord; and there are varieties of working, but it is the same God who inspires them all in every one. . . . For just as the body is one and has many members, and all the members of the body, though many, are one body, so it is with Christ. . . . Now you are the body of Christ and individually members of it.[36]

This text highlights the division of labor as well as the unity of the body of Christ. Can the whole be more than the sum of the parts? I believe that it can. Reinhold Niebuhr's aphorism "moral man and immoral society" can be reversed to read "immoral (or incomplete) man and moral (mature or whole) society." Put in faith development language, a community with a majority of stage 2, 3, and 4 persons, and a remnant of stage 4, 5, and 6 persons can become a stage 5 or 6 church. (I believe that stages 5 and 6 are idealistic for most individuals, but can be normative for the Christian community.) Crucial to this suggestion is an interpretation of stage 3 as that stage in which grace can first be recognized and participation in the community becomes dialogical. Consequently, persons can benefit from the contributions of others who have special callings (stage 4, 5, and 6 persons). Such a church could occur through the synergy of Christian community with its discernment and affirmation of "callings" on the basis of stages. Individuals perform special and catalytic functions; persons and leadership, in turn, open to the Spirit and to one another, lead to a more complete use of the talents and resources of the body of Christ. We have done for us what we are not able to do for ourselves. We do for others what they are not able to do for themselves. Individual developmental journeys are shared within the interdependent unity of the body of Christ.

Thus faith development within the community as a whole

becomes as important as the faith development of the individuals within it, a realization that overcomes the implicit elitism of stage analysis and affirms the central importance of the stage 2 to 3 transition for all Christians. Within the greater economy of the community, individual Christians have specific, unique callings related to the stage of their faith development for which they are to be freed, called, and trained.

In summary, three implications of reference group theory for faith development emerge from the previous analysis: (1) Individual persons are members of more than one reference community, each with its center of value. Whether these centers are manifest or hidden, the first task of Christian reflection is to name the real situation. (2) The Christian community becomes the key interpreter for the private lives of its members, but also for the ordering and subordinating of the centers of value of individual public lives. (3) Making the body of Christ the basic unit of faith development has major implications for the church.

ROOT METAPHOR THEORY

Increasingly, the use of root metaphors as a way of talking about religious and ethical matters is finding a niche in theological-ethical literature.[37] Niebuhr employed a loose typology of metaphors (which he called ideas, theories, and symbolic forms, as well as metaphors) that facilitated his analysis.[38] He used such metaphors as organism, mechanism, contract, man-the-maker, man-the-citizen, as well as some variants of covenant. In a short article, entitled "Metaphors and Morals," Niebuhr said:

> Now we understand, for instance, what a mighty though often unacknowledged role in guiding scientific experiment and theory during the last three hundred years the image of the machine has played. . . . And so, with metaphysics the root-metaphors of generating substance, of the republic, of the organism, of the machine, of the event, and of the mathematical system have exercised a deep-going influence on the construction of great systems which those great artists, the metaphysical philosophers, have set before us as images of being itself.[39]

Fowler, reflecting Niebuhr, sees the metaphor of covenant as central: "The patterns of faith that make selfhood possible and sustain our identities are covenantal (triadic) in form."[40] Beyond this initial assertion he goes on to say, "Some of these covenants are tacit, informal, and taken-for-granted. Nonetheless they are vital and real. Other of our covenants are explicit. These we formalize, celebrate, review and occasionally dissolve."[41]

The argument which I propose, however, extends Fowler's argument with the assertion that the covenantal metaphor is distinctive and needs to be distinguished from the organic, which neither Niebuhr nor Fowler fully recognize. As a result, they overlook some of the richness of the biblical tradition, and Fowler, in particular, makes himself unnecessarily vulnerable to criticism.

Piaget and the developmentalists operate basically out of an organic metaphor. Fowler has combined Niebuhr's theology, which is fundamentally covenantal, with developmental theory. The result has been an amalgamation of covenantal and organic thought, significantly integrated, yet with some distinctive aspects of the covenantal remaining to be worked through.[42]

The critical distinctions between covenantal and organic metaphors are three. First, harmony and unity are the norm in the organic metaphor; struggle and conflict of a certain kind, as well as harmony and unity, in the covenantal. Second, forgiveness, or its functional equivalent, is essential to covenant. While present in the organic view, it does not have the "breakthrough" or "new beginning" quality it exhibits in covenantal thinking. Rather, problems tend to be solved through normal growth and development. Third, the organic perspective views time primarily in terms of movement from the past to the present, with a narrow view of the future as the unfolding of essential form. The covenantal, on the other hand, stresses the future while also including the past and present.

Both Fowler and Niebuhr incorporate many aspects of covenantal thinking. Both employ an actional/relational ontology; both have a covenantal understanding of time. Still, neither affirms the role of struggle and conflict as an aspect of love nor the centrality of forgiveness in reconstituting relationships (though Niebuhr acknowledges its importance). What implications for faith development emerge when aspects of covenantal thinking are worked through?

First, the form and dynamic of encounter—between person-and-person, person-and-community, God-and-person—needs to be viewed in more vigorous terms. This happens through recognizing struggle and conflict as a normal aspect of interpersonal love, community transformation, and the God-person relationship. Struggle as integral to love needs to be accepted as normative along with the recognition and practice of forgiveness, grounded in a transcendent center of value.

Second, the view of transcendent grace or forgiveness as "breaking through," disrupting the regularities of a developmental model, need not destroy the essential insights of stage development but rather punctures a kind of determinism and false predictability. Furthermore, grace or disjunctive impulses do not come only from the "transcendent" but also through the community, or from the "transcendent" through the community.[43] Caution or accepting only moderate tension characterizes normal developmental expectations, while the rough encounter with a sustaining, accepting, and forgiving community frees persons to experience and experiment with life which entails struggle.

Third, the language of equilibrium, equilibration, and balance, used to refer to the processes of assimilation and accommodation, is essentially a language of the organic metaphor; and it is a limiting one by the criteria of the covenantal metaphor. The concept of stages may appropriately mark the regular and distinctive changes in the way the world and personal relationships are accessed. But more attention needs to be paid to the complexity of the process. Perhaps visions, stories, and models of persons who have stage 5 and 6 capacities perform important functions to challenge those not yet conceptually or relationally prepared for that way of being-in-the-world. Likewise, memories and recapitulated aspects of stages 1 and 2, in their own right and not yet reinterpreted into "higher" stages, provide important insights for accomplishing subsequent developmental tasks.

Fourth, rather than positing a harmony of whole selves and souls, universally related, the stage 6 vision needs to be modified to include a community of incomplete souls who, in their brokenness, are able to identify with all persons and creatures and who realize the ambiguities and tragedies of existence. Encounter and struggle still continue, and awareness of finitude is poignant, but the identifying image is of one who participates in universal community with others, who struggles for love and justice among the marginalized and alienated. Universality of vision and identification is conjoined with particularity and the ability to relate to concrete persons at each stage of pilgrimage. It is a vision in marked contrast to the Kantian and Kohlbergian universal. The hierarchical stages are not replaced but are given a radically different relational structure because of the basic ontology of the covenantal metaphor and the dialectical-dialogical manner of relating particularity and universality. Integration, unity, and wholeness also assume radically different forms as they relate to the community more than the individual.

Fifth, if historical and formal thinking does become a possibility at stage 3, then perhaps developmental theory should acknowledge and anticipate a variety of developmental options in each stage thereafter. For example, while continuing to think of stage 4 in systemic terms, the substages of stage 4 may be governed by a variety of root metaphors—systemic organic, systemic covenantal, systemic power, systemic mechanistic.

Insights from the covenantal root metaphor can critique and supplement faith development theory, which presently is influenced predominantly by the organic metaphor, in the following ways: (1) The encounters between persons-and-persons and persons-and-God need to be understood to include struggle and conflict. (2) "Transcendent" forgiveness can be seen as a possibility which "breaks through" the regularities of developmental expectations. (3) The language of equilibrium and balance, based on the organic metaphor, should be replaced by a more adequate account of the complexity of the actual processes. (4) The stage 6 vision needs to be modified to include brokenness, tragedy, and participation with the marginalized. (5) Stage 4 systemic thinking needs to be expanded to include systems based on a variety of root metaphors.

The interface of theology and developmental theory is complex. Nevertheless, if the combined insights of both survive the critical fire, an expanded faith development theory can enrich our ability to discern, and respond creatively to, what is going on in a complex world. Awareness of that world as governed and redeemed by a center of value and power can grow through the enlarged understanding of our communal and personal experience that results from the creative application of covenantal thought.

NOTES

1. James Fowler, *To See the Kingdom: The Theological Vision of H. Richard Niebuhr* (Nashville: Abingdon, 1974).

2. James Fowler, *Becoming Adult, Becoming Christian* (San Francisco: Harper & Row, 1984).

3. H. Richard Niebuhr, *Radical Monotheism and Western Culture* (New York: Harper & Bros., 1960), pp. 16-18.

4. Quoted in H. Richard Niebuhr, *The Meaning of Revelation* (New York: Macmillan, 1952), p. 23.

5. Erik Erikson, *Insight and Responsibility* (New York: Norton, 1964), p. 105; italics added.

6. Even here the value stance of Fowler's and Niebuhr's phenomenological approach is present. Polytheism is a negative value in Niebuhr's theory, leading to fragmentation. Monotheism (radical) is the implied positive value. But value stances are intrinsic to all social science. All data is organized into facts by theory. And theory entails a worldview. So values are embedded in all social scientific descriptions, most often unacknowledged. See Stuart D. McLean, "Ethics, Reference Group Theory and Root Metaphor Analysis," *Andover Newton Quarterly* 8 (March, 1978) 4, pp. 211-221. This insight does not negate the distinctive role of social science. Rather, it points to how values not only function "above board" and explicitly in theology and ethics, but also implicitly in the processes of description itself. Awareness of this insight is another contribution of Niebuhr. He states that we increase our objectivity about social facts by acknowledging the values assumed by the theory used to order the data.

7. H. Richard Niebuhr, *The Responsible Self* (New York: Harper & Row, 1963), chaps. 1 and 2.

8. In a later section of the book, Niebuhr reintegrates the values of each of these approaches within his dialogical anthropology and ontology.

9. Ibid., pp. 61-65.

10. Fowler, *To See the Kingdom,* p. 207.

11. Paul Tillich, *Systematic Theology,* Vol. I (Chicago: University of Chicago Press, 1951), p. 165.

12. See Robert Wuthnow, "A Sociological Perspective on Faith Development," in *Faith Development in the Life Cycle,* ed. Kenneth Stokes (New York: Sadlier, 1982), p. 218, and John Broughton, "The Political Psychology of Faith Development Theory," in the present volume.

13. James Fowler, *Stages of Faith* (San Francisco: Harper & Row, 1981), p. 273.

14. Ibid., p. 272.

15. Ibid., p. 92.

16. Ibid., p. 98.

17. Ibid., p. 102.

18. Ibid., p. 103.

19. Ibid., pp. 103-104.

20. Ibid., p. 104.

21. Ibid., pp. 281-282.

22. Ibid., pp. 285-286.

23. Niebuhr, *The Meaning of Revelation,* p. 114.

24. Ibid., p. 121.

25. Niebuhr, *The Responsible Self,* p. 104 (italics added).

26. Ibid., pp. 104-105.

27. Ibid., pp. 84-85; but also in principle on pp. 65, 94-95, 98-99.

28. See Jerome G. Manis and Bernard N. Meltzer, eds., *Symbolic Interactionism: A Reader in Social Psychology* (Boston: Allyn and Bacon, 1967), especially chaps. 9, 13, and 14; and Paul E. Pfuetze, *Self, Society and Existence: Human Nature and Dialogue in the Thought of George Herbert Mead and Martin Buber,* foreword by H. Richard Niebuhr (New York: Harper Bros., 1954). Pfuetze argues that there is a significant overlap in the thought of Buber and Mead. Buber functioned in European theological thought much as Mead did in American theological thought.

29. Niebuhr, *The Responsible Self,* p. 84.

30. Ibid., pp. 84-85.

31. "Transcendent reference groups" refer, not only to those beyond face-to-face contact, but also to those participated in through memory and anticipation. God can be understood as a "transcendent reference person," or a "transcendent reference group," if one has a social understanding of God.

32. Ibid., p. 98.

33. Ibid. The role that reference group theory plays in understanding God, sin, and salvation is developed in chaps. 4 and 5.

34. But, see McLean, "Ethics, Reference Group Theory, and Root Metaphor Analysis."

35. Niebuhr, *The Responsible Self,* p. 155.

36. Vv. 4-27; RSV.

37. See Sallie McFague, *Metaphorical Theology* (Philadelphia: Fortress Press, 1982); Gibson Winter, *Liberating Creation* (New York: Crossroad, 1981).

38. In H. Richard Niebuhr, "The Idea of Covenant and American Democracy," *Church History* 23 (1954) 2, Niebuhr used the metaphors of field of forces, mechanism, hierarchy, organism, and covenant. In "Metaphors and Morals," *The Responsible Self,* pp. 149-60, he used the metaphors of organism, the machine, the republic, generating substance, warfare, pilgrimage, contract, *homo faber, homo politicus, homo dialogicus.* While the language of root metaphor surfaced explicitly in "Metaphors and Morals," the functional equivalent of metaphor was present as early as 1954 in "The Idea of Covenant and American Democracy" with the use of such terms as "ideas," "conceptions," "models," "images," and "great common patterns." Also, the functional equivalent of covenant (at least various aspects of covenant) appears under the guise of terms such as "federal," "relational," "trust and loyalty," *"homo dialogicus,"* "responsibility," "promise making and keeping." From my perspective, none of these by themselves, nor all of them collectively, plumb the richness of the concept of covenant; nevertheless, Niebuhr juxtaposed this relational concept to other metaphors or basic ideas.

39. Niebuhr, "Metaphors and Morals," p. 153.

40. Fowler, *Stages of Faith,* p. 33.

41. Ibid., p. 292.

42. See Stuart D. McLean, "A Functional-Relational Understanding of Covenant as a Distinctive Metaphor" (unpublished). There I argue that the concept of covenant encompasses at least seven interdependent aspects. First, it presupposes that persons are social and symbolic and live in communities, as Niebuhr and Fowler both emphasize. Second, within community, persons are understood as relational and interactional beings, the relationship being understood in dialectical-dialogical terms (again, as Niebuhr and Fowler agree). Third, normative love and relationship entail struggle and conflict, of a certain kind, *as well as* harmony and unity. Both Niebuhr and Fowler, I believe, have an *inadequate* grasp of this point. Fourth, forgiveness is essential for the continuation of speech and action. Niebuhr discusses this theme, Fowler is less clear. Fifth, bondedness, loyalty, and commitment (God-to-persons, persons-to-persons) are as important as freedom in describing the will and purposes of God—a significant part of Niebuhr's and Fowler's theories. Sixth, law, expressed through personal and communal structures, is *essential* but *relative* to God's vision for whole persons in a just society. Both Niebuhr and Fowler are strong on the relational and relative, but less clear on the essential role of law. Seventh, all three modes of time are important—memory of the past, living in the existential present, and anticipation of the future. The future in terms of God's promises and human hope is an extremely important aspect of covenant, but so also is the reinterpretation of the past and the transformation of present personal histories and social systems, aspects affirmed by both Niebuhr and Fowler.

43. See Joseph Haroutunian, "Grace and Freedom Reconsidered" and "Three Dimensions of Will and Willing," *God With Us* (Philadelphia: Westminster, 1965); and Gustavo Gutierrez, *A Theology of Liberation* (Maryknoll, N.Y.: Orbis, 1973).

Chapter 8

Research in Faith Development

C. ELLIS NELSON AND
DANIEL ALESHIRE

> If we want to know how people feel, what they expe-
> rience, and what they remember, what their emotions
> and motives are . . . why not ask them?
> —Gordon Allport

> "I did that," says my memory. "I could not have
> done that," says my pride, and remains inexorable.
> Eventually—the memory yields.
> —Friedrich Nietzsche

The above quotations were used by Pauline V. Young as an
introduction to her discussion of the interview as a research
method.[1] The two observations are at the heart of the research
enterprise in the social sciences. If we want to know, we have to
ask; but the respondent is a person with an ego that knows how to
enhance or defend its self-esteem. Information coming to the
individual passes through a variety of influences before it ever
registers. Information coming from the individual passes through
controls—of which the individual may not even be aware. No
research method has resolved this dilemma.

When the social sciences were formed as fields of study and
research in the early nineteenth century, the idea that there was a
scientific method which could produce—or come close to—absolute objectivity was assumed. Emile Durkheim's *The Rules of
Sociological Method* is a classic example of that spirit, which
endured in all branches of the social sciences.

Modern research has viewed the possibility of objectivity with greater suspicion. Gunnar Myrdal, the Swedish researcher who made his remarkable study of race relations in the United States, writes:

> How can a biased view be avoided? More specifically, how can the student of social problems liberate himself from (1) the powerful heritage of earlier writings in his field of inquiry. . . (2) the influence of the entire cultural, social, economic, and political milieu of the society where he lives, works, and earns his living and his status, and (3) the influence stemming from his own personality as molded not only by traditions and environment but also by his individual history, constitution, and inclinations?

Since objective understanding cannot be guaranteed, Myrdal recommends that researchers bring their biases into "full awareness" and then analyze them in relation to the society under study so that others can judge the extent to which bias has influenced the data gathered and interpreted.[2]

PROBLEMS IN EMPIRICAL RESEARCH

Objectivity is a primary problem with research that derives its data from individuals' reports and reflections on life experience. The investigator and the person being questioned partake of a human condition that makes for imprecision. People exist amid a constellation of forces—many they do not control and some they do not understand—which require the individual to act or think about situations as they occur. Even the most precise social research method—voting behavior—makes no claim except that the data are true within certain limits at the time the interview took place. Thus pollsters have to re-do their work every week or so before an election because people change their views in the light of developments. When we move from one measurable act such as voting, which takes place on a certain day, and go to research dealing with people's beliefs, motives, hopes, fears, or ability to endure a lifestyle in spite of opposition, then we are into an area that is vague even to the person who responds to the questions.

There are research methods which increase objectivity. If objectivity were the only research issue, those methods would cure most of the problems. But objectivity is not the only issue. A measurement device can be objective and still elicit the wrong information, with consistency and reliability. Objective data must still be interpreted—a process which always requires logic and frequently reveals conviction. Objectivity cannot be the only consideration. Research must also provide some guarantee that complexity, interaction, and affect are as ably represented in the data as is objectivity. It is apparently this aggregate of concerns that led Fowler to choose the interview method of gathering data. Like any method, it reflects trade-offs and introduces biases. Myrdal's recommendation about awareness of bias is important.

THE INTERVIEW METHOD

Recent study of bias in interviewing sorts out many issues. For example, some obvious errors can be eliminated by the training of interviewers. But bias remains, and it comes about "through (1) the respondent's perception of the interviewer, and (2) the interviewer's perception of the respondent." Example:

> In one study, 50% of a sample of non-Jewish respondents told non-Jewish interviewers that they thought Jews had too much influence in the business world, whereas only 22% of an equivalent sample voiced that opinion to Jewish interviewers. Similar experiments have shown that blacks will frequently answer differently when interviewed by white people and that working class respondents are less likely to talk freely to middle class interviewers.

The part of the bias coming from the respondent is not easily controlled. There is evidence that some respondents "appear to be totally immune to even the most flagrant biasing characteristics of the interviewer." But others are more evasive as the questions get closer to matters that are precious to them. If the interviewers are given little freedom to explain wording of questions and are held to a set standard of procedure and interview, the result will produce responses with less bias. But the more freedom interviewers are given to explain questions and to get at the real attitudes, values, or motives of the respondent, the more the interviewer's presuppositions and perceptions of the interviewee will become a part of the interchange. Thus the interviewer with more freedom may produce more objective data, but the data may also reflect more bias.[3]

Sociologist Jack Douglas likens good research to detective work or to investigative reporting. All data from people must be checked and rechecked from various sources and with different methods in order to obtain data which are usable.[4]

The interview approach to data gathering provides for rich and varied information. It can tap complex areas of life where thought and feeling, memory and hope intersect. But it is riddled with problems that are not easily eliminated. Interviewee subjectivity and bias is compounded with researcher bias and subjectivity. Each influences the other, as do the questions asked in the interview. At best the interview identifies the rich tapestry of human experience. At worst it is little more than an artifact created by interviewee and researcher.

DEVELOPMENTAL RESEARCH

Gathering data by interview has a variety of problems. When the interview is used to obtain data about developmental phenomena, an even lengthier list of potential problems emerges. Consider, for example, some of the more obvious ones.

When the developmentalist interviews people at different ages, the questions may vary in meaning as a function of the interviewee's age. "Tell me about your father," for example, may mean fundamentally different things at age eight than age forty-eight. The effect of the interviewer may vary with the age of a respondent. A twenty-eight-year-old interviewer may be seen as a parent to a six-year-old interviewee and as a child to a fifty-year-old respondent.

There are other problems, too. If the researcher is to develop a theory over a relatively short time period, he or she must interview people of different ages, evaluate their responses, and assume that the differences in responses reflect a progression; that is, that a thirty-five-year-old respondent thought the way the eight-year-old respondent now thinks, only twenty-seven years earlier. Differences in culture, history, and patterns of upbringing can make that assumption very difficult. If the researcher seeks to avoid this problem, he or she must take a lifetime to develop a theory by asking individuals questions during childhood, adolescence, young adulthood, middle adulthood, and later adulthood. But even a sixty-year longitudinal study has problems. For example, the process of asking the same people the same questions consistently through life may influence how they perceive and reflect on life. The interview in this case *creates* a part of life experience rather than simply measuring it. Such a study also depends on a single cohort sample—everybody is from the same generation and shares a common history. Their common history confounds the data. Would a study about beliefs and values that began in 1917 and ended in 1972 identify the developmental process by which beliefs and values emerge, or would it trace the impact of events—World War I, the Great Depression, World War II, the Korean Conflict, the American anticommunist sentiments of the '50s, the student movement of the '60s, and the Vietnam war—on the beliefs and values of the people who experienced them?

Developmental research is a very difficult kind of research. So, for Fowler, the problems of interview research are compounded by the problems of inquiry into the nature of human development. If that were not enough, Fowler's subject of inquiry—belief, values, and faith—includes some of the most difficult human phenomena to operationalize and investigate.

ROLE OF RESEARCH

Given the complexity of obtaining information from people by interviews, the difficulty of using that information to construct a developmental paradigm, and the subtlety of the human phenomenon of faith, of what value is research? The answer is that research, properly done, produces more reliable information than a person can obtain by guess, hunch, or even by experience accumulated over a period of time. With more reliable information, one can develop hypotheses about human life which will help understand human situations. We in the church could develop more effective educational programs, counseling work, or family nurturing processes if we would submit the assumptions informing our present practice to research. Unfortunately, we do not do so because good research is expensive and is often restricted to small parts of the problem.

Research also makes it possible to identify the biases that are being introduced into a study. It provides a standard for judging biases and estimating their impact on conclusions. Research, at least the better attempts at it, disciplines the interpretation of data and catalogues alternative hypotheses.

Research is a series of trade-offs. We can get either lots of data with little understanding of dynamic elements or much understanding with little ability to generalize the findings. We can use one method because we do it well, but we may have to accept limitations on our findings due to the limitation of the method employed. We can carefully control the accuracy of data from persons but at the sacrifice of people's telling us what is true in their own idiom and from their own perspective. Because the choices made influence the conduct of inquiry and interpretation of results, investigators usually explain in great detail what they plan to do, the safeguards they will employ, and the instruments they will use in their data gathering. This is partly so that readers can make an independent judgment about the worth of the project, and partly it is to encourage others to try their research on their own to see if they can get similar results.

FOWLER'S RESEARCH

These general statements about social-developmental research aid an understanding of James Fowler's attempt to identify six stages through which he believes the faith of a person may progress. The data he has assembled are used through his book, *Stages of Faith;* and an explanation of his method and a copy of the items used in the interview are included as Appendix A and B. Parts of a sample interview with judgments about Mary's stage development are in chapter 22 of the book.

The purpose of this chapter is to respond to the data-gathering aspects of Fowler's larger program. Therefore what is said here has a rather narrow focus.[5] It is assumed that the readers of this chapter have read Fowler's book, including Appendices A and B. Our response is at three levels. The first concerns the gathering of the data; the second is the nature of instrumentation; and the third is the interpretations drawn from the data. The nature of scientific inquiry makes it undesirable to deal with one of these dimensions without the others.

THE DATA GATHERING

The data reported in *Stages of Faith* do not come from a scientifically chosen sample. Because of this, Fowler states that "we may make no attempt to suggest that this group of respondents is like any other" (p. 315).[6] In other words, this is a collection of interviews from a select, not necessarily representative, group of individuals. Furthermore, the data have been collected *according* to a stage theory of human development. The theory guided the process of data collection; it did not emerge after all the data were gathered.

The method is that of a controlled interview. This is a pleasingly appropriate method. It gives the investigators an opportunity to get the story of individuals' faith in their terms. Faith is personal, and, if we can get any data from individuals, it must come from their life situations. For this purpose the interview method is superior to the tests, questionnaires, or responses to prefabricated, stylized human situations. Furthermore, the way the investigator is expected to "set" the interview experience by focusing on the person's life is excellent. The expectation of trying to get the person to relate events in his or her life keeps the conversation on the dynamic elements in a person's life. Moreover, the interview method assumes that a person may decline to answer questions or, at the end, may cancel the whole thing by asking for the tape. These procedures give an openness to the interview experience which should enhance confidence in what is said. This structuring of the interview and the mood it evokes is so well worked out that it should produce significant data quite apart from the follow-through questions in Part II and Part III. (See the top half of page 308.)

Enough has been said already about the assets and liabilities of the interview method. Fowler recognizes that people change as they live. "Past, present, and future are dynamically interrelated and all three are continually undergoing reimaging and reinterpretation" (p. 308). He is using this principle to get the respondents to "deal with the way the past appears and feels to you *now.*" But the principle affirms that the data are true as of a certain time, so it would require other interviews at later times with the expectation that the "reimaging and reinterpretation" may be different. Fowler is aware of this because he has begun follow-up interviews (p. 315). Such interviews should be useful in understanding how and why a person changes.

The two appendices on data gathering do not go into detail on the exact method of the interview. Since the interviewers were paid and functioned under supervision, we assume they were coached to minimize interview bias. However, coaching cannot reduce the bias introduced by the respondent's perception of the interviewer. It is difficult to tell how the interviewers were introduced, but the study was given the prestige of a long-term, university-based project (p. 308). Whether the interviewers were perceived as professors or ministers was not noted. In the only fully reported case (Mary), the interview was conducted for purposes of possible pastoral counseling rather than for research (p. 239). It would be important to know the perception the respondents had of the interviewers and what effect those perceptions may have had on their responses. A reliable accounting of the nature and the extent of these effects would be as significant and informative as the follow-up interviews which have already begun.

Something important happened to the American psyche in the late 1960s and early 1970s: We became more aware of the way deception has become a part of our national life. Probably one of the best examinations of this matter was done by Sissela Bok, for she looked at the whole range of problems in her book, *Lying.* Her chapter on "Deceptive Social Science Research" revealed the extent to which deception is commonplace. It does not take a very wide reading in sociological or social psychological research to find studies which withheld information or in other ways failed to be truthful with participants. Bok makes a strong case for being truthful with respondents in social research projects.[7]

Stuart W. Cook points out that most scientific societies formulated codes of ethics in the early 1970s to guide researchers. Most of the ten practices Cook discusses as unethical (such as "coercing people to participate" or "exposing the research participant to physical or mental stress") are readily recognized as such. But the category of "withholding from the participants the true nature of the research" is more of a borderline problem. The wording of this issue about "informed consent" in the American Psychological Association's ethical principles (1973) requires researchers to inform participants about all features of the research which might influence their "willingness to participate and to explain all other aspects of the research about which the participants inquire."[8] By this rule, the respondents in the faith study were adequately informed according to the briefing guide (p. 307). Certainly their rights were protected, for they were told they could request the tape at the end of the interview. One is left with a nagging suspicion, however, that the data supplied by respondents would have been significantly different if they had known how it would be used. Fowler, posed with this question soon after the book was published, said he did not know what difference full disclosure would make. It is quite plausible that respondents from mid-adolescence upward would tell their stories differently if they knew in advance the characteristics of the six stages and that they were going to be placed in one of the stages on the basis of their story.

It would be helpful to test this hunch. This might be done by interviewing some of the respondents a second time by someone who did not have a professional investment in the six-stage theory. The second interviewer would explain the stage theory to the interviewees and the way their story would be judged to place them in a stage. Another way to test this hunch would match pairs of people on the basis of relevant information, such as age, sex, church affiliation or not, social status, etc. One party would be interviewed with the typical Fowler introduction, the other with the explanation of stage theory introduction. We might be able to tell whether the data from the fully informed person in the pair were different from that of the person who was not informed.

Thomas Achenbach has identified several sources of bias in development research data. They provide some appropriate criteria for a summary review of Fowler's data gathering. The first is the influences which are present when individuals are aware their responses are being used for research purposes. For example, people who have been interviewed by ministers may talk as if they have a more enlightened religion than they really have. Or people talking to university professors may characterize their religion in more intellectual terms than they actually use. The more open-ended a data collecting process, the more potential there is for these subtle influences to affect participants' responses. The lack of a systematic variation of these influences in Fowler's research makes it impossible to conclude what effect they may have had on the data. Second, response sets—"dispositions to respond in certain stereotyped ways regardless of what they are asked to do"—could have influenced the results. The free-floating nature of the interview reduces this to some extent. But participants, particularly younger ones, may have answered with pro-religion responses even though the questions encourage them to respond differently. Third, subject-selection factors can influence the resulting data. Fowler's data are very sensitive to whatever biases a nonscientifically chosen sample may have introduced. Fourth, the instrument can introduce its own bias by the character of the responses it elicits. For example, how does Fowler's instrument influence people who are less articulate and find self-expression very difficult? Fifth, and perhaps most interesting, Achenbach suggests that bias can be introduced by the researcher's expectancy. For example, how much did interviewers wish to provide helpful data for Fowler or for their own studies? How much does their questioning bend toward their hopes for the study of faith development?[9]

Fowler's data gathering leaves something to be desired at each of these five points. The possibility of bias is so great, at least at this point, that data must be treated very tentatively—*which is precisely what Fowler does.*

The limitations in the data gathering raise questions about the reliability of the data, but not their usefulness. The investigators are aware of these potential biases and clearly warn the reader:

> This description of the data collected to this point is provided not to confirm or refute the theory developed herein. The data are in rough form, and we hope that we have urged the necessary caution and exercised the necessary restraint in our examination. It has been encouraging to find that the preliminary evidence does reveal the

predicted pattern for this sample. It is impossible to determine, at this point, the extent to which bias and error account for the observations. These findings are offered to provoke thought and comment from the readers and to provide a glimpse at the evidence that does now exist (p. 323).

The limitations inherent in the gathering of data make the present study more useful as heuristic information than definitive, empirical evidence. The study succeeds in making information available to a wide community with adequate detail to test and evaluate it with better sampling and more variation in experimental design. The research is adequate for the proposal of a theory, but it is not adequate for the confirmation of a theory. Fowler has introduced his biases, been self-conscious about them, and told his readers about them. That is at least as much as Myrdal suggested should be done.

THE INSTRUMENTATION

Fowler's interview protocol provides the process by which constructs become operational. Before examining each of the main parts, a general word about the construct of faith is in order.

Researchers strive for elegance in their designs. That is, they want to eliminate extraneous or uncontrollable factors in order to keep the variable under observation as uncontaminated as possible. In this case, the object of study is human faith unrelated to any religion. The subtitle of *Stages of Faith,* "The Psychology of Human Development and the Quest for Meaning," accurately reflects Fowler's definition of faith as "a human universal" (p. xiii). In chapter 2, following his discussion of the thought of Wilfred Cantwell Smith, Fowler carefully separates faith as a human quality from faith as a religion or beliefs.

Fowler has the option to research this human universal in one of two ways. He can define the most generic nature of the phenomenon and invent a way to sort through particularity in order to assess the generic construct. Or he can assess particular expressions of the phenomenon and make inferences about the generic quality they reflect.

The first option is the one Fowler has chosen, and it is a very difficult research strategy. It creates problems with both measurement and sample. The measurement concern is that more general or abstract constructs are more difficult to measure. The problem with sample is that almost all of his respondents are related to some religious tradition. If there really is a human universal to be assessed, a better design would include a majority of respondents who are not affiliated with any religion. They may, of course, have a religion. But if they were not under the influence of a congregation, minister, or recent memories of religious beliefs, such respondents would be freer to explore faith as a human aptitude and would produce less cluttered data. As it is, the investigators have to go through "God language"—translating it into human equivalents—or the interview data will not serve the purpose of the study.

The second option would not only provide for easier measurement; it may be more philosophically acceptable. While faith may be a human universal, it may not be possible or desirable to isolate faith from religion—at least at this stage of the research. While faith may exist apart from some concrete system in which it is anchored and through which it is interpreted, it may not be measurable in its more pure, abstract form. Fowler could have interviewed Christians to identify a developmental sequence in Christian believers, then have interviewed Jewish believers to assess developmental stages in that tradition, then have interviewed Buddhist believers to assess the stages in their faith development. The results of these separate studies could be compared, and inferences about similar generic qualities drawn. This method would make for more precise measurement, eliminate the need to be translating particularistic language, and provide a broader data base for the assertion that faith is, indeed, a human universal.

It cannot be determined from these data if faith as a human universal has been measured. Ultimately what has been measured is that part of reality evoked by the interview questions. Therefore an evaluation of the research method must deal with the instrument's questions.

Interview Part I. This chapter has already commented favorably on this section of the interview. It is designed to put respondents at ease and to suggest topics around which they might tell

their story. It is open-ended and should produce good, spontaneous data.

Interview Part II. The second part of the interview is designed
to give a "more in-depth life review" by asking questions about
persons, events, relationships, and crises which might help the
respondents open up areas they have not covered in the more
free-form opening section. As a method, this seems entirely appropriate. If rapport has developed, the respondent may dig in
for a fuller discussion. If the interviewer is able to link the prepared topic questions to responses from Part I, then respondents
should feel that their life is of importance to the project.

The research issue here has to do with the use of the information solicited. The questions seek data about the respondent's
relationships to parents and other significant adults. Questions
about taboos are presumably an effort to get at the substance of
the negative conscience. This cluster of questions deals with facets of personality which tend to endure rather than change with
increased capacity of a growing person's ability to reason. Perhaps
"human relation" type questions are here because investigators
wanted to apply psychosocial stage theory to the six faith stages,
and they needed data which could be interpreted psychoanalytically (pp. 106-114). This is a commendable goal, but it presents a
formidable research problem. To get proper psychoanalytic data
would require interviewers trained from that point of view. After
such data are obtained, it would be necessary to find a way to
relate this view and its theory of mental activity supporting the
structural-developmental notion of stages. Using data from different perspectives is often done in the case method, so there are
ways to deal with the inherent problems. But these faith interviews are the only source of data, not part of a collection of data
from many sources—as used in the case method.

Interview Part III. The interview questions in this section deal
with the way human faith operates within a person, producing
beliefs about life. It probes the respondent's beliefs about matters
such as the value of groups, the way decisions should be made,
evil, death, and social justice.

This section is, quite commendably, in complete harmony with
the purpose of the study. It assumes there is a faith-attitude at
work and then proceeds to pose life situations everyone has to

face. Data from these questions should get at the respondent's true beliefs, because the questions avoid reference to religion or to social expectations. From a research point of view, Part I—the open-ended solicitation of one's faith story—plus a few questions in Part II and this part form a rather "elegant" cluster of questions which sticks to the purpose of the study.

The problem with the questions in this part is the uncertain meaning of the terms used. Questions such as "What is the purpose of life?" are abstract. To answer other questions, the respondent would need a working definition of these words: symbol, ritual, value, true, and image. Respondents probably have a definition, but whether it conforms to the investigator's is something that would have to be worked out in the interviews. However, this should not be interpreted as a negative appraisal of the questions. It is simply a recognition that care must be taken to obtain valid data.

Interview Part IV. We have already suggested that a consideration of religion in a study concerned with faith as "human quality" creates unnecessary complications. That respondents would probably use religious language and concepts in replying to questions is to be expected. If the research is to gain information about the human universal dimension, interviewers must probe the answers to yield nonreligious equivalents so that such data could be compared with answers of respondents who do not use religious language. The interview could thus follow to the logical conclusion the role of faith apart from specific beliefs or religious communities, as Smith proposes, and as Fowler concurs (pp. xii-xiv, 4-15). This would allow religion whatever role and value the respondent chooses, if such can be measured.

Fowler, however, elects to include religion as a category for appraising human faith. We will not comment on the wide range of questions in this section, but do want to point out the complication of using data from these questions. Take question number 7: "Some people believe that without religion morality breaks down. What do you feel about this?" Replies could lead to some significant data about the quality of a person's thoughts about ethics. How will those thoughts be judged? Ethicists have produced a small library on this issue, and there are at least four and maybe five schools of thought about the relation of religion to morals. Each position is logical, given the ethicist's presuppositions. From which school of thought will Fowler make judgments? It is not possible to determine from the book how respondents answered this question or how the answers to other religious questions were used to place people in stages—except in the case of Mary which is given in some detail.

SCORING AND INTERPRETING THE INFORMATION

A typical interview lasted two-and-a-half hours and yielded a thirty-five to forty page verbatim transcript (p. 315). Interviews were read at least three times and the substance judged according to seven aspects: form of logic, perspective-taking, form of moral judgment, bounds of social awareness, locus of authority, form of world coherence, and symbolic functions (pp. 244-245). When all judgments are brought together around one aspect, a stage of development is assigned. Then the aspects are averaged to produce an overall stage location for the respondent.

Scoring interview protocols is tricky business. Too loose a grid precludes reliable assessment, while too tight a grid may eliminate the richness of information the interview was intended to obtain. Early efforts, such a psychoanalytic interviews, attempted very little coding. Judgments were as much a work of art—frequently a good work—as they were a technical assessment. Lawrence Kohlberg has been thirty years attempting to develop an adequate system of coding moral dilemma interviews.[10] It has been an elusive task, even though he is concentrating on responses to a standard set of dilemmas. Fowler's interview is more expansive, less focused, and likely to be even more difficult to code than Kohlberg's.

The scoring process can be evaluated in a variety of ways. The first standard is reliability: Can more than one person assign the same codes to the same protocol? Fowler answers this question positively. Inter-rater agreement is reported between 85-90 percent. This reliability should be expected, since the raters are trained to look for the same things within the same theory of development (p. 314). But coder reliability is not enough. If people are instructed to code black as red, and they reliably code red every time they see black, they still have not generated a great degree of truth. A second issue is the consistency or clarity of interpretation available from the codes: Once similar information has been scored, will similar scores produce similar interpretations? One goal of research is systematically to eliminate alternative hypotheses. The evaluation of Mary's interview later in this chapter relates to this standard. A third issue concerns validity: Do the variables derived from the properly coded interview distinguish among people and relate in logically consistent ways with other, related variables? Fowler does not move toward this third issue in the present study so there is no basis for evaluation. However, the issue underscores the kind of work that yet needs to be done before all the initial data for the theory are in.

Fowler illustrates the process of judging the interview data through the case of Mary. All of the interview is not printed, but enough is reproduced to show how the investigators analyzed her story and why they placed her in developmental stage 3.

Mary was chosen even though Fowler records that she is not a case (the interview was not complete, and the encounter was in a context of counseling rather than research). Apparently she was of special interest to the investigators (p. 239-240).

The analysis is first done on Mary's *locus of authority.* After reviewing the episodes in Mary's life, they conclude that during the age period of twenty-two to twenty-seven authority was located externally to herself in terms of God's will, scripture, and the consensus of groups where she felt accepted and loved. According to the definition of stages (Table 5.1), this places her at stage 3—a rather conventional place where a person accepts authority. Persons not trained in the stage system of classification can read the data differently. Mary uses the norms of the various groups with which she is associated during those years as the *substance* of authority, but she is constantly rejecting the group as the locus of authority—she was literally ousted from strong groups because she would not accept their authority (p. 226, note 27). She also saw through the pretensions of group leaders (p. 226, note 28; see also page 228). She even helped her brother, Ron, her spiritual mentor, see through the deception of a group (p. 229, note 39). In fact, she spoke specifically of her fear of the Daytona group's authority over her life (p. 235, note 57). There are more examples which could lead to placing her emotionally in stage 1—"attachment/dependence relationship." Her mind helped her to see the reality of the authority situation, so she struggled to be free. When free, she started the process all over again. Out of a number of these experiences, she developed some internal confidence and felt less need for group support. One could judge that the underlying dynamic is a struggle for authentic selfhood and that during this five-year period she may have moved from stage 1 to stage 4, using the stage definition of authority.

It is not possible to propose judgments about all aspects of Mary's inner life since the whole interview is not provided. But one comment about God language is in order. In an explanatory paragraph, Fowler makes a careful distinction between *structure* and *content* of faith. Content is what one believes about God, church, sin, etc., while structure has to do with the "set" of the mind or how the mind sees or understands religious works. For example: People can be dogmatic about various religions or about having no religion. This is clear and correct. Given the theoretical constructs for faithing, the research would have been more elegant if it had stuck to structure and had not attempted to interpret the meaning of religious words to the respondent. However, the investigators did deal with religious words, even though they did not ask Mary to explain what she meant by the religious words she used. As a result, they were forced to make "tentative judgments" with a "lack of data" (see top of page 250). These speculations place her in stage 3 (p. 252).

The problem with this section is not with the liberties the investigators have taken, for they reported what they were doing, but with their judgment about Mary. Again, the information can be read differently. A summary statement reads:

> In any event, it is clear that in Mary's account of her faith "the Lord" is a powerful, multidimensional symbol, filled with highly personal and subjective emotive content. I think it is equally clear that Mary, properly speaking, has sharply delineated no *concept* of God. That is to say, she has not questioned the powerful symbol "the Lord," either in its meanings for her or for others, so as to clarify, reflect upon and draw together explicitly its many dimensions of meaning (p. 251).

This is an odd judgment in the light of the previous explanation of the importance of content. Mary had used God language throughout the interview, but she is judged to have no *concept* of God. In this instance the symbolic function aspect of stage theory has a place for people who respond like Mary: It is stage 2, "one dimensional, literal." Stage 2 is for people who have not yet "questioned the powerful symbol 'the Lord' " (pp. 244 and 251). Why not place her there, since the above quote judges her to be at that place?

The form of logic aspect of Mary's life is judged to be at stage 3, though the writer explains that tests were not administered (p. 252). The perspective-taking and the forms of moral judgment aspects were judged to be at stage 3, although no data were available for analysis (pp. 254-257).

These reflections illustrate the problems of determining valid codes and deriving meaningful interpretations from them. The difficulty is further illustrated in another use of the case. Mary's case is also used to show how the investigators used psychosocial stage theory to relate to the structural stage theory which forms the basis of this study. Two comments about this enterprise are called for.

First, from a research point of view, this is an extremely complex venture. Psychosocial data—as Erikson has developed this scheme—are made from a psychoanalytic perspective.[11] The structural-developmental data, as developed by Piaget and Kohlberg, are made from an epistemological perspective. Some of the differences are reviewed by Fowler in Part II of *Stages of Faith.* The data we have from Mary are from one interview and from an interview with her brother, Ron, three years later (pp. 266-268). There are no data from an interview done by a person trained in psychotherapy and interpreted from that perspective. So what we have in this section are "reflections." The investigator states that "our data are too limited to do more than hypothesize" (p. 259). A sample of such hypothesizing is contained in the following sentences:

> In this period, from ages three to six, she tells us, "There were two little boys up on the corner who were very naughty, and I used to play with them" (20). She remembers in that era "hearing the minister preach a sermon about death, [and] about how there was no place to hide from it." And she adds, "I remember that I was suicidal from a

very early age, and it was always a reaction to my relationship with my mother" (21). Those scant windows into the world of a bright and active but lonely preschooler do not give us a very comprehensive picture of her way of dealing with the crisis of initiative vs. guilt. There is enough, however, to suggest that the fantasies of suicide and the probably accompanying childhood depressions had a good deal to do with the contemplation of angry initiatives toward the mother. Playing with the "naughty" boys may have involved sex-play or other activities that led to feelings of guilt. Expressed in ways that were unacceptable and punished or kept within in a stubborn secretiveness, it seems likely that these gave rise to guilt, depression, and the ambivalent aggression of the suicide fantasies (p. 259).

Second, although this may surprise the reader, we like this section of the study because it does not claim to be scientific (p. 257-268). It is interesting, for the writer is trying to make sense out of Mary's story in human terms and from the perspective of one who can sympathize with her struggle. There is a search for underlying themes or traits which exist throughout Mary's life cycle.

Perhaps this change in mood is occasioned by the influence of Erikson, who in his epigenetic principle stated that each stage is a development in the light of the way a person managed the previous stages. In Erikson's plan, stages do not signify "mere succession" but a "progression through time of a differentiation of parts." Thus a person has a history with memories, conscious and unconscious, which are factors throughout the lifespan.[12]

Three years after Mary's interview there was a contact with Ron, Mary's influential brother. After Ron had read the interview with Mary and Fowler's commentary, he wrote a response. Ron filled in facts about Mary during the three years that showed a lot of settling down, training for a vocation, and an engagement to be married. But what is particularly fascinating about this part of Mary's story is the persistence of struggle with herself, about her relation to her mother, and the way "the Lord" spoke to her so she would have strength to resist Ron's advice about a place to live (pp. 266-268). In Erikson's terms, some segments of her authority problem seem to be unresolved from her early childhood. But now we are beginning to hypothesize, so we must stop; for this is a review of research methods.

CONCLUSION

At each point of his research Fowler has opted for the difficult. He deals with a complex concept (faith); theorizes about it from some of the more complex approaches to understanding human development (Piaget and Erikson); and conducts the research with very difficult methods (coded, life-oriented interviews). Critics could plead the case for plausible alternative hypotheses that explain some of Fowler's data more precisely and systematically than the hypotheses forwarded in this study. But Fowler has an interesting advantage for his case which the critics do not yet possess—ten to twelve thousand pages of transcribed data. The best evaluation of empirical research—even tentative, heuristic research—is more empirical research. Chapters like this one are necessary, but they cannot ascertain the credibility of the data by raising research issues. Ultimately, the only convincing evaluation of empirical research is more research. That research should deal with the concerns raised in this chapter, but the concerns themselves do not invalidate a single conclusion.

Murray Thomas provides some interesting criteria for evaluating developmental theories. They provide some questions relevant for a summary of many of the issues dealt with in this chapter.[13]

1. Does the developmental theory accurately reflect the real world? Fowler's work attempts to deal with the real world of faithing people. The interview elicits personal reality and likely accomplishes its task.

2. Is the theory stated in ways that make it clearly understandable to any who are reasonably competent? Fowler's constructions are clearly more complex than simple. Whether the complexity represents accuracy or fuzziness is unknown. It may be overly complex at points. Theories do tend to simplify as they mature, so we withhold judgment on this count.

3. Is the theory internally consistent? Fowler's work must be commended at this point. He is a structuralist, and that shows in the care and consistency with which themes are developed and set forth in the theory. His research methods are, by and large, quite consistent with his structuralist approach.

4. Is the theory founded on as few unproved assumptions as

possible? Fowler's work does not do as well on this count. The content, focus, and emotion of the research grow out of philosophical and theological reflection. We would not want it any other way. But it does complicate the scientific theory-building process. It may not be possible to prove some of the assumptions (like faith as a human universal).

5. Can the theory be falsified or disconfirmed? This is a fundamental issue in scientific inquiry. To some extent this theory can be disconfirmed, but it is debatable just how much. Caution is needed for theories with an answer for everything; and psychodynamic theories, in particular, have a tendency to do this.

6. Does the theory contribute to new ways of thinking and the discovery of new knowledge? Fowler gets high marks here. This work represents an innovation in the understanding of faith of paradigmatic proportions. Few researchers as productively incite speculation, response, even whole collections of essays like this one.

7. Is the theory self-satisfying? This may be the most important criteria at this stage of the research. Does the developmental journey Fowler traces "ring true" with people who take seriously their constructions of meaning, values, relationships, and centers of power? These answers, like the research, will be highly individualistic.

NOTES

1. Pauline V. Young, *Scientific Social Surveys and Research* (Englewood Cliffs, N.J.: Prentice-Hall, 1963), p. 205.

2. Gunnar Myrdal, *Objectivity in Social Research* (New York: Random House, 1969), pp. 3-5.

3. Claire Selltiz, Lawrence S. Wrightsman, and Stuart W. Cook, *Research Methods in Social Relations* (New York: Holt, Rinehart & Winston, 1976), pp. 570-573.

4. See Jack D. Douglas, *Investigative Social Research* (Beverly Hills, Calif.: Sage Publications, 1976), pp. ix-xv.

5. See C. Ellis Nelson, "Does Faith Develop? An Evaluation of Fowler's Position," *The Living Light* 19 (Summer, 1982), pp. 162-174, for an evaluation of other aspects of Fowler's theory.

6. All page references in parenthesis are to James W. Fowler, *Stages of Faith* (San Francisco: Harper & Row, 1981).

7. Sissela Bok, *Lying: Moral Choice in Public and Private Life* (New York: Pantheon Books, 1978). See chap. XIII, "Deceptive Social Science Research."

8. See Selltiz et al., *Research Methods in Social Relations,* pp. 200-249. The quotation is on p. 212.

9. Thomas Achenbach, *Research in Developmental Psychology* (New York: The Free Press, 1978). See pp. 180-190.

10. See Lawrence Kohlberg, *The Psychology of Moral Development, Essays on Moral Development,* Vol. 2 (San Francisco: Harper & Row, 1984).

11. See Erik H. Erikson, "Elements of a Psychoanalytic Theory of Psychosocial Development," in *Toward Understanding Personality Development, Vol. 1: Infancy and Early Childhood,* ed. S. I. Greenspan and G. H. Pollock (Adelphi, Md.: Mental Health Study Center, Division of Mental Health Service Programs, National Institute of Mental Health, U.S. G.P.O., 1980-81).

12. Ibid., p. 19.

13. See R. Murray Thomas, *Comparing Theories of Child Development* (Belmont, Calif.: Wadsworth, 1979), pp. 19-24.

PART IV

Faith Development Theory and Ministry

Chapter 9

Faith Development and the
Requirements of Care

K. BRYNOLF LYON AND
DON S. BROWNING

As with most other dimensions of religious thought and practice, the hermeneutics of suspicion has made an indelible impact on the pastoral care of the contemporary church. We have learned, for example, that the language of faith emerges from a developmental praxis, that, like all discourse, it expresses multiple conscious and unconscious intentions, and that its reaching expression is governed by the requirements of compromise given, in Roy Schafer's words, the "highly unfavorable conditions of the human psyche." Since the language of faith holds no distinctive position in this respect from any other discourse, we have tended to move away from faith itself as an interpretive category in pastoral care. Faith has been, if you will, less an interpretive category than an interpreted category in situations of pastoral care.

There have, of course, been good reasons for this (as well as some not-so-good reasons). The demands of therapeutic neutrality, the difficulty of making sense of "faith" and "faith development" in the increasingly pluralistic world which pastoral care addresses, and the suspicion that the idea of faith development carries more of an apologetic than a therapeutic intent up its sleeve have all mitigated against faith development as an interpretive lens in helping relationships. The recent, powerful work of James Fowler in articulating stages of faith development, however, provides us with an opportunity to wonder again about the complex of issues involved here. In this essay we will examine certain of these issues as they relate to a dialogue between Fowler's developmental epistemology of faith and the requirements of care, particularly in relation to pastoral counseling or therapy. Our intention in this is simply to make preliminary comments about some potentially fruitful areas of this dialogue. To begin this discussion, however, it will be necessary to discern precisely what Fowler's theory of faith development is meant to be a theory of. That is, what is his understanding of the meaning of that faith which he also hopes to understand developmentally?

THE MEANING OF FAITH

Fowler's discussion of the meaning of "faith" is highly nuanced. While it is not entirely clear at points how all the nuances and rephrasings fit together, the basic outlines of his understanding seem relatively clear. Three characteristics of faith as Fowler is studying it seem of particular relevance for our purposes. First, faith is a dimension of the activity of knowing. In line with Baldwin, Dewey, Piaget, Kohlberg, and other cognitive-developmentalists, Fowler sees knowing as an activity: the composing, construing, or constructing that an active subject engages in, wherein both self and other are "known." Faith, then, for Fowler, is a particular dimension of this activity of knowing.

The importance of this point in Fowler's scheme is twofold. On the one hand, it suggests that faith is less something one *has* than something one *does.* As he is fond of saying, faith is a verb. On the other hand, it suggests that the core of his interest in faith is not so much with variations in content (or beliefs) but with the various structures of this dimension of knowing. His interest is in the developmental "epistemology of faith."[1] For Fowler, in other words, the stages of faith development are meant principally to refer, not to changes in the content of what is believed, but to changes in the process of knowing or construing that which is believed. The contents of faith may or may not change with stage transition, but the way in which those contents are made meaningful does change. And it is this change in the form or structure of the activity of meaning-making that Fowler has in mind by faith development.

Second, for Fowler faith is a knowing which involves both self-formation and rational analysis. This distinction with respect to dimensions of knowing, Fowler tells us, is that between "constitutive-knowing in which *the identity or worth of the person is not directly at stake* and constitutive-knowing in which it is."[2] Faith-knowing here inevitably entails, not only the construction of the object(s) of faith, but also an "extension, modification, or reconstitution of the *knower in* relation to the known."[3] In faith, as an activity of knowing, the constitution of the self is always at issue. Faith, in this sense, is not a dispassionate construing but rather one which entails commitment and loyalty—a passional stance in relation to that which is known.

Fowler grounds this discussion in a distinction between what he calls the logic of rational certainty and the logic of conviction. The logic of rational certainty refers to the predominant Piagetian interest in knowing as "impersonal, propositional, demonstrable, and replicable."[4] The logic of conviction, on the other hand, is that knowing in which the "self is continually being confirmed or modified in the knowing."[5] The logic of conviction, which Fowler sees as the broader of the two (and, indeed, as encompassing and contextualizing the logic of rational certainty), is the cornerstone of that kind of knowing which faith is. This is not to say, however, that Fowler sees no place for the logic of rational certainty in faith-knowing. Indeed, Fowler does see a place for rational knowing in "conceptualizing, questioning, and evaluating the products of other modes of imaginal and generative knowing."[6]

The third characteristic of faith as Fowler is studying it is its relational character. This is in some ways, of course, already implied by the first two characteristics mentioned above. To know at all, in Fowler's sense, is to be formatively related to that which is known. The developmentally earliest manifestation of the relational character of faith that Fowler distinguishes, citing Erikson, is found in the parent-infant relationship. Through parental patterns of care, prelinguistic experiences of the world as trustworthy or capricious, present to the self or absent to the self, caring or indifferent, form the nascent (but forever powerful) faith-knowing of the child.

Drawing on the work of Josiah Royce and H. Richard Niebuhr, Fowler observes that the relational character of faith is essentially triadic in structure. In other words, the self is related, not only to the other, but also to those "shared centers of supraordinate value and power" which inform the relation. It is, therefore, not only through the parental patterns of care but also through the broader meanings and values which those patterns themselves express that we come to sense "what the world is like . . . how it regards us and . . . whether we can be 'at home' here."[7]

FAITH DEVELOPMENT AND ITS ASSESSMENT IN PASTORAL CARE

This approach to the meaning of faith with regard to stages of faith development suggests several important things relevant to pastoral care. Two of these, both having to do with questions of assessment in pastoral care, bear particular mention. First, Fowler's general intent would seem to enable us to assess faith development while yet avoiding the Scylla and Charybdis of reductionism, on the one hand, and the generation of criteria of development from a set of beliefs of a particular faith community, on the other. The banishment of attempts to assess faith development in pastoral care has frequently been based on these two problems. Fowler's approach to the question of faith development, however, addresses both of these forthrightly.

With respect to reductionism, Fowler's theory suggests that faith knowing is, if the phrase is allowable in this context, a line of development.[8] That is, faith knowing has its regular developmental vicissitudes which can be understood and charted. Thus, just as we assess psychosexual development, ego development, and object-relations development, so Fowler provides us a means of assessing faith development. We must not misunderstand this, however. It is not just a morale booster for pastoral care (injecting something that at least sounds more traditionally "religious" into pastoral care than the development of "ego" or "object-relations"). Indeed, if Fowler is correct in this, faith development would be a relevant dimension of assessment for *any* therapeutic enterprise, pastoral or otherwise. Whether it does us any good to be able to make such an assessment in helping relationships, however, will be a question we will later address.

With respect to the generation of the criteria of development, Fowler's scheme also seems fruitful. The question here is whether, in pastoral care, it is possible to assess faith development in a way that is neutral with respect to the contents of faith or the particular faith community (or apparent lack thereof) to which the agent of pastoral care or the client, family, etc., belong. If it is not, then attempts to assess faith development in pastoral care would smack of either heavy-handed imposition or dishonesty.[9] Yet, Fowler's theory helps to resolve this problem through the differentiation of structure and content. Good (or bad) Marxists, Muslims, Jews, Christians, Buddhists, materialists—all, apparently, except good nihilists—can be assessed with regard to faith development, irrespective of the content of their beliefs. If pluralism is to be affirmed and yet faith development acknowledged (and pastoral care is richer for both of these), then the differentiation of structure and content in faith knowing seems a vital issue. How well the "content" of Fowler's stages maintain this distinction—particularly at the higher stages—remains to be seen. While this is an important question, we must leave it for others to discuss. The more pressing foundational question is precisely what *kind* of neutrality is possible in Fowler's developmental epistemology of faith. We will turn to this question shortly.

Second, Fowler's theory of faith development also promises eventually to enrich assessment in pastoral care since, unlike traditional cognitive-developmental theories, it intends to embrace dynamic psychological understanding. As Robert Kegan has noted, "cognitive-developmentalism has had a robust life in the university and almost no influence whatever in the clinic."[10] Attracting more attention from educators than clinicians, the cognitive-developmental theories of Piaget and Kohlberg, for example, have had profound impact on religious education theory and practice but little substantive effect on pastoral care. Fowler's explicit attempt to incorporate the passional dimensions of the person in his faith development theory, however, makes this potentially far more fruitful territory for pastoral care.

Yet the link Fowler draws in this regard is weaker than it might be. It never becomes quite clear what the relationship is between faith viewed structurally and the emotional or depth-psychological dimensions of human development. This issue is especially crucial for pastoral care since the usefulness of the structural model in that context hinges on our ability to make sense of it in relation to the broader dynamics of change.

This brief outline of some of Fowler's contributions to the assessment of faith development in pastoral care has also raised questions for further dialogue. We can group these into two general areas: (1) the question of the parameters of neutrality and (2) the question of the relation between the structural and the emotional or depth-psychological dimensions of the theory (which we will refer to as the object-relations context of faith). Since both of these bear directly on the issue of faith as an interpretive category (as well as an interpreted category) in pastoral care, some further sketching of the issues involved may prove useful.

THE PARAMETERS OF NEUTRALITY

To say that Fowler's distinction between structure and content allows the stage placement in a manner neutral with regard to the particular contents of faith does not mean that the theory lacks practical-moral intent. As with any such theory, its neutrality is defined by and limited to the parameters of its practical-moral intention.[11] We can see this most clearly in faith development theory in the criteria of assessment that underlie stage structure. In other words, what Fowler understands as counting as aspects of stage structure (form of world coherence, locus of authority, role-taking, etc.) and his articulation of their hierarchical differentiations embody within them a particular normative vision within the context of which the idea of "neutral" stage placement gains its particular meaning.

The basic thrust of this vision is nicely captured in Fowler's comment on the general movement of stage progression: "Overall, there is a movement outward toward individuation, culminating in stage 4. Then the movement doubles back, in stages 5 and 6, toward the participation and oneness of earlier stages, though at quite different levels of complexity, differentiation, and inclusiveness."[12] It is this movement between individuation and participation that forms the criteriological boundaries of the neutrality of stage placement in Fowler's scheme. Since those criteria (and their hierarchical differentiations) express the underlying—in Fowler's words—"normativity" of the theory, we may say, perhaps, that it is within the context of this normative vision that "neutral" stage placement is possible. The parameters of neutrality, as a requirement of care, in other words, are defined by the practical-moral intent of Fowler's developmental epistemology of faith.

The theory is, of course, not neutral with respect to alternative normative visions *at this level.* This is problematic, it should be noted, only to the extent that it is shown that the particular practical-moral intent underlying Fowler's faith development scheme is not relatively more adequate than alternatives. Our point here, though, is simply to underscore that the neutrality available to the individual engaged in pastoral care in this assessment procedure (as in any other) is limited to the parameters of its practical-moral intention, which therefore highlights the importance of critically reflecting on the validity claims of the procedure at this level. It may be helpful, then, to see precisely how Fowler himself understands some of the issues relevant to this.

Fowler notes, as we have said, that his faith development theory embodies a certain "normativity." Citing Kohlberg's pioneering use of structural theory in moral development, Fowler suggests that in similar fashion each subsequent faith stage (as is the case in moral development) is not only developmentally later, but normatively better. He carefully notes, however, that the "criteria of adequacy for faith include, but are not limited to, the formal structure of the faith stage."[13] Nonetheless, while it may not be sufficient in itself to assess the relative adequacy of faith, the structural stage progression does evince a normative hierarchy.

The question that arises in this is on what grounds one can say that successive stages are *normatively* more adequate than previous ones? Kohlberg, of course, could argue that the higher moral stages were more adequate on *moral* grounds (in addition to cognitive-logical ones).[14] What grounds are there, though, internal to faith (understood in Fowler's structural sense), that could serve as *normative* criteria in this regard? Fowler appeals here to John Chirban's work on intrinsic and extrinsic forms of religious motivation, where higher faith stages show greater intrinsic motivation. This seems to beg the question, however. On the one hand, it is not clear what the *conceptual* relation is between "religious motivation" and faith-knowing. On the other hand, even if this was clarified, it would be necessary to show that intrinsic forms of religious motivation are more adequate than extrinsic forms of motivation on normative grounds. To do this, of course, it would be necessary to suggest the nature of the normative criteria one has in mind.

The only criteria that Fowler cites appear to be quasi-moral ones: "a widened, more inclusive accounting for the interests, stories, and visions of others"; "qualitative increase in choice, awareness, and commitment"; "qualitative new degree of self-responsibility." Fowler himself, however, does not tell us precisely on *what type of normative grounds* he thinks developmental increments in these things are relatively more adequate. Our suspicion, though, is that the grounds are moral ones.

If what we have suggested here is correct, then the normativity inherent in this developmental epistemology of faith is essentially a moral one. But if *this* is true, then the relation Fowler conceives between faith knowing and moral knowing needs to be rethought. Since the normative validity claims of the theory itself require moral justification, it becomes difficult to understand how they could be meaningfully justified if morality was not, in a sense stronger than Fowler will allow, at least somewhat autonomous from faith.[15] In other words, one cannot really justify the normative validity claims of the theory if the means of justification are derivative from and dependent upon that which is to be justified.

We may seem to have wandered a long way from the question of the parameters of neutrality in pastoral care. Yet the foundational clarification of the meaning of neutrality in assessing faith development requires that such questions come to the fore. That addressing these questions leads us to seemingly disparate aspects of Fowler's theory suggests, we hope, the potential fruitfulness for both pastoral care and faith development theory of such a dialogue. Much more could be said about this particular issue, of course. However, since our intent in this essay is simply to highlight some areas of mutual concern in this dialogue, we will turn to the second issue relevant to assessment mentioned above: the object-relations context of faith.

THE OBJECT-RELATIONS CONTEXT OF FAITH

As we have noted, it never becomes quite clear what Fowler thinks is the relation between the depth-psychological and the structural dimensions of faith development. We can see the dimensions of this problem hinted at in one of Fowler's attempts to give a concise definition of faith. Faith, Fowler says, is:

The process of constitutive-knowing

Underlying a person's composition and maintenance of a comprehensive frame (or frames) of meaning

Generated from the person's attachments or commitments to centers of supraordinate value which have power to unify his or her experiences of the world

Thereby endowing the relationships, contexts, and patterns of everyday life, past and future, with significance.[16]

This attempt to be concise about the matter, however, serves to highlight the ambiguity noted above. It is an ambiguity that goes to the heart of the theory's potential fruitfulness for pastoral care.

The difficulty might be put this way: Having suggested the fundamentally relational character of faith, Fowler here implies an undialectical relation between the "centers of supraordinate value and power" and the "relationships, contexts, and patterns of everyday life." In other words, Fowler's definition of faith here focuses on the ways in which the centers of supraordinate value and power endow everyday interpersonal relationships with significance but does not focus on the reverse movement. He does not discuss the ways in which those centers are themselves constructed and construed through the intrapsychic and interpersonal dynamics of everyday life.

The issue is not that Fowler does not know this is the case. His discussion of the relational character of faith surely appeals to just such an understanding at points. Yet it is precisely this dimension that finally fails to find adequate and consistent expression in the theory. Fowler's structural-developmental interests tend to override the more dynamically oriented concerns that inevitably come to the fore in pastoral care and that, frankly, must be appropriately integrated into any understanding of the development of faith. This tendency not fully to integrate the object-relations context and source of faith-knowing imbues the understanding of human nature embodied in the theory with an unfortunately undialectical understanding of the origins of faith knowing. Faith informs our interpersonal relations, but these same relations seem not to inform our faith.

We can see a particular instance of this in his discussion of the passions. Fowler, of course, seeks to integrate the passional and affective dimensions of the person into his theory. For example, his interpretation of the logic of conviction commits his theory, at the deepest levels, to a recognition of the dynamics of the passions in understanding faith development. This is incorporated into the theory, it should be noted, not simply as an issue of content, but as a foundational issue of the *structure* of faith-knowing. Having stated all this, however, Fowler tends to leave his understanding of the dynamics of the passions (with respect to the structural dimensions of faith) unsystematized and not fully integrated with the rest of the theory. His appeals to Erikson in this regard, as he himself notes, tend to lapse into background considerations.

This need not necessarily be the case. There is an option that might be pursued to incorporate more fully the concerns of depth psychology into faith development theory. The idea here would be to acknowledge forthrightly that faith, as Fowler is studying it, *is* our object-relations when viewed with respect to their implications for understanding the broader horizons of our experience as this is interpreted by one's particular level of cognitive development functioning. Or to say it differently, faith is our value knowing of what our object-relations (our deeply felt and internalized interpersonal relations) seem to imply about the ultimate context of experience. Faith is not our experience of these object-relations themselves. Faith is our comprehension of what these relations imply or suggest about things beyond themselves, particularly about the ultimate and enduring aspects of reality as a whole. In addition, faith is not simply the experiencing of these relations in terms of what they imply about the ultimate context of experience; faith entails, as well, our *intellectual operations on* the broader felt implications of these relations.

Because our intellectual operations change, evolve, and undergo a variety of revolutions through the course of development in ways well described by Piaget, Kohlberg, and other structuralists, our knowing and comprehension of the broader implications of these relations will also change. In short, our knowing of the implications of these object relations will shift from undifferentiated to highly differentiated. For example, the intellectual operations, and the value-knowing that they permit, which a five-year-old can bring to discerning the implications of a mother's trust is vastly more limited than the kind of intellectual operations a forty-year-old individual can bring to the same task of discernment. The mother's capacity for trust may be much the same, but intellectual comprehension of both the trust and its implications for the way the world *is* will likely be far more nuanced, differentiated, and complicated at the later age.

Looked at this way, the difference between faith development and emotional development is primarily a matter of interpretative perspective. When development is viewed strictly from the perspective of our experience of, internalization of, and response to our object relations (what we will later call "self objects"), we can be said to be studying or observing emotional development. This is often called the depth or dynamic perspective of human development. When we are viewing human development from the perspective of how these same object relations both affect us yet imply a broader vision of the ultimate context of experience, then it can be said we are observing faith development.

Making the distinction between emotional development (which we might study with the use of our dynamic or depth psychologies) and faith development (which we might understand with the use of Fowler's structural views) in the ways we have done here greatly lessens the distance between these two perspectives on development. The pastor and pastoral counselor can readily use both perspectives with the understanding that they are simply two perspectives on many of the same human processes.[17]

The recent psychological work of Robert Kegan may help us overcome dichotomous ways of thinking about the relation of faith development to emotional or object-relations development. The psychological vicissitudes of both might be regrounded, as Kegan has suggested, in the more fundamental movement of the "emergence from embeddedness."[18] In other words, both object-relations development and cognitive development would be seen as aspects of the psychological movement and interplay between symbiotic, autonomous, and interdependent modes of experiencing and relating to self and others. Faith, in Fowler's scheme, would here be seen as a developmental line within the vicissitudes of this matrix of meaning-making. There are a variety of issues that would need to be sorted out before knowing whether this regrounding would suffice. Yet it might well provide a way of organizing, in a fashion conducive to the requirements of care, the object-relations and cognitive-developmental dimensions of faith-knowing.

Whether this would be acceptable to Fowler or not is difficult to tell. At times he seems to want more independence between faith stages and object-relations than this option would seem to allow. The way he discusses the fact that people at different faith stages experience, perceive, and reflect on Erikson's psychosocial crises in different ways implies as much. Thus, for example, he cites Richard Shulik's work suggesting that older adults at differing faith stages construct their experience of aging differently. Fowler expands on his general point with reference to another example:

> Research is likely to show that a person of twenty-two whose moral and faith structuring is best characterized by stage 2 will indeed encounter the physical, social and emotional issues of the crisis of intimacy. But he or she will "construct" and experience them without benefit of a capacity for mutual interpersonal perspective taking, without a self-reflective sense of identity, and with a construction of the ultimate environment likely based on intuitions of cosmic reciprocity. As will become clear in subsequent sections of the book, other twenty-two-year-olds, structurally operating at stage 3 or 4, will construct, interpret, and respond to the issues of the intimacy crisis in qualitatively different ways than one at stage 2. In some respects, we might say, it is not even the same crisis for persons at these three different stages.[19]

The idea here is that Erikson's "developmental eras" will be experienced differently by people at different faith stages. There would be no argument from Erikson, of course, that people will experience the crises of intimacy vs. isolation, or integrity vs. despair, for example, in different ways. The reason they will experience them differently, Erikson might suggest, is at least in part because of the diverse ways in which the different people adapted to and experienced the previous stages. If we might be allowed to reformulate this somewhat in line with our previous comments, Fowler's hypothetical twenty-two-year-olds will experience the crisis of intimacy vs. isolation differently because of the variant object-relations contexts, and variant cognitive development, that informs the experiential-reflective matrix of their lives. What Fowler has isolated in his faith stages, then, is a particular line of development generated by the vicissitudes of this object-relations/cognitive-development interplay. In this sense, it should not be surprising that people at different faith stages may experience and reflect on psychosocial crises in different ways. The reason for this, however, would have to do with the fact that the faith stages themselves reflect a certain dimension of object-relations development.

PASSIONAL ALIGNMENT AND SELF PSYCHOLOGY

In order to clarify what this reformulation of the meaning of faith might entail, it may be helpful to examine a particular example of the way in which Fowler's formulations open out into this fuller incorporation of object-relations development. To do so we will examine an aspect of the logic of commitment and suggest a way in which a recent development in psychoanalytic theory, called "self psychology," might illuminate some of the structural issues involved in this.

Faith-knowing, for Fowler, is a dimension of the formulation of the self. In faith, we do not just abstractly or "intellectually" know the objects, ideas, or persons that come to form the content of faith. Rather, we are committed to, loyal to, and passionally aligned with those centers of supraordinate value and power. Thus Fowler's theory would seem to require an analysis of the psychological dynamics of commitment, loyalty, and passional alignment to such centers of value and power. No systematic analysis is offered, however. The closest Fowler seems to get to such an analysis is in his brief comments on faith and identity. He writes, for example, that "the centers of value and power that have good value for us, therefore, are those that confer meaning and worth on us and promise to sustain us in a dangerous world of power."[20] Later, he suggests that "in a real sense, we become part of that which we love and trust."[21] How are we to understand how this happens and the dynamic developmental character of such commitment and loyalty? Our question here, we must be clear, is not that of the content of the particular centers of value and power that are chosen, but rather the more "structural" concerns regarding the developmental forms of ways *any* such centers evolve.

While Fowler offers no systematic exploration of this, his discussion of this dimension of faith-knowing does seem to open directly into the concerns of self psychology—that aspect of psychoanalytic thought most thoroughly explored by Heinz Kohut. Kohut's thought is concerned with the developmental line of, what he calls, self-object relations. Self-objects are those persons, ideas, and objects that we experience as a part of ourselves. Our experiences of and relation to self objects, Kohut says, have their developmental vicissitudes throughout life. The self-object line of development, in this sense, is not a pathological phenomenon, but rather constitutes a normal aspect of development, which may nonetheless become disturbed or distorted in various ways.

Developmentally, as Kohut explains, there are two major varieties of self-objects: the idealized parent imago and the mirroring self-object. Mirroring self-objects refer to those self-objects "who respond to and confirm the child's innate sense of vigor, greatness, and perfection."[22] Idealized parent imago self-objects, on the other hand, are those "to whom the child can look up and with whom he can merge as an image of calmness, infallibility, and omnipotence."[23] It is within this matrix of ideals and ambitions (and the tension arc established between them) that the self is formed. This highly schematic presentation of Kohut's thought cannot do justice to the range and richness of his work, but it may be sufficient to note how aspects of Fowler's discussion open into these concerns.

To put it most forthrightly, what we mean by bringing Kohut's work into this discussion is that faith, as Fowler is studying it, seems to refer in part to the implications of our self-object relations for our understanding of the broader horizons of our experience, as these are shaped and articulated through the particular cognitive-developmental lens of the individual. Fowler's discussion of the relation of faith and identity seems to imply as much at points. When he says, for instance, that we choose those centers of supraordinate value and power, not because we "ought" to, but because they "confer meaning and worth on us and promise to sustain us in a dangerous world of power," the self-object dimensions of this (particularly with reference to its idealizational components) seem clear. Likewise, when he says that "we become part of that which we love and trust," self psychology helps us understand the dynamics and vicissitudes of merger with idealized objects, persons, and ideals which this implies. Thus our *way* of constructing our centers of supraordinate value and power (not just their contents) in part arises from and reflects the infrastructure of our self-object relations, just as those centers, when their dynamics are made conscious and reflected upon, may in turn possibly modify, contextualize, or rationalize our self-object relations. Fowler's understanding of faith development seems to open out into these concerns and, if more fully developed, would enable us to understand the dynamic aspects of structure.

CONCLUDING COMMENTS

This essay has sought to explore, in preliminary fashion, some avenues of dialogue between the requirements of care and Fowler's developmental epistemology of faith. While Fowler's work was not written specifically with the requirements of care in mind, the richness of his discussion and the importance of the nurture and challenge of care in our world suggest that such an encounter is necessary and may bear unexpected fruit. Our attempt to delineate some areas of mutual concern is meant to further this dialogue in the hopes that others may find reasons to join the conversation.

NOTES

1. James Fowler, "Stages in Faith: The Structural-Developmental Approach," in *Values and Moral Development,* ed. Thomas Hennessey (New York: Paulist Press, 1967), p. 186.

2. James Fowler, "Faith and the Structuring of Meaning," in *Toward Moral and Religious Maturity,* ed. J. Fowler and A. Vergote (Morristown, N.J.: Silver Burdett, 1980), p. 60.

3. Ibid., p. 61.

4. James Fowler, *Stages of Faith* (San Francisco: Harper & Row, 1981), p. 102.

5. Ibid.

6. Fowler, "Faith and the Structuring of Meaning," p. 64.

7. Fowler, *Stages of Faith*, p. 16.

8. For fuller discussion of this concept, see Anna Freud, *Normality and Pathology in Childhood* (New York: International Universities Press, 1965); and John Gedo and Arnold Goldberg, *Models of the Mind* (Chicago: University of Chicago Press, 1973).

9. We are provisionally applying the traditional approach to this issue in pastoral care by separating the question of the validity claims of the "content" of faith and the question of their developmental genesis and function. We will qualify this somewhat below.

10. Robert Kegan, *The Evolving Self* (Cambridge, Mass.: Harvard University Press, 1982), p. 14.

11. A helpful discussion of related points is found in Charles Taylor, "Neutrality in Political Science," in *The Philosophy of Social Explanation,* ed. Alan Ryan (Oxford: Oxford University Press, 1973).

12. Fowler, *Stages of Faith*, p. 274.

13. Ibid., p. 301.

14. Lawrence Kohlberg, "The Claim to Moral Adequacy of a Highest Stage of Moral Judgment," *Journal of Philosophy* 70 (October 25, 1973), pp. 630-646.

15. See also, from a different perspective, the argument of Ernest Wallwork, "Morality, Religion, and Kohlberg's Theory," in *Moral Development, Moral Education, and Kohlberg,* ed. B. Munsey (Birmingham, Ala.: Religious Education Press, 1980).

16. Fowler, "Faith and the Structuring of Meaning," pp. 64-65.

17. For an extended discussion of these issues, and especially how faith development and emotional development converge in pastoral diagnosis, see Don Browning, *Religious Ethics and Pastoral Care* (Philadelphia: Fortress, 1983), pp. 102-4, 107-113. For an extended discussion of the possible identity yet perspectival differences between object relations development and faith development, see Browning's "Review of Fowler's *Stages of Faith,*" *Anglican Theological Review* 65 (July, 1983) 3, pp. 124-127.

18. See Kegan, *The Evolving Self.*

19. Fowler, *Stages of Faith*, p. 107.

20. Ibid., p. 18.

21. Ibid.

22. Heinz Kohut and Ernest Wolf, "The Disorders of the Self and Their Treatment: An Outline," *International Journal of Psychoanalysis* 59 (1978), p. 414.

23. Ibid.

Chapter 10

Faith Development and Pastoral Diagnosis

CARL D. SCHNEIDER

One way to pursue the potential contribution of the faith development framework to pastoral counseling is to investigate its capacity to help with the task of generating a systematic approach to pastoral diagnosis. This is an area of great need and controversy in the field at the present time, and one in which faith development theory has promise to be useful. There are also some problems, however, and this essay will investigate both.

Paul Pruyser wrote his book, *The Minister as Diagnostician,* to plead for the importance of pastoral diagnosis in pastoral care. It is, he said, "a jarring note when any professional person no longer knows what his basic science is, or finds no use for it."[1] But this, he argues, is the situation in pastoral counseling. He lists a number of crucial questions that pastors must be able to answer, not at all convinced that the means are available by which to respond:

> In what way, with what concepts, in what words, with what outlook does a practicing pastor assess the problem of a client who seeks his pastoral help? What, if anything, distinguishes a pastoral from a psychological assessment? In what terms does he describe his client and size up his problems? In making his pastoral help available, how does he proceed to heal, guide, or sustain the person who is turning to him for assistance. . . .
>
> If he makes a diagnosis, how does he do so? And does his diagnosis have any bearing upon his helping moves, his counseling techniques or goals, his advice-giving, his encouragements, his pastoral interventions? Does he know what his clients seek of him, and does he realize

what they hope to attain in selecting their pastor rather than a lawyer, doctor, or social worker as their prospective helper?[2]

Pruyser is not alone in his call for a pastoral-theological diagnostic system. His plea has received a broad response of agreement. But what one should consist of is still a major unresolved question.

PREVIOUS ATTEMPTS AT PASTORAL DIAGNOSIS

Although systematic approaches to pastoral diagnosis are not widely available today, several attempts have emerged during the twentieth century which deserve some attention. By looking at two of the most important of these we will be in a better position to assess the promise of Fowler's work for this vital task. Historically, one of the more significant attempts to develop a systematic interview schedule and set of categories for assessing people comes from that root figure in the modern pastoral care movement, Anton Boisen. Glenn Asquith reports on three extended interview schedules which Boisen developed over the years.[3] Asquith simply labels them Form A, Form B, and Form C.

Asquith believes that Form A was used by Boisen throughout his career, since it appears in many different places in his files. Under each of his categories, there are many detailed questions, but it will suffice to list here his basic categories (see Table 1).

Table 1: Boisen's Diagnostic Interview Schedule (Form A)

I. Preliminary Orientation
   [A brief description of the patient, including age, sex, and previous admissions to the hospital.]

II. Social and Religious Background
   [The outstanding features of the patient's heredity and environment, including the social, economic, and religious status of parents, grandparents, and other family members.]

III. Personal History (Previous to Illness)

   A. Early Childhood
      1. Prenatal Influence
      2. Birth Conditions
      3. Disposition
      4. Walking, Talking, Weaning (if breast-fed), Sphincter-control
      5. Physical Health and Vigor

B. School Years
   1. Studies
   2. Special Abilities and Disabilities
   3. Health
   4. Social Relationships
      a. With members of the home group
      b. With teachers
      c. With school-mates
      d. With pets
   5. Work and Play
      a. Leisure time
      b. Chores and duties at home
   6. Personality

C. Adolescence and Maturity
   1. Social Adjustments
      a. Primary Loyalties (with parents and other groups)
      b. Social Contacts
      c. Accomplishments
      d. Recreations and Satisfactions
      e. Religion (church affiliation, attendance, attitudes)
      f. Personality (12 characteristics listed)
   2. Sex Adjustments
      a. Childhood and Adolescent Difficulties
      b. Attitude toward the Same or toward Opposite Sex
      c. Special Attachment or Antagonism toward Either Parent or Other Member of Family
      d. Love Affairs and Disappointments
      e. Sex Irregularities Before and After Marriage
      f. Marriage (facts concerning courtship, wife, children)
   3. Vocational Adjustments
      a. Plans and Ambitions
      b. Industrial Record
      c. Attitude toward Work
      d. Relationship with Employers and Fellow Workers
      e. Opportunity for Self-expression
   4. Physical Condition and Health

D. Later Years
An examination of any major changes in the person's life situation and current health condition.

IV. History of Present Illness (previous to present admission)
Includes symptoms, changes in behavior, religious concern, attitudes of family toward illness.

V. Characteristics of the Disorder (during period of observation in hospital)

A. Changes in Condition
B. General Appearance and Behavior
C. Intellectual Functions
D. Content of Thought
   1. Sense of the Mysterious and Uncanny
   2. Sense of Peril
   3. Personal Responsibility
   4. Erotic Involvement
   5. Philosophy of Life
   6. Plans and Ambitions

VI. Diagnostic Impressions

    A. An Appraisal of the Life Situation
    B. An Analysis of the' Reaction Patterns
    C. An Analysis of the Personality Organization
    D. A Consideration of the Clinical Label
    E. A Forecast of the Outcome
    F. A Plan of Treatment

VII. Interpretation
The diagnostic impression is a consideration of the patient's problem in light of his previous history and of our knowledge of other cases of mental disorder. It is directed specifically toward the problems of classification, prognosis, and treatment, and it seeks to do this as concisely as possible. From the standpoint of our general problem it is of great value to follow this with an attempt to relate our findings to the experiences of normal persons and to constructive religious experience. More important still is the attempt to review the patient's experience in the light of certain general hypotheses to see how far these hypotheses will explain the phenomena. In any such attempt it is hardly worthwhile to begin with any fixed categories. The question before us is: What is there in this man's particular experience which becomes intelligible when we consider it in the light of certain leads or theories? What light does this case throw upon the laws of the spiritual life with which we are all concerned?

VIII. Observations and Progress Notes
Good case records append the primary data upon which the case record has been based. Such data should include the daily notes and observations both before and after the case has been written up and the diagnostic summary made.

After the completion of the report, the daily or weekly notes and observations should from time to time be supplemented by diagnostic and interpretive comments.

The interview schedule which Asquith labels Form B differs in two major areas from Form A. First, Boisen has a section labeled "Religious Concern" which appears under "Characteristics of the Disorder" (Segment V in Form A). It reads as follows:

RELIGIOUS CONCERN

Degree of concern about vital issues
Forces upon which he conceives himself to be
    dependent—personal or impersonal? human or superhuman? friendly or unfriendly? monistic or dualistic?
Practice of prayer, Bible reading, attendance at religious services
Self-estimate—exalted or self-depreciative?
Ideas of—communication with God
    conflict with evil spirits
    remorse over sins

expiation
cosmic identification
rebirth
previous incarnation
prophetic mission

Second, a separate section labeled "Religious Attitude and Orientation" also appears in Form B but not in Form A. It follows the section labeled "present condition" and comes before the Diagnostic Summary:

RELIGIOUS ATTITUDE ORIENTATION

Present concern about vital issues
His interpretation of the disturbance
Attendance at—church services and mental health conferences
Practice of prayer and Bible reading
Reasons given for attendance or nonattendance at church
His concept of the Bible
His idea of the chief end of life
His concept of God
His concept of the cross

Asquith labels as Form C the schedule which Boisen used to gather his data for the cases in his book, *The Exploration of the Inner World*. This questionnaire, developed in cooperation with Helen Flanders Dunbar, included two sections of particular interest, one titled "Philosophy of Life" and one "Religious Concern."

PHILOSOPHY OF LIFE

26. How much serious thinking do you do? What is your idea of what we are in the world for?
27. What is your idea of God? What reason do you have for believing in God? Have you ever seen him? heard him? What is your attitude toward him? his attitude toward you? How do you think we can please God most?
28. Do you believe in other superhuman beings besides God?
29. What is your idea of this universe in which we live? What do you think of when you see a) the sun? b) the moon? c) the stars d) water? e) fire? f) flowers? g) trees? h) rocks?

RELIGIOUS CONCERN

30. What does church mean to you? Have you been accustomed to attending it? To what church do you belong? How often do you go to the services here? What is your reason for going, or not going?
31. What does prayer mean to you? Has it given you any special comfort or help? Have you received any special answer to prayer? For what kind of things should one pray?
32. What does the Bible mean to you?
33. What ups and downs have you had in your religious life? What attempts have you made to turn over a new leaf? Have you had any periods of marked awakening? of back-sliding? When were you at your best?

A review of Boisen's questions makes it clear that many of the items on Fowler's schedule were raised by Boisen: the meaning of life; the focus of transcendent beauty, value, or power; objects of reverence or awe; religious experiences; religious beliefs and practice; specific meaningful religious symbols, etc. It is also interesting to note how similar Fowler and Boisen are on their views of the potential religious significance of all experience. Pruyser points out that it was Boisen's work which led him to alter the fundamental question of his own diagnostic inquiry from "which are the significant data of religious experience?" to "which data of experience are of religious significance?"[4] This perspectival shift accounts, I believe, for the simultaneous presence in both Boisen's and Fowler's schedules of multiple explicitly religious questions coupled with extensive life history questions which are *not* explicitly "religious." The shift that Pruyser identifies permits a fresh approach to the problem of "overdetermination." Material already interpreted from a dynamic, social, sexual, political framework may also yield religious meaning.

A second important figure is Edgar Draper, a psychiatrist who wrote an article for the *Archives of General Psychiatry* with the suggestive title, "On the Diagnostic Value of Religious Ideation,"[5] as well as a chapter on "Pastoral Diagnosis" in his helpful book *Psychiatry and Pastoral Care.*[6] Draper reports on research in which fifty patients were first given a "religious interview" involving a series of projective questions concerning religious issues (see Table 2)[7] and then seen by a separate team for independent psychiatric evaluations. Draper attempted to test the hypothesis that on the basis of religious material alone symptomatic, characterologic, and genetic diagnoses could be made, along with a psychodynamic formulation including prominent defenses used.[8] Draper claimed a predictive rate of 92 percent in scoring for symptom and character diagnoses.[9]

Table 2:
Draper's Projective Religious Questions

1. What is your earliest memory of a religious experience or belief?
2. What is your favorite Bible story? Why?
3. What is your favorite Bible verse? Why?
4. Who is your favorite Bible character? Why?
5. What does prayer mean to you? If you pray, what do you pray about?
6. A. What does religious mean to you?
   B. How does God function in your personal life?
7. A. In what way is God meaningful to other people besides yourself?
   B. How is God meaningful to father or mother?
8. What religious idea or concept is most important to you now?
9. What is the most religious action one can perform?
10. What do you consider the greatest sin one could commit?
11. What do you think of evil in the world?
12. What are your ideas of the after-life?
13. If God could grant you any three wishes, what would they be?

Draper made major advances over previous psychoanalytic studies of religion in this study. He provided a balanced assessment of the role of religion organized around the basic metapsychological perspective. Witness the extensive revision of and improvement upon Freud's early formulations about religion in the following statement:

> In the religious sphere, Freud's early contributions focused psychiatric attention on the oedipal struggle developmentally and on the superego structurally. Our findings, however, indicate that religious or cathected philosophies offer a broad base as well for expression of pregenital manifestation, developmentally, and for ego and id functions,

structurally. For some patients, religion offered distinctly an external trapping for operations of the superego. For others, it offered ideation and activity based clearly in the service of the ego or its defenses. For a few patients, religion served as an external framework for erotization, for various primitive impulse gratifications, and for primary process thinking. In all three cases cited . . . the variety of developmental, structural, and psychodynamic potential that religious ideation offers is clearly manifested. In these cases, too, adaptive as well as defensive functions can be discerned. Heinz Hartmann indicated that "the continued influence and synthetic achievements of religions rest on their being tradition saturated, socially unifying wholes, which are fed by the contributions of all the three mental institutions and provide a pattern, accessible to many people, for satisfying the demands of all these three institutions."[10]

Boisen was persistent in his efforts to comprehend religious experience in a constructive fashion. He lacked, however, an adequately systematic, dynamic framework. Psychoanalysis has had the systematic, dynamic framework, but in classical analysis religious experience was consistently construed in negative and pathological terms. Draper manages to redress this bias, while perserving the systematic framework.

There are problems, however. Though Draper's *psychological evaluation* of religious experience is a significant achievement, it is still an example of a reductionistic model. Religion is construed only in terms of psychodynamics and is reduced to a psychological process. When Draper writes about "the diagnostic value of religious ideation," he is not yet speaking in a way which makes possible *pastoral* diagnosis. He is, as he is clearly aware, speaking only of "the *psychological* diagnostic value of patients' religious beliefs and activities."[11] Again, when he speaks of a "developmental theory of religion" (which, we note, Boisen failed to provide), it turns out that he means by that "the psychosexual developmental correlates of religious expression."[12]

FOWLER'S WORK AS A MAJOR ADVANCE

This critical limitation is important for our understanding, because it helps us to see clearly the scope and significance of Fowler's achievement. Let me make the comparison directly. I believe that Fowler's work is a major advance over alternative attempts to develop a pastoral diagnostic framework for five reasons:

1. Fowler's theory *organizes* a variety of aspects of human existence into a coherent framework which permits reliable comparison among subjects, and thereby permits research;
2. The organizing category in Fowler's theory is *faith* itself, rather than some other category to which faith is reduced;
3. Fowler's theory gives us a fully elaborated *developmental* approach;
4. The various *aspects* of faith development are delineated in multidimensional and interdisciplinary analysis;
5. Fowler's model is *structural* rather than thematic, and thus universally applicable.

Fowler has, in my opinion, incorporated major achievements of previous research on pastoral diagnosis and then gone well beyond earlier formulations. He gives us an organized framework for viewing persons from the perspective of faith. The stage/aspect theory enables us to go beyond earlier hit-and-miss, idiosyncratic, *ad hoc* diagnoses. This is a major contribution because it allows for reliability among subjects. There is an inclusive typology which permits us to relate subject A to subject B to subject C. Not only does every subject fall into one of the six stages which, Fowler claims, are sequential and invariant. It is also possible to compare all individuals in terms of the seven "aspects" (form of logic, role-taking, form of moral judgment, etc.) which together constitute the various stages. What this permits is *research.* It enables us to have consistent terminology and an overall frame which is fixed. This is what Freud provided in a different way with his metapsychological framework for the study of psychodynamics. Fowler provides it for the study of faith.

This points to the second and third reasons. Fowler has provided at once a powerful framework for understanding the *development* of *faith.* Psychological developmental stages have been used widely in the study of religion and faith, and there have been many studies of the nature of faith. But Fowler is alone in having provided a theory which at the same time is developmental and has faith as its organizing category. This is a major contribution to pastoral diagnosis because faith itself is the ultimate pastoral concern and because the developmental understanding is so central to the practice of diagnosis.

Third, because Fowler has delineated the "aspects" or component elements of the various stages, he has greatly increased the
sophistication of the model. It identifies dimensions of human
existence which are related but which still have their own discrete
lines of development. This strategy is reminiscent of a similar one
in psychoanalytic model building. Such a multidimensional analysis of lines of development has been proposed by Anna Freud in
her concept of the "developmental line,"[13] by Blanck and
Blanck,[14] and by Gedo and Goldberg in their effort to construct a
comprehensive model of psychological development.[15] Because
Fowler uses the same strategy, interdisciplinary integration from
various fields can be correlated to the study of faith development
and used in pastoral diagnosis without necessarily reducing faith
and faith development to the phenomenon being studied in another field.

Fourth, Fowler has given us a structuralist approach to faith.
The roots of this approach stem not only from Fowler's psychological sources in Piaget and Kohlberg. They are found equally in
the understanding of faith that he appropriates from H. Richard
Niebuhr. As John McDargh notes, Niebuhr and Fowler are more
interested in the "*how* of faith as a universal phenomenon as
opposed to the *what* of faith in terms of particular dogmatic
contents."[16] In a structural approach, faith is construed as an
activity having to do with what we regard as our centers of value,
images of power, and master stories. It is an attempt to define
how we *position* ourselves in the world rather than any *fides quae
creditur.* This has two positive consequences for pastoral diagnosis. First, it forces us to investigate faith as a person's own action
and not just as an external reality to which a person responds.
When we look at faith, we are looking at the "faithing" person's
own action. Pastoral diagnosis, then, is personal diagnosis just as
diagnosis from a reductionistically psychological perspective
would be, but without the reductionism. Second, because faith is
defined structurally, it can be seen as a universal phenomenon.
Not all people are explicitly religious, but all people must position themselves in the world in some way. This approach is not
content-bound to any particular tradition or creed or denomination. It is a way of understanding faith that will work for any
content. Thus pastoral diagnosis is not something that is appro-

priate for some people but not others. Pastoral diagnosis, informed by Fowler's theory, will be an appropriate part of the pastoral care of all people.

PROBLEMS WITH FOWLER'S APPROACH

These are virtues of Fowler's theory and points at which Fowler shows promise for providing a framework for pastoral diagnosis that advances beyond anything we have had to this point. But there are also problems. The most significant problem is the obverse of one of the theory's central virtues. Because it is a cognitive-structural theory, it does not finally deal with content. Thus it does not offer us much help in understanding the role, origins, and dynamics of the personal images that even Fowler claims are so central to faith. This is the area in which psychoanalytic perspectives have been particularly fruitful. Because Fowler's is most fundamentally a structuralist theory which abstracts from such contents, a crucial gap appears in the theory which both makes it inadequate as a fundamental paradigm for pastoral diagnosis and causes internal problems within the theory itself. McDargh identifies this gap as "the influence of unconscious elements in the constellation of any given faith position, the mediating role of personal images of the transcendent in the reasoning of faith, and the interaction between significant personal relationships past and present and the structure of faith." By focusing on this gap, as it is identified and illuminated by psychoanalytic insight, it may be possible for us to provide some suggestions for ways in which Fowler's own theory could be further developed and made more useful for pastoral diagnosis. A thorough study of the major faith development "case" that Fowler provides will make this possible.

"MARY'S" CASE

Fowler claims that his theory rests upon an empirical base. He and his associates, he reports, have conducted 359 interviews between 1972 and 1981. Strange, then, that in a decade in which Fowler has published something on faith development almost yearly, there is, to my knowledge, only one extended report of a faith interview: the case of Mary, reported in chapter 22 of *Stages of Faith*.[17] This fact alone would warrant giving it considerable attention. But there are other reasons it deserves scrutiny. In a "case conference" at the institution where I work, a group of us spent almost a month on this case. We found ourselves in considerable disagreement with Fowler, who has offered his own staging for this woman. And yet our group had previously developed considerable intragroup reliability in scoring faith development interviews. How shall we account for this divergence? I believe there is a set of reasons why our group viewed Mary differently from Fowler, and they point to basic issues with regard to an assessment of the character and validity of Fowler's theory. I would like, then, to look at this case in some detail.

It would be entirely too cumbersome to recap the interview here in any depth. A brief synopsis may be helpful, however. Mary is a twenty-eight-year-old Caucasian female, the oldest of four children, and particularly close to her youngest brother (3; numbers refer to those given in the interview in *Stages of Faith*). Her father is almost totally absent from the interview material. He is a man "closed in" in his feelings (16), and who works hard and spends a lot of time by himself. Mary says, "I really don't feel like I know my father very well" (17). Mary and her mother have a very difficult relationship. Mary reports that she "was suicidal from a very early age, and it was always a reaction to my relationship with my mother" (21).

Mary describes her years from twenty-two to twenty-seven as her "lost years," during which time she dropped out of a Midwest college and subsequently left a university in the West. By the end of this period, she was suicidal, on drugs (LSD), involved in various fads and cults (yoga, the occult), had a serious car accident, was arrested for shoplifting, and finally made a serious suicide attempt. She identifies two related turning points following the attempt. Three weeks afterward, she had a spiritual experience, while on LSD, in which "it was revealed to me" that "our only purpose on earth is to worship and glorify the Lord" (7). Then eight months later her younger brother Ron, who was converted to Christianity, came home unexpectedly for Christmas and "witnessed" to her. She "made a decision that I was going to believe in Jesus Christ and follow him" (11).

The years that follow are a repetitive story of Mary's involvement in a succession of cults and ill-chosen men. As she said, "the only thing I wanted from the Lord, other than to know him and to do his will, was a husband. I became very obsessed with that idea" (27). Following three months with the Followers of God, she then joined a "Logan Road ministry" where "I felt that God had showed me that I was going to marry a certain brother in that house" (31). The man, however, rejected her, and the Church fellowship asked her to leave. She then went to a house church in Florida where her brother was. This group, she reports, was really into "submission" and she was "kicked out" of the house for some angry remarks to the leader. Mary perceived this experience not only as a rejection by this evangelical group; it also involved a rejection by her brother, as well as by God. The experience was so traumatic that Mary reports that hospitalization was being considered for her (though it is not said by whom).

Mary's work history is spotty. Having dropped out of school, without skills, she was doing temporary office work for a fast-food corporation. Fowler's interview revolves around her involvement with "the Lord," but a summary of the other areas of her life—personal relations, work history, schooling, family life—reflect an otherwise bleak picture of failure.

Mary became involved with another evangelical group in Florida for three months. Then a professor at her brother's Bible Institute recommended another evangelical group, and she moved to Bethel House in Wisconsin, where she met her husband. Her explanation of their attraction: "I had had such a history of rejection, and both of us felt that we had such a need for a relationship. I guess that's what really drew us together, just our common need" (46). They married four months after they met, partially out of guilt around premarital sex. Almost immediately her husband became involved in drugs and a series of affairs and was physically abusive. Mary became pregnant and the couple soon separated. Mary meanwhile became involved with still another evangelical group called "Pilgrim's Way," an outgrowth of a Lutheran house church. She moved in with another family, had her child, then moved back in with Harry, her husband.

Nothing changed. He failed repeatedly at several business ventures and sent her back to Florida. She returned, feeling, after reading *The Total Woman,* she would try to patch up the marriage. He moved out again. She began to get a hold of her life, got child care, took junior college courses. But then she accepted him back again. This led to another break with her "Pilgrim's Way" fellowship. They moved to yet another charismatic church, "Agape." Harry and she continued for another six months until he became flagrantly and publicly abusive, and finally she moved out and divorced him. Pregnant with her second child, she agreed, again against the advice of her religious fellowship, to move home with her parents. Back in Georgia, she joined another religious fellowship, one associated with another in Birmingham, Alabama, where the fellow she had originally fallen in love with was. She still hoped to marry him.

AN ALTERNATIVE ANALYSIS

This is a very brief summary of the course of Mary's life as it emerges in Fowler's interview with her. It is on several counts a strange interview for Fowler to choose to put forward as the only clinical example he offers in hundreds of pages of writing on faith development. It is an incomplete interview, not conducted for research purposes, but rather with someone who had come to Fowler for counseling. It is a puzzling choice also because, in all his work, Fowler is so at pains to insist that he is studying *faith,* not just religion—above all, not just "conventional" religion. Yet this case does not direct us toward thinking about the nature of the faith of individuals who do not exhibit a manifest religiosity. Instead, we are thrust back into the most clichéd and stereotyped form of religious faith. Of course, in Fowler's approach all people have a faith. But to make this case the centerpiece of his approach seems to me to be at best confusing.

Fowler alludes to the personal motivation that led him to choose this interview, saying, "I have found it a *troublingly compelling* interview."[18] What is "troubling" for Fowler seems to be that Mary is a "highly intelligent" woman, yet exhibits "repetitive patterns that were destructive to her." I think that Fowler's being troubled by this fact is deserving of commentary and reflects a basic deficiency in his theory. The form in which Fowler presents this case, however, is that of an invitation to the reader to do his or her own staging of Mary. Thus, he writes, "After you have answered all the questions for yourself, you can read my answers to them, comparing and contrasting your perceptions and judgments with mine."[19] Fowler invites a dialogue. He has also told us that he stays with this case because he himself does not fully comprehend it—it is still *troublingly compelling.* We will accept Fowler's invitation and attempt to engage him in serious dialogue.

Fowler takes each of his seven "aspects" and argues that in each of them Mary occupies a *Synthetic-Conventional* position. For example, with regard to "locus of authority," he writes:

> Clearly, the description of stage 3 most aptly characterized the way Mary then constituted and relied upon authority. The stage 2 description of incumbents of authority roles does not fit. Mary's conventional counterculture posture had emerged to negate that locus of authority. On the other hand, in those years she clearly lacked the internalized locus of authority described in stage 4, "one's own judgment, as informed by a self-ratified (self-chosen) ideological perspective."[20]

With regard to the "role of symbols," Fowler similarly writes:

> I think it is clear that in this respect also Mary's faith structuring in her postconversion period also fits best the description given in stage 3. . . . Regardless of the lack of adequate data for determining the level of the symbolic function, however, I think it is easy to see that Mary's way of using her central symbols and images in those years went beyond either the magical-numinous quality of stage 1, or the one-dimensional and literal quality of stage 2. And I would be surprised indeed if further probing of her use of symbols at the time of the interview would have disclosed the kind of critical distance from and conceptual translation of symbolic meanings that characterize stage 4.[21]

Our case conference, on the other hand, thought that Mary was possibly a stage 1, or, at best, a stage 2 individual. The group quarreled with Fowler's reading. Fowler, for example, argues that Mary's countercultural "posture" negated stage 2 as an accurate description of Mary's locus of authority. It is not clear, however, that Fowler's description of stage 2 locus of authority would not describe Mary well:

> The claims of authorities, insofar as they relate to areas of the boy's or girl's sensory experience, will be subjected to the child's own forming

canons of judgment in that area. But in other areas, and for the validation of conclusions drawn from their own experience, children look to trusted adults—teachers or parents—or to older siblings. The question of authority is not a conscious issue at stage 2. Choices are made and preferences are expressed and relied upon, but the criteria by which these are made are not yet matters of conscious reflection.[22]

As Fowler notes, Mary held a countercultural "posture," which led to a "negating" of parental authority. But it is not at all obvious that Mary has in any meaningful way gone beyond her parents' authority. Mary's view of herself is impossible to differentiate from that of her parents. When she refers to herself as a "rebellious brat"(15) one wonders whether that is her view or that of her parents. Mary, though in her late twenties, has at the time of the interview just moved back into her parents' home. She may negate her mother's ideas, but it is never clear that she is *free* of them. The account has more the oppositional quality of a two-year-old. Furthermore, it seems that Mary consistently looks to "siblings"—her brother Ron—"for the validation of conclusions drawn from her own experiences." In this respect, she remains dependent on her family from the beginning to the end of this account. Indeed, the central event of her conversion is utterly involved with her relation to Ron. Ron came home unexpectedly at Christmas, witnessed to her, and, as she says, "he was able to answer my questions and really pin me down"(11).

With regard to "form of world coherence," Fowler simply states: "Hers was clearly not the 'explicit system, conceptually mediated . . .' of stage 4. Nor was it the 'Episodic' or 'Narrative-Dramatic' forms of stages 1 and 2. Again, the structuring pattern of stage 3 best describes this aspect of Mary's faith."[23]

Fowler doesn't argue this point here; he simply states it. But it is not so "clear." It would seem that his description of the stage 2 "form of world coherence" applies to Mary better:

Stage 2 achieves mastery of the *narrative* mode for giving coherence to experience. Without the capacity—or the need yet—to interrupt the stream of life and reflect more abstractly upon its meaning or direction, the individual best described by stage 2 employs stories or myths, whether personal or cultural-religious, to express his or her sense of an ultimate environment.[24]

Mary's life cetainly is primarily characterized by its *narrative* quality. Indeed, Fowler notes he never got to other parts of her life because the interview was taken up with her narrative account of the last several years of her life. Fowler says Mary is past stage 2 because she can answer the question about dividing her life into chapters without difficulty. That reflects a capacity to stand *outside* the flow of her life, at least a stage 3 competence. But I would think that, at best, Mary might be a stage 2 trying to achieve a stage 3, a person in stage-transition. She may *try* to reflect on her life, but in fact the extended account of her many repeated communal involvements has precisely the quality of a shaggy dog story that goes nowhere and has no point.[25]

I would quarrel in the same way with Fowler's appeal to intuitive recognition that "it is easy to see that Mary's way of using her central symbols and images in those years went beyond either the magical-numinous quality of stage 1, or the one-dimensional and literal quality of stage 2."[26] Mary in fact exhibits several examples of a magical-numinous approach to symbols. Witness her idea that the airplane flight number 777 confirmed her decision to go to Wisconsin as "auspicious" (44). Similarly, her use of symbols seems to be often very literal and concrete:

> During this time when I was really praying for the will of God, three different people who had no relationship with one another gave me a word about stepping out like Abraham. You know, it says in Hebrews 11, that he went to a place where he didn't know anybody, and he left everything familiar behind (43). . . . So I really believed that that was the word of the Lord to me, to do as Abraham had done and just step out on faith. . . . So I did, and it was rather frightening since I didn't know a soul in Wisconsin (44).

This seems to be a classic example of conservative religious groups using biblical imagery and myth in a literalistic, proof-texting fashion.

"IDEALIZING" IN FAITH DEVELOPMENT THEORY

What are we to make of this discrepant reading which Fowler and we give? Is one of us simply mistaken? I think the truth is rather that our disagreement reflects a basic problem in Fowler's system. Fowler's approach to staging is characterized by *intellectualizing* and *idealizing* in the psychodynamic sense of those terms. Let me attempt to document this.

When Fowler looks at Mary's use of symbols, he notes, correctly, that Mary uses the phrase "the Lord" in two quite distinct ways:

> I speak of images in the plural because the coherence of Mary's faith world at that time involved at least two major images of God. On the one hand, there was the God who gives guidance and sanctions initiatives. When these initiatives turned out to have been mistakes or to have had extremely painful consequences, the goodness, fidelity, or authenticity of this God were never questioned. On the other hand, there was God the rescuer—the one whom she saw as meeting her when she was at the end of her rope, the one who never forsook her.[27]

Speaking of what he calls these "two dominant *personae* or masks of the Lord," Fowler uses them to establish that for Mary " 'the Lord' is a powerful, multidimensional symbol, filled with highly personal and subjective emotive content."[28]

This seems to me to reflect the confusing circularity of Fowler's staging. He has mixed description and evaluation as he talks about the "coherence" of Mary's faith. "Coherence" becomes for him evidence for assigning Mary to a stage 3 level with regard to the category of "symbolic function." But the coherence is something that Fowler *attributes*. It would seem to be more accurate to say that what we are faced with is precisely a *lack* of coherence.

When Fowler speaks of this as "two personae" or "masks," and of the "tacit system" of strongly felt meanings, a dynamically oriented clinician might suggest that Mary's treatment of God would be better described as a primitive form of *object splitting,* in which good and bad objects are not able to be integrated but are held side by side. Fowler places under the umbrella of the "coherence of Mary's faith world" data that suggest just the opposite: the failure of Mary to achieve integration.

This process of inversion and relabeling recurs with unsettling frequency. Speaking again of the symbolic function in Mary, Fowler says that we lack data to make judgments concerning "this aspect of her faith structuring."[29] But "faith structuring," while it is faithful to Fowler's concept that faith is a verb, an active process, lends a more active sense of agency to Mary than is appropriate, given her "pattern of passivity."[30]

This idealizing cast appears even in the midst of the interview. Fowler, in an aside, comments on the "priestly role" of Ron, Mary's brother, in helping Mary reach a decision (59). This seems to me to be a gussied-up way to speak of Mary's inability to make her own decisions and her dependency on others.

More than once Fowler interprets Ron and Mary's relation in this strained matter. Referring to Mary's report that Ron was given "supernatural wisdom" by the Lord which enabled him to answer her questions and "really pin me down," Fowler says: "Ron is established by virtue of the crucial role he played in bringing her to Christ, and by virtue of the fidelity of his love and care for her, as the most consistent and lasting mediator of divine authority she has during most of the time covered by the interview."[31]

But Ron's love is not simply faithful; he in fact breaks with Mary. Fowler reverses the relation. It is not because of his role in bringing her to Christ that Ron is the mediator of authority; it is because Mary depends on him that he brings her to Christ! It is just such unjustified reversals that result in Fowler's scoring Mary higher in his staging than our case conference did.

Once one begins to scrutinize Fowler's idealizing language, it becomes clear that a clinician's eye would offer a leaner and more parsimonious account. Fowler, for example, writes expansively of Mary's use of Scripture as authority. Authority, he says, "was located in Scripture (in highly selective passages, which usually are brought to her attention by valued others and made salient by their response with her immediate existential situation)."[32] This is fancy language for what a clinician would call her impulsiveness and lack of ego strength. She responds less in terms of "salience" (i.e., valuing) and more in terms of intensity of impulse and external pressure.

This pattern continues throughout Fowler's description of each of the categories of the faith stages. Fowler, in speaking of the bounds of social awareness, asks: "Who are the significant others in relation to whom Mary maintains her sense of identity and the vitality of her faith? Whose questions and criticism—intellectual and/or social and existential—must her faith 'stand'?"[33] The very question attributes qualities to her faith (e.g., "vitality" and the "ability to withstand existential criticism") that are mainly noted by their absence.

Why does Fowler fall into this pattern? Fowler does not deny the importance of a psychodynamic perspective. Rather, he devotes half of his comments to an attempt to relate the structural perspective to a dynamic perspective (à la Erikson) on Mary. But Fowler seems to me never to face clearly the *defensive* function of Mary's faith. Thus, even when what he says is not inaccurate, it is inadequate. Speaking of the bounds of social awareness in terms of the stage 3 interpersonally constructed world, he says, "the bonds of community are constituted by friendship, love, and emotional solidarity in faith."[34] This is true, as far as it goes. It names the positive qualities of an interpersonally constructed (and limited) world. But it does not go far enough. It does not name the way in which such a stage 3 is a defense against the threat implicit in a stage 4 construction.

NEED FOR A "HERMENEUTIC OF SUSPICION"

As we noted, Fowler has the apparatus for a major advance in pastoral diagnosis. But his actual use of his instrument, in this case at least, is more a reversal of the classical Freudian position than an advance upon it. The classical Freudian interpretation of religious material was skewed toward a pathological interpretation, construed mainly in terms of its defensive function. Ego psychology has attempted to improve upon this formulation by reminding us that an adequate formulation would have to include both defensive and adaptive functions. *But Fowler often seems to see only the adaptive function and neglects the defensive.* To utilize his theory in this manner seems to me a mistake. It is not adequate to the dynamics of faith or religion. It is rather a relapse to predynamic formulations.

Paul Ricoeur, the French philosopher, has been deeply interested in the integration of the social sciences and religious studies. Ricoeur suggests that there is a necessary dialectic between two contrasting hermeneutics, the *"hermeneutics of suspicion"* and the *"hermeneutics of restoration."* In his monumental and profound study of Freud, Ricoeur argues that a proper reading of Freud would place him primarily in the camp of what he terms the "hermeneutic of suspicion." This role is a demystifying, debunking one. But, argues Ricoeur, such a discipline is essential to religion. It has been a mistake to regard such sciences as the enemy of religion. There is a "positive benefit of the ascesis required by a reductive and destructive interpretation."[35] Among its positive benefits are that it functions as a corrective to the unbridled fancy and imagination of the "hermeneutics of restoration." This latter, best exemplified by figures such as Eliade, Van der Leeuw, and Ricoeur himself, is given to excess and idolatry. This school of hermeneutics as "recollection of meaning" needs the chastening of a hermeneutics of suspicion.

Formulated in terms of our discussion, this suggests that Fowler's hermeneutical idealization needs the chastening of the hermeneutics of suspicion exercised by a psychodynamic approach. Ego psychology has given a central place to understanding such defensive dynamics. One of the seminal books of ego psychology remains Anna Freud's, *The Ego and the Mechanisms of Defense.*[36] To bring the two frameworks into confrontation would be bracing. It would, I believe, lead to a winnowing and toughening of Fowler's theory.

My own experience of Fowler is that he would subject a faith such as Mary embodies to a strong critical scrutiny when he encounters it in corporate form.[37] But one-on-one, he seems reluctant to temper his appreciative hermeneutic with an astringent hermeneutic of suspicion. James Fowler is a gentleman in person. In his theory he has embodied the same considerateness, the same concern to be respectful of the faith of every person. But his reticence here, while a personal virtue, is a theoretical fault. He has incorporated personal virtues in an explanatory theory which thus lacks, at critical points, "bite" and power.

Let me suggest three places where that is so. First, *Fowler lacks an adequate instrument to account for the discrepancy between a person's words, affect, and behavior.* Words are overvalued by Fowler. In the interviews Fowler offers us, he analyzes only the verbal productions of the interviewee. He fails to give us a parallel analysis of the interviewee's affect and behavior. Clinicians typically utilize not only a client's report *about* their everyday life and their history, but also a client's direct interaction with the therapist. Freud identifies transference as the mechanism involved in curing a patient. Robert J. Langs corrects the emphasis on transference to focus instead on the therapeutic *relationship.* But Fowler pays no attention to this dynamic at all.

We may see this in his introduction to the Mary interview:

> Mary is a neatly dressed young woman who seems a bit younger than her twenty-eight years. I have never met her before. We spend thirty minutes or so getting acquainted. *I explain to her* that for some years I have been conducting interviews of this kind. *My interest is* to invite people to share with us . . . something about their ways of seeing life, their values, what's important to them and so on. *I explain* that our work is part of the field of life span developmental psychology and that we are interested in knowing something about the life experiences and the important relationships that have helped to shape peoples' perspectives, their values, and their lifestyles. *I make it clear* that in this interview there are no right or wrong answers, only her answers. She is free to decline to answer any question with which she does not feel comfortable. *I promise* to keep the information she shares with me confidential and assure her that in the event of its use in any publication, her anonymity and that of any persons she mentions in the interview will be carefully protected. The interview begins.[38]

Note that Fowler reports only what *he* said: "My interest is. . . ," "I explain. . . ," "I make it clear. . . ," "I promise. . . ." Of Mary, we hear only that she seems "a bit younger than her twenty-eight years."[39]

Even without any direct information from Fowler concerning the interview relationship and Mary's demeanor, the interview itself provides disturbing clues. In our group we found ourselves assessing an individual whose verbal productions might at times seem to qualify her as a stage 3 intellectually, but her emotional responses were more appropriately described by stage 1 or 2. We did not believe her words. Or, better, her words betrayed, at an emotional level, something they do not when looked at just intellectually. Emotionally, they seemed to be less developed.

Fowler seems to employ a consistently intellectual criterion across the stages in his assessment. In spite of his claim to be concerned with both intellect and volition, mind and heart, willing and loving as well as thinking, he appeals repeatedly to intellectual/cognitive criteria and seems still in the Piaget/Kohlberg tradition. For example, when speaking of the "form of world coherence" which Mary displays, he asks: "To what degree is Mary *critically self-conscious* about the meanings which sustain her and about how they differ from those of other persons or other groups? How concerned is she about *internal consistency* between elements of her system of meanings and values?"[40] Both are intellectual criteria. What Fowler does not ask about here is coherence in terms of cognitive/*emotional* integration. A theory that does not deal with that issue is handicapped at best.

At one point Fowler makes the following fascinating observations: "Initially in the interview, and afterwards as I have read and reread it, I have been impressed by a kind of gentleness with which Mary attempted to see things as her mother saw them. A quality of fairness—and the ability to differentiate her mother's perspective from her own—marked her way of saying, 'My mother is an extremely giving person. She's always faithfully served her family, far above what most women would do.' "[41] This seems to me a serious failure to recognize dynamically what is going on and again accounts for Fowler's arriving at a higher stage level than our group.

Fowler identifies Mary's comment just quoted as an example of her "fairness" and "gentleness," as well as of her "ability to differentiate her mother's perspective from her own." To the contrary, I would suggest that these comments reflect Mary's undigested incorporation of her parents' self-report and precisely her *failure* to differentiate her mother's perspective from her own. One senses here that this is a self-flattering description of a demanding and guilt-inducing woman resentfully suffering from a martyr complex.

I claim this because the next words Mary utters after saying this belie the reality of mother as a "giving person":

MARY: And yet, I've always felt that her attitude toward me was very negative and critical. Like she didn't accept me. . . . It always comes out in the form of irritation or anger and disgust toward me and the way I do things (14).

INTERVIEWER: So nothing you could ever do was very pleasing?

MARY: Right. I could never please her (15).

This exchange hardly depicts an "extremely giving person." Rather than illustrating Mary's ability to differentiate, as Fowler proposes, I would take this passage as evidence of Mary's merger and lack of differentiation. To use a psychological construct from a different school, Mary is still *embedded.*

Robert Kegan suggests that stage-theory ought to be seen as a series of rebalancings in which the self becomes increasingly distinguished from its perceptions, its feelings, its community, and ideology. But Mary is unable to distance herself adequately from her mother's perceptions. She is still tied to mother's attributions.

Fowler himself recognizes this. At one point he talks, not of Mary's fairness and gentleness in her perceptions of others, but about the "empty" quality of the characterizations she gives of her parents and about her self-absorption. Fowler, although he does not use this language himself, points to the primitive and narcissistic quality of Mary's relationships with others. Talking about the absence of mutuality in her perspective-taking in relation to others, he concludes:

> Apart from roles and relationships in an intense group or in a marriage relationship, Mary felt that she could have no self or self-worth. She had no third-person perspective from which she could coordinate and evaluate her interactions with others. There was no transcendent "cognitive ego" that could hold Mary's reflective sense of herself constant, while comparing it with the assessments or evaluations of others in such a way that the assessor and assessment could be evaluated as well as Mary.[42]

Although earlier Fowler had argued that Mary had achieved formal operational thinking (and thus, again, is at stage 3 in terms of "form of logic"), is this not a statement from him that she is unable to sustain detached, objective thinking in relation to other persons? In ego psychology language, she lacks an adequate observing ego, operates out of superego, and has weak ego strength together with a fragile and provisional sense of self. Fowler's theory seems to have difficulty distinguishing between activity that is ego-motivated and that which is superego dominated.

LACK OF ATTENTION TO EARLY CHILDHOOD

Fowler's failure to describe adequately Mary's embeddedness may in turn issue from a second deficiency in his theory: *the nonstatus of the first three years of life.* He gives us a six-stage theory, but stage 1, which he calls "intuitive-projective," he assigns to the four- to eight-year-old group![43] This is an extraordinary fact, because it relegates the critical first three years of life, those years of fundamental interest to psychoanalytically oriented theorists, to a nonstage.

Fowler doesn't even mention it in some of his writings (for example, in *Life Maps*). In *Stages of Faith,* he devotes three brief and unsatisfactory pages to "Infancy and Undifferentiated Faith."[44] Of this "prestage," he says:

> In the prestage called Undifferentiated Faith the seeds of trust, courage, hope and love are fused in an undifferentiated way and contend with sensed threats of abandonment, inconsistencies and deprivations in an infant's environment. Though really a prestage and largely inaccessible to empirical research of the kind we pursue, the quality of mutuality and the strength of trust, autonomy, hope and courage (or their opposites) developed in this phase underlie (or threaten to undermine) all that comes later in faith development.[45]

But surely, even if Fowler's own instrument—the interview—does not give him access to this stage, it should nevertheless not be relegated to the status of a "prestage." Psychoanalysis also discovered that its primary instrument—free association—was unable to give it access to the preoedipal period. It concluded, however, that its method had to be supplemented with other modes of inquiry. So, it seems to me, Fowler's theory must also be supplemented at this point if it is to be adequate.

STAGES AS ACHIEVEMENTS AND
THE PROBLEM OF SIN

The final point I have to make relates to Fowler's modification of the work of Erik Erikson. Fowler compares his theory with that of Erikson in the latter half of his Mary chapter. I would like to suggest that his theory, as much as it draws upon and derives from Erikson's work, has altered Erikson's approach at a critical point, and suffered thereby. Both, of course, are developmental theories, and both describe a series of stages a human being goes through. But Fowler gives us a theory in which each stage is an *achievement.* It is precisely this quality of his theory which makes it so vulnerable to the charge of many that the theory is hierarchically value-laden.

Fowler argues unconvincingly that the theory is not value-laden. He does this by pointing out that he does not claim that everyone should move ultimately to stage 5, say, or even to the next stage. But movement is not the issue. The issue is the kind of stages Fowler's are. Each stage in this theory is tied to a specific achievement which is described only in positive terms. Thus the idealization which we witnessed above is not an accident or a *faux pas.* It is intrinsic to the theory.

Erikson, in contrast, has a maturationist developmental theory in which a person must go through each stage and face a series of developmental tasks. At each stage, a person can handle it well or poorly. Each state identifies a task to be mastered (trust, shame, doubt, guilt, etc.) *and* the result of failing to master that task (distrust, shame, doubt, guilt, etc.) In Erikson's theory, one can come through stage 1 having failed to achieve a sense of basic trust, maintaining a position of basic distrust, while going on to the next stage of autonomy vs. doubt/shame. Such polarities are absent from Fowler's theory. McDargh suggests it may result from the influence on Fowler of the structural-developmental mode "with its characteristic avoidance of depth psychology's preoccupation with pathology."[46]

Fowler, in earlier versions of his theory, had developed a set of "prototypical challenges" with which faith would struggle at each stage. But recent statements of the theory have omitted these.[47] As McDargh so incisively notes, "This reluctance to describe faith in terms of a life trauma or inquiry that must be overcome or a challenge that must be mastered seems to be the influence of the more ameliorative bent of structural developmental thought. . . . *The language of developmental fixation, immaturity or repression is never evoked because of its presumed invidious connotations."*[48]

This is a blind spot, indeed, of this theory. When Fowler does turn to the difference between psychoanalytic and structural-developmental theories, the discussion tends to focus around the issue of the inability to *regress* stages in structural-developmental formulations. But even that comparison is the most innocuous one possible. One talks merely of going forward or backward; not of the possibilities of being warped, bent, misshapen.

Theologically, we might state this in terms of *the inadequate doctrine of evil and sin in Fowler's theory.* Fowler is very committed to a theory which deals with structural evil in the world. But his discussion of personal and intrapsychic destructiveness is so weak as to be nonexistent. Although Fowler *says,* in his discussion of the protostage of primal faith, that "the quality of mutuality and the strength of trust, autonomy, hope, and courage (or *their opposites*) developed in this phase underlie (or *threaten to undermine*) all that comes later in faith development,"[49] he fails with almost phobic avoidance to even name those opposites. Nor does he describe the "psychic processes by which this *undermining* might take place or call much attention to it in discussion of subsequent faith development."[50] Again, this is an interesting twist of this theory, since it fails to pursue the discussion of "inner manyness" that so occupied the interest of Fowler's mentor, H. Richard Niebuhr.[51]

It might be interesting to speculate at this point whether the mechanisms at work in this theory which we have noted above— of idealization and intellectualization and, I would add, of displacement and suppression, if not denial and repression—might not be seen as defenses against intrapsychic forces and dynamics of negativity. This would include, not only the libidinal and aggressive drives of classic psychoanalytic theory, but also the destructive character of the "higher" aspects of the individual, such as ego psychology has documented.[52] It is, however, enough to note simply the distortions discussed above—both in the theory itself and in its clinical application in the case of Mary—in order to propose that Fowler's theory would be strengthened in important respects by a more adequate understanding of evil, a more active dialogue with ego psychology, and the recognition of a need for a hermeneutic of *both* suspicion and restoration.

NOTES

1. Paul Pruyser, *The Minister As Diagnostician: Personal Problems in Pastoral Perspective* (Philadelphia: Westminster Press, 1976), p. 28.

2. Ibid., pp. 21-22.

3. Glenn H. Asquith, Jr., "The Case Study Method of Anton T. Boisen," *The Journal of Pastoral Care* 34 (June, 1980) 2, pp. 89ff. See this article also in reference to Table 1.

4. Paul Pruyser, "The Minister as Diagnostician," *Perkins School of Theology Journal* (Winter, 1973), p. 13.

5. Edgar Draper, George Meyer, Zene Parzen, and Gene Samuelson, "On the Diagnostic Value of Religious Ideation," *Archives of General Psychiatry* 13 (September, 1965), pp. 202-207.

6. Edgar Draper, *Psychiatry and Pastoral Care* (Philadelphia: Fortress, 1968), pp. 25-72.

7. Draper et al., "On the Diagnostic Value," p. 203.

8. Ibid., p. 116.

9. Apparently, however, his test design was not "clean."

10. Ibid., p. 206.

11. Draper, *Psychiatry and Pastoral Care,* p. 115.

12. Ibid., p. 116.

13. Anna Freud, *Normality and Pathology in Childhood* (New York: International Universities Press, 1965).

14. Blanck and Blanck trace not only psychosexual maturation, but also "drive-taming processes, object relations, adaptive function, anxiety level, defensive function, identity formation, and processes of internalization." Gertrude and Rubin Blanck, *Ego Psychology: Theory and Practice* (New York: Columbia University Press, 1974), pp. 114-115.

15. John E. Gedo and Arnold Holdberg, *Models of the Mind: A Psychoanalytic Theory* (Chicago: University of Chicago Press, 1973).

16. H. John McDargh, *Faith and the Imaging of God* (Cambridge, Mass.: Harvard University, 1980; doctoral dissertation), p. 60.

17. Fowler has offered other psychohistorical studies, such as his treatment of Malcolm X and the other cases, in James W. Fowler, Robin W. Lovin et al., *Trajectories of Faith* (Nashville: Abingdon, 1980), but Mary is the only firsthand interview he has published.

18. James W. Fowler, *Stages of Faith* (San Francisco: Harper & Row, 1981), p. 239.

19. Ibid., p. 217.

20. Ibid., p. 243.

21. Ibid., p. 252.

22. Jim Fowler and Sam Keen, *Life Maps: Conversations on the Journey of Faith* (Waco, Tex.: Word Books, 1978), p. 50.

23. Fowler, *Stages of Faith*, p. 247.

24. Fowler and Keen, *Life Maps*, p. 50.

25. Perhaps it would be more accurate to say that Mary gives it a point: she construes it as "the Lord . . . really working in my life to draw me to himself. . . ." But this "point" seems so inadequate as a description of her experience that perhaps our objection is that Mary is unable to see the main point. She misses the point. Fowler, talking about stage 1, says, "It does not matter how often you take a child at this stage to the refreshment stand or restroom at a movie. He or she will, in any case, remember from the film only episodes and not the narrative line of the story. These considerations mean that the child's sense of coherence vis-à-vis the environment is largely derived from the *external* patterns of sameness and continuity provided by others in the context of home and play" (*Life Maps*, p. 43). But Mary similarly gets the "wrong point." She fails to perceive her repeated pattern of passivity, dependency, and destructive choices.

26. Fowler, *Stages of Faith*, p. 252.

27. Ibid., p. 247.

28. Ibid., p. 151.

29. Ibid., p. 250.

30. Ibid., p. 243.

31. Ibid., p. 242.

32. Ibid., p. 243.

33. Ibid., pp. 247-48.

34. Ibid., p. 248.

35. Paul Ricoeur, *Freud and Philosophy: An Essay on Interpretation,* trans. Denis Savage (New Haven, Conn.: Yale University Press, 1970), p. 35. See chapter 2, "The Conflict of Interpretations."

36. Anna Freud, *The Ego and the Mechanisms of Defense* (London: Hogarth Press, 1937).

37. See Fowler's exchange with Sam Keen in *Life Maps,* esp. ch. 4.

38. Fowler, *Stages of Faith*, p. 218; italics mine.

39. It is difficult in this instance to make any independent assessment of Mary and her relationship with Fowler, since we have only a verbal transcript, and that has been edited. Fowler, however, did show a videotape of another interview at his workshop at our Center, and it was clear from that tape that the client had powerful reactions to the process of being interviewed. The major spontaneous anecdote in that interview, which was otherwise somewhat flat, was the client talking of a priest who didn't realize the impact he was having, and who, furthermore, *used* the client in a public setting. The symbolic reference to the video-taping and the meaning it held for her subjectively was unmistakable. Robert Langs, in his various writings, has been most eloquent about attending to such interaction and what he terms "the bipersonal field and the adaptive context." See Robert J. Langs, *The Bipersonal Field* (New York: Jason Aronson, 1976).

40. Fowler, *Stages of Faith*, p. 246; italics mine.

41. Ibid., p. 255.

42. Ibid., p. 257.
43. Fowler and Keen, *Life Maps,* p. 42.
44. Fowler, *Stages of Faith,* pp. 119-121.
45. Ibid., p. 121.
46. McDargh, *Faith and the Imaging of God,* p. 68.
47. See ibid.
48. Ibid.; italics mine.
49. Fowler, *Stages of Faith,* p. 121; italics mine.
50. McDargh, *Faith and the Imaging of God,* pp. 68-69.
51. See ibid., p. 68.
52. See, for example, a model of such analysis in Erikson's classic work, *Young Man Luther* (New York: Norton, 1958), with its discussion of the destructive aspects of morality and "goodness."

Chapter 11

Faith Development and Religious Education

CRAIG DYKSTRA

Among the people who have taken most notice of James Fowler's work on faith development are religious educators. His works have been widely read by us since the first articles began coming out, and continual reference is made to his faith development theory in books and articles in the field of religious education. This is not surprising. The fundamental concerns of religious educators overlap considerably with the concerns that faith development theory addresses. And Fowler himself has, at various points, addressed religious educators directly on those concerns.

Religious education is most fundamentally a practice. It is something that people do for and with one another. And, at its best, it is always a disciplined practice. This means at least two things. First, it is action with purpose and intention and not just inchoate, random activity. What is done is done toward some end. There is some point to all the activity. Second, it is a practice imbued with thought and reasons. It is "mindful" activity. As a mindful activity, religious education asks of itself a number of key questions.

One set of questions has to do with the *aims* of religious education. What are, in fact, the purposes of this enterprise? Why do we do it? What do we really hope will come from it all? What can we really expect to happen as a result of it? And how do we make judgments about whether what we hope for has come or is coming about? How do we evaluate this activity and its fruitfulness? A second set of questions concerns the *participants* involved in religious educational activity. What can we know about them as

251

persons? Especially, how do people learn and grow? What goes on within them when this happens? What are they able to do and when? Are there consistent and fundamental similarities among people at certain times in their lives that are important for educators to know? And are there consistent and fundamental patterns of changes that take place in most people as they "develop" that call for various educational approaches? If so, what are they and what are their implications? And then a third set of questions has to do with the *processes* involved in religious education. What kinds of experiences are important for people to have in order for them to learn and grow in ways that are consistent with our hopes? What can we do for each other, particularly through teaching, to help each other learn and grow in these ways? In what kinds of contexts can this best happen?

Because religious educators ask all of these kinds of questions, because they must ask them and answer them more or less fully in order to carry out this practice at all intelligently, Fowler's theory has attracted a good deal of attention. It has attracted that attention because it shows promise of providing some answers to these very questions. Our task in this essay is to explore Fowler's theory with these questions in mind, to see what answers his theory either explicitly or implicitly provides, and to subject those answers to some critical scrutiny in order to determine how helpful the theory may ultimately be to us and at what points.

FAITH DEVELOPMENT THEORY AND THE AIMS OF RELIGIOUS EDUCATION

Religious education normally takes place within and from the point of view of particular religious faiths and communities. Thus we have Christian religious education, Jewish religious education, Islamic religious education, and Hindu religious education, and so on. Within each such religious faith may usually be found some constellation of normative images of maturity in that faith's way of life. This constellation includes such dimensions as the desirable beliefs and convictions, patterns of perception and understanding, attitudes and affections, values and ethical norms, skills and competences, and commitments and behaviors that are integral to that way of life. These usually are not left separated from one another but are pulled together into some integrated style of life. This style of life normally has both personal and interpersonal, individual and communal, dimensions. It refers both to the kinds of people the faith community hopes individuals will ultimately become and to the kind of communal life the community hopes for itself. The theologies or ideologies of the religious faith have names and symbols which help to capture the essence of these images of maturity. In Christian faith, for example, "disciple" and "saint" are two traditional key terms. In Jewish faith, to take another, "the righteous one" *(tsedek)* would be central.

The aims of religious education in any particular faith usually draw heavily upon such constellations of images, whether the traditional terms are used or not. The fundamental aim of religious education is more often than not stated in terms of helping people to live ever more fully into the maturity imaged in the faith's tradition, theology, or philosophy. Because these constellations of images are complex, and because in different historical circumstances they may actually change to some degree, the aims may be stated in somewhat different ways. Thus, to take some recent work in Christian religious education as an example, one thinker might say that the aim of Christian religious education is "to lead people out to the Kingdom of God" and to "lived Christian faith,"[1] while another might articulate it in terms of "radical life in the world as followers of Jesus Christ."[2] Others will state it still differently. Nonetheless, all turn in one way or another to the normative vision of maturity found in the faith's tradition and/or community as a fundamental source for the articulation of the aims of religious education. The aims of education are almost always linked up with the overarching aims of the faith itself.

Implicit to this connection between the aims of religious education and the images of maturity in religious faith are two assumptions which are important for our discussion. First, religious maturity understood as an *aim* implies that it is something that must be moved toward. It is not given at birth or at any other time. The notion of maturity in faith implies a corresponding notion of growth or development toward it. Maturity looks backward to antecedents, to earlier forms of life which may anticipate maturity but do not yet achieve it. Second, religious maturity as an aim of *education* suggests that education has something important to do with this growth toward maturity. Religious maturity does not just come out of the blue or as a result of sheerly random experience. If it did, religious education would not be necessary. Thus, any religious faith community that involves itself in religious education assumes, at least implicitly, that maturity is something that one moves toward and grows into and that education is in some way an important and necessary element in that movement.

Now, what does this all have to do with Fowler's faith development theory and what help might this theory provide in helping religious educators with understanding what their aims should be and how they should operate?

Many have taken Fowler's theory to be a description of aims appropriate to religious education. This is not at all surprising, since Fowler's theory lays out a series of stages that move from images of relative immaturity to images of maturity. The theory provides normative images of maturity and looks backward to its antecedents, describing in some detail what the movements toward this maturity involve. Furthermore, the stages through which one moves are described by Fowler as stages of *faith*. This would seem to be precisely what religious educators are looking for: a description of the *telos* or purpose of religious education defined in terms of maturity of faith. What we might hope for as a result of religious education is that people will move through the stages and eventually become people who could be described in terms of the higher stages, and hopefully, ultimately by "stage 6." We could evaluate the fruitfulness of our educational efforts by whether they do help people become like this.

Reading Fowler this way is especially tempting for Christians, because Fowler's presentation of his theory is often loaded with images that come from this theological tradition. He describes his sixth stage, for example, in terms of the image of "the Kingdom of God," and uses a sizable number of religious metaphors that come from the Jewish and Christian traditions throughout his writing. He has also repeatedly stressed the normative dimension of his theory, claiming that it goes beyond mere description of changes that take place in people's faith to a statement of the direction toward which faith ought to move. Thus it would not be difficult to come to the conclusion that Fowler is describing a set of aims that could simply be appropriated by religious educators.

But Fowler himself does not quite make this move. He does not really argue that the stages provide aims for religious education. And it would be a mistake for us to think that they do. Fowler's proposal is more subtle. He argues that faith development theory can provide a helpful and illuminating *perspective* on faith and thus be a useful *partner* with religious educators in identifying aims. But he does not say that the theory *provides* those aims.

When Fowler writes about religious education (specifically, Christian religious education), he states the aims without recourse to his faith development theory. In an essay entitled "Future Christians and Church Education," Fowler defined church education as "education for creative discipleship in the context of the coming kingdom of God."[3] He argued that this definition could not be translated without serious loss into other common definitions including "intentional religious socialization" and "education for faith development" because these do not "contain the normativity and radicality" intended by the "creative discipleship" definition.[4] Fowler understands creative discipleship here in terms of response to and faithfulness in the light of the kingdom of God, the dimensions of which are seen not in faith development theory itself, but in the history of Israel and most particularly in the mission and ministry of Jesus—his actions and stories, his teachings and miracles, his calling and sending.[5] Jesus, Fowler says, "beckoned people forward into the in-breaking grace of God's powerful future."[6] In the light of the nearness and presence of the kingdom seen in him, people are called to a radical change of their ways, values, and lifestyles—radical enough to be called repentance and metanoia. These aims all come directly from the constellation of images of the Christian faith tradition itself. Faith development theory is not necessary for the statement of them. These aims can be discovered and articulated without reference to that theory at all.

Nor, for Fowler, does faith development theory provide the articulation of a "spiritual path" toward maturity. In explaining how this is so, Fowler says:

Usually spiritual paths prescribe particular disciplines and contemplative exercises that have evolved in a given tradition. They are transmitted and taught because they have proven efficacious in fostering the progress of practitioners toward an ideal state of culminating enlightenment. Typically there is a more or less developed ideological or theological perspective informing and justifying the approach and its desired end-state. In most instances phases or steps in spiritual progress have been identified. . . . Stages or phases in spiritual paths are, then, blazes or stopping places on particular trails leading toward the goal of ideal spirituality as epitomized by a specific tradition or by a particular pioneer of a subtradition within it.[7]

Faith stages, according to Fowler, are something different from this. "It would be awkward or peculiar," he says, "for a person to claim stage 5 or stage 6 as the goal of his or her spiritual aspiration"; it would make perfect sense, though, "for a Zennist to characterize the goal of his or her spiritual quest as *satori,* or for a Christian to speak with St. Teresa of 'mystical marriage' with God the King as the goal of prayer."[8]

If faith development theory is not, even for Fowler, the source for the aims of religious education, what help can it provide religious educators with the question of aims? The best clue comes in one of Fowler's early essays, "Faith Development Theory and the Aims of Religious Socialization." In that essay, Fowler argued that norms by which a religious community may set its educational goals and standards are available from within. But he feared that no standpoint is provided there by which to *critique* those norms. This, Fowler thought, was something that faith development theory could provide. It could make available "exogenous standards against which users of the theory may evaluate their own tradition's internal goals and norms"[9] and provide "a valid, normative trans-religious perspective on religious socialization," while "avoiding blatant or subtle religious imperialism."[10]

The constructive role for faith development theory in relation to aims for religious education, then, is to be a conversation partner with a religious community in its own critical inquiry into the norms embedded in its tradition. In this conversation, faith development theory has a particular role to play. It does not raise the question of *what* beliefs, attitudes, values, and ways of living are to be normative for a community, much less what (or who) the object of one's believing, knowing, trusting, and love is to be. Rather, it is to help us to discern the various *ways* in which such "contents" of faith are "structured" and "processed" by various people in a faith community. As Fowler puts it, "The focus of our stages is on the 'how' of faith as a dynamic but structured process, as opposed to the 'what' of faith, i.e., that which is believed, known, trusted, or loved in faith."[11]

Faith development theory provides two angles of critical vision on the dynamic process of faith which, he believes, will be useful to us. First, it can help us to articulate what human competences are required for the realization of our traditional norms at various levels (insofar, of course, as these aims have to do with "faith" as here understood). Second, it can provide a perspective by which to evaluate those norms qualitatively.

The first angle of vision is made possible since Fowler says that, like Kohlberg, he is describing "a set of necessary *underlying competences*";[12] "an integrated set of operations . . . a patterned process or *structure* underlying and giving form to the *contents* of believing, valuing, knowing and committing."[13] These competences are described in terms of the familiar six categories, or aspects.[14] As each of these competences develop through their sequence and in relation to one another, they form integrated sets of competences, or stages. Each stage is an integrated set of structured competences which make possible certain ways of believing, valuing, loving, and living in faith.

The second angle of vision is made possible because the descriptions of the competences issue is certain "qualities." This is what makes it possible for Fowler to suggest that "through its work in and with the contents of a particular religious tradition, [religious education] should help develop persons whose faith manifests the qualities described by stage 5 or stage 6."[15] Such qualities include: "recognizing the integrity and truth in positions other than [one's] own," readiness "for community of identification beyond tribal, racial, class, or ideological boundaries," espoused "values and beliefs" which are "congruent with risk, and action taken," and the ability to "relate to [people] affirmingly, never condescendingly, yet with pricks to our pretense and with genuine bread of life."[16]

These "qualities" do provide a kind of norm and may be taken up into the aims of religious education. But before they are, Fowler says, they need to undergo a "theological validation" which "will involve testing whether the characteristics of the culminating stages of the theory capture and describe structures necessary for fulfilling the highest normative intentionality of the great, particular religious traditions."[17] Still, he hopes that this testing will be reciprocal so that the structural theory might "contribute to the ongoing, renewal, reform, and extension of the highest normative intentionality of those traditions, and to the guidance of their efforts in religious socialization."[18] The theory offers, in other words, a perspective by means of which a religious community can ask itself questions.

Thus Fowler argues that while his theory cannot, and should not, provide specific norms of belief, value, affection, and life-style for a religious community, it can provide important perspectives on the operations of the dynamics of faith which specific traditions should take seriously in understanding and critiquing its own norms and in articulating its aims for religious education.

The appropriate use of faith development theory in relation to the articulation of aims for religious education would, then, be something like this. Religious educators would turn first to their own religious tradition as the primary source for its understanding of maturity in that religious life and construct the aims of religious education primarily on those grounds. Then they would ask, with the help of faith development theory, what competences are necessary for people to grow into the kind of maturity articulated in those aims. In doing so religious educators may find that some (or many, or perhaps all) of the competences described in faith development theory are important for growth in faith as their tradition understands it. The use of faith development theory here will help them to be clearer about what these competences involve and how they arise, and their development may in themselves well become subordinate aims of religious education in the community. Finally, they would look critically at the aims they have articulated, using the qualitative norms of faith development theory to help them inquire as to whether their aims are adequate, or whether, under the stimulus of faith development theory, their aims might be renewed, reformed, and extended. The testing here, though, is thoroughly dialogical, and faith development theory does not provide the final criteria. But it may be a very helpful partner.

When faith development theory is used in this way, how helpful a conversation partner is it for thinking through the aims of religious education? Different educators will have their own views on this, but I think it has been and can be a very helpful resource. For one thing, this work has already functioned to help us see again, and perhaps more clearly now, that faith involves human action. As Fowler puts it, it can be thought of as a verb. Faith, rather than primarily a thing that one has (a set of beliefs, say), is a way of living and being in the world. Furthermore, faith is a way of "having a world." We do not all live in the same "world" in the sense that we all see, understand, and experience it in the same way. And faith has to do with what "world" we live in just as much as it does with how we live there. Faith development theory has helped us to see this more clearly, too, while at the same time drawing our attention to the fact that the development of certain competences may be necessary conditions for and elements in being active in faith and in having a world in certain ways. Likewise, faith development theory has been careful to point out that people's "faiths" differ in ways that are much more complex than those described in terms of differences between denominations or religious traditions, and that there are commonalities among people across such differences that are important for faith. It has also, and in a fresh way, made evident how compelling a concern and dynamic faith is in human beings just as human beings, even for those whose beliefs and practices do not fit the standard definitions.

When faith development theory is a conversation partner with us in thinking through the aims of religious education, we find ourselves compelled to find ways to deal with these issues and insights. And even if we would state things in different terms, we realize that what we say will have to make sense of the things which faith development theory makes sense of. The use of faith development theory in thinking through aims is problematic only when the theory is no longer seen to be a *partner* in conversation and becomes *the* basis for the articulation of aims. Because the theory provides so many fruitful insights that are relevant to the educator's problems and questions, it may be easy to stop really asking questions and simply to substitute the theory's conclusions for answers that we must come to in our own context and in relation to multiple conversation partners.

WHAT FAITH DEVELOPMENT THEORY HELPS US TO KNOW ABOUT PEOPLE

Religious education is an activity among people, and religious educators need to know many things about the participants in the enterprise in order to be able to understand them and respond to them appropriately. We especially need to know how people learn and grow and what goes on within them when this happens. We also need to know what they are able to do, and when, and what consistent similarities and differences there may be among people that can be accounted for developmentally and that are relevant to our work.

In the twentieth century we have gotten many of our answers to questions about what people are like from psychology, particularly developmental psychology. The use of faith development theory to help answer such questions seems perfectly natural, then, and perhaps particularly so since its focus is on people's faith. We need to recognize, however, that developmental theories are not written with religious educators particularly in mind or in response to our particular questions. Therefore we cannot expect them to provide all the answers.

Developmental theories do not focus on learning, so we cannot expect them to be learning theories. Nor do they focus heavily on the social and cultural forces which shape us, so we cannot expect them to answer many of our questions about how various circumstances and situations affect people's learning and growth. Furthermore, no theories of any kind can give us the knowledge we need of any particular person, the kind of knowledge that makes it possible for us to be appropriately responsive to the particular people we teach and learn with. This can only happen through face-to-face interaction. We can only really know particular persons as we attend to them personally and as they reveal themselves to us.

Because of all this, we cannot expect that faith development theory is going to tell us all we need to know about people. But developmental theories, and this one in particular, can tell us some very important things that we need to know. And they can provide what Dwayne Huebner once called "scaffoldings of understanding"[19] by means of which we ourselves can be prepared to see more deeply into what is going on with people. There are far too many important insights about people in Fowler's work to be able to summarize them here, but we can pick out a few areas of insight that are particularly important.

The first is Fowler's general conception of the human being as one who is inevitably and essentially involved in the task of making sense of things.[20] Fowler argues that meaning is essential to being human and that the quest for meaning is fundamental to all of our other activities. He also argues that we are active agents in the search for and creation of meaning, that this happens in and through our relationships in the world, particularly relationships with other human beings and the meanings that are important to them, and that the most significant such relationships are relationships of trust and loyalty. This general view of what human beings are like and what they are up to, what makes them tick, is foundational to any appropriate understanding of who the participants are in religious education. It helps us to see others at levels that run deeper than we ordinarily go, but at levels that are crucial for making the educational enterprise at all alive. And whether one agrees with Fowler or not that this is the heart of what faith itself is, it is certainly a basic dimension of human life.[21]

A second important contribution to our understanding of people is Fowler's articulation of the various "aspects" of the structures he describes with his stages. Some of these aspects have been previously (and more fully) described by others (Piaget, Selman, Kohlberg, and in some respects Erikson), but Fowler puts them in relation to each other and to other aspects that he himself has identified.[22] Simply being aware of these aspects and their meaning provides a set of categories we can use with which to discipline ourselves in paying attention to others. Usually we attend to one another in rather general ways. This is good and important, but it often has the effect of restricting the range of our vision. We often do not attend to enough dimensions of people. Fowler's aspects provide a kind of "hermeneutic device" which opens up dimensions to which we might not otherwise attend and respect. Fowler's aspects are not, of course, exhaustive, so we should not limit ourselves to these, but they are significant and we should not ignore them.

Third, there are the stage descriptions themselves. These descriptions are useful as reminders that people in particular areas of their lives are in some important and regular ways similar to others who are "at the same stage" in the manner in which they think, feel, comprehend, evaluate, and act. In order to make use of Fowler's insights into these commonalities, however, it is not nearly enough simply to know the names or general features of each stage description. This, in fact, can be quite dangerous, for then we are tempted simply to caricature and label others. The important thing is to see the reality—in actual human beings—of the phenomena that the stage descriptions are an attempt to describe. In order to do this we must attend to particular people in the light of the descriptions (and, then, to the descriptions in the light of the people) to see if the language Fowler uses actually helps us to see others more clearly and profoundly. When it does, the descriptions are immensely useful. When it does not, they should be ignored or improved. In other words, we should not just listen to what the theory says, but engage in the same empirical-analytical process that Fowler does in developing and refining these descriptions.

Similarly, the stage descriptions, when taken in sequence, point out some of the important patterns of change that more or less naturally take place in people as they develop. These are not, of course, all of the important changes that take place, because not all changes are developmental. Some important changes in people's lives are due to circumstances, events, and social forces that impinge only on particular individuals or groups and, therefore, cannot be said to be developmental (at least in the universal, structural sense). Nevertheless, Fowler has pointed to ways in which all people seem to move, if they move at all, toward increasingly more complex, differentiated, and integrative patterns of "making sense" in their lives.[23] Again, the usefulness of these insights for religious education does not come from just a general comprehension of the fact that people develop. It comes from a rather detailed knowledge of what each more complex, differentiated, and integrative pattern makes possible that the previous one(s) did not. For since these stages each describe new patterns of competency, they are of little use until we can see in some fullness what each new pattern makes a person competent to be and do. When Fowler himself discusses the usefulness of his developmental stages for religious education, he usually does so in terms of "readiness"—of how each new pattern of competence makes people increasingly more ready and *able* to do and be and respond in new ways.[24] Religious educators will benefit most from a knowledge of these stages when they are able to study each in terms of what people at those stages are ready for in relation to the kinds of experiences that they as educators can make possible for them. The task is not so much to get people to move through the stages as to understand what, educationally speaking, would be helpful to those people as they are already (more or less naturally) moving in and through them.

A fourth important area of insight is Fowler's articulation of the whole complex web of relationships between "structure" and "content," "stage transition" and "conversion," and "imagination" and "revelation."[25] Through his discussion of this complex of ideas, some of the suggestiveness of his work concerning the kinds of change that may take place in people that are important for religious education become apparent. Fowler is concerned, not just with faith *development,* but more broadly with *transformations* in faith. "Development" is one kind of transformation but not the only one. "Conversion" is another.

For Fowler, development is the kind of transformation that takes place when there are transitions from one stage to the next. He says that "a structural stage change represents a qualitative transformation in the ways faith appropriates the contents of religious or ideological traditions."[26] "Conversion" is, for him, something quite different from this. It is not so much a shift in the way one appropriates, but a shift in the fundamental contents themselves. "Conversion is a significant recentering of one's previous conscious or unconscious images of value and power and the conscious adoption of a new set of master stories in the commitment to reshape one's life in a new community of interpretation and action."[27] The one kind of change may happen without the other, or they may precipitate one another, or they may correlate with one another.[28]

That there are two kinds of change or transformation is important for religious educators to see and discriminate between, because both are important for our understanding of what is going on in people as they change. But it is also important to see what the processes of change are in each of these cases, for these provide the clues Fowler offers toward an understanding of educational processes.

Developmental change takes place when a person's present structures are experienced by them (at least tacitly) as no longer complex and flexible enough to deal with perplexing dimensions of one's environment. Development happens as a result of a combination of (1) an increasing frustration in one's ability to make sense in the *way* one has been making sense, (2) a structural readiness or competence to begin to try to make sense in new ways, and (3) a (largely preconscious) willingness both to give up the older way and to struggle toward a new one—all in relation to (4) some "content" that one is really invested in making better sense of.[29] A new stage appears as a new, more adequate fundamental way of making sense becomes consolidated over time and replaces the former.

Note the features involved in this kind of change: some sense of frustration or conflict plus some struggle toward a new way in relation to some significant "content." A similar pattern arises when Fowler deals with conversion, but here the themes of imagination and revelation come into prominent play.[30] Conversion is most fundamentally a transformation of the imagination that takes place when "revelatory events and experience" work on the image structure of a person in three movements.

First, such events and experience act as a "solvent." "The struggle for a decisively new image, which can honor and conserve the impact of revelatory experience, involves first the dissolution or the disintegration of previous images. Put another way, the first imaginative response to a revelatory event is a *making strange and distant* of that which had been familiar, powerful, taken for granted."[31] Note here how the starting point of change is, as before, a strangeness, a lack of being at ease with the way things are understood, but also an engagement which brings with it a concomitant struggle toward some new pattern. Here, however, there also seems to be something of an "event" quality to experience that is not so evident in developmental change. Something happens that seems to provoke a struggle, that "makes" strange the old pattern.

Following the first, "a second movement in the imaginative response to revelatory events is the composition of new images by which to understand God, the neighbor, and the self. Jesus' ministry and parabolic communication were full of narratives and dramatic actions which evoke new images."[32] Here, again as before, something new arises. But this time it is not so much new ways of making sense but new images by which to make sense. On how these arise and from where, Fowler is not very clear. In one sentence, he says that we compose them, suggesting that we somehow actively create them. In the next, however, he says they are evoked, suggesting that they somehow come *to* us from beyond our (at least conscious) selves and at the stimulus of another. Perhaps it is not a matter of one *or* the other, but an interplay between the two.

The third movement involves a synthesizing process "in which bodies and souls, activated by new images, begin to march in accordance with a new comprehensive master-image of life and reality."[33] The result, then, is a transformation of the imagination in which one comes to live one's life and make sense of reality in the light of a whole new set of orienting images.

"Development" and "conversion," then, are two different kinds of transformation, participating however in somewhat similar kinds of dynamics. Fowler suggests that the capacities and competences of different stages make possible somewhat different forms of conversion. "Life-span research into what we have come to call 'faith development,' " he says, "has begun to shed light on the quality and shape of the imagination's capacity to respond to revelatory events at different developmental stages."[34] It clarifies "what human beings bring, by way of readiness to respond, to the encounter with the record of revelatory events and to tradition."[35]

FAITH DEVELOPMENT THEORY AND EDUCATIONAL PROCESS

The question of educational process is one which, at its most general level, asks what fundamental patterns of interaction among people can and ought to be structured, deliberately and systematically, in order to foster the kinds of changes in people that our aims call for and that our understanding of human beings shows us are possible. More simply, what kinds of experiences are important for people to have in order for them to learn and grow in ways that are consistent with our aims? And what can we do, for and with one another, to make these kinds of experiences possible? What this boils down to at the more concrete and practical level is the concern for educational methods and curriculum.

Fowler's faith development theory does not treat these questions directly. It should not be expected to. It is neither a learning theory nor a theory of education, but a theory of development. Nevertheless, Fowler has addressed some educational questions briefly himself, and there are other implications from his developmental theory that can be surfaced.

It must first be said that there are many kinds of change that are of interest to educators that are neither developmental changes or conversions. Learning new ideas, perspectives, skills, patterns of behavior, being introduced to and appreciating in new ways new features and dimensions of reality—none of these necessarily involve either developmental change or conversion, though they surely involve learning and even growth. Nonetheless, the kinds of changes that Fowler does discuss, and the dynamics through which they take place, suggest some of the conditions for learning and growth of any kind that may be important.

Some of Fowler's insights into these conditions include the constructive power of frustration, dissatisfaction, or conflict; the importance of the relevance or engaging power of the "contents" of the educational process to the learners' own lives and imaginations; and the need to make room for and encourage the learners' own struggles with the images and experiences that they engage. In other words, the kinds of experiences that promote learning are experiences in which the learners themselves are engaged in inquiry and struggle in relation to "contents" that pose questions for them in their own lives and that allow them to make discoveries of their own through this process. It is this conviction about the kinds of educational experiences that are most fruitful that leads Fowler to say that faith development theory can help religious educators "avoid trying to provide comprehensive answers for questions [people are] not yet asking," "avoid playing broken records when [they] are ready to compose new songs," and "overcome the tendency to think of faith as separate from everyday life."[36]

From another perspective, the kinds of experiences that would be crucial for religious education, from the point of view of Fowler's theory, would be those that draw the learners' attention to particular dimensions of the faith tradition and community in which the education is taking place. These are: (1) the centers of value that the faith community finds worthy of worship, allegiance, and trust, (2) the images of power by which a community aligns itself in relation to the world, and (3) the master-stories that characterize "the patterns of power-in-action that disclose the ultimate meanings of our lives."[37] Experiences that made learners aware of these would be essential and focusing elements in the religious education curriculum, and any curriculum that did not pay considerable attention to these would be inadequate.

Fowler sometimes talks about religious education in terms of "sponsorship." Because growth in faith happens through personal relationship, for Fowler, religious education would have to make possible experiences of personal relationship in which "sponsors" provide

> affirmation, encouragement, guidance, and models for growth and development. The sponsor is one who walks with you; one who knows the path and can provide guidance. The sponsor is one who engenders trust and proves trustworthy in supporting you in difficult passages and turns. The sponsor may, as needed, confront you, insisting that difficult issues be faced and that self-deceptions or sloth be avoided. The sponsor or sponsoring community should be able to provide both models and experiences in education and spiritual direction that deepen and expand one's initial commitments and provide the nurture for strong and continuing growth.[38]

"Sponsorship" may be something broader than religious education in the strictest sense, but this kind and quality of relationship would need to infuse the educational process as well as other dimensions of ministry.

One further aspect of the relational nature of the kinds of

experiences Fowler's theory points to has to do with the communal context of religious education. Fowler has suggested that particular communities have "modal developmental levels." That is, a given community may have an "average expectable level of development for adults" which acts both as a kind of magnet which pulls people up to it, but also a kind of limit which tends to keep people from moving beyond it.[39] Presumably, ordinary socialization patterns in a community involve qualities and competences that have stage-like characteristics. If the patterned-processes of interaction in a community tend to have, say, stage 3 characteristics embedded in them, it will be difficult for many people to develop qualities and competences that are more complex. If this is true, it presents an issue and perhaps also a problem to religious educators. The issue is that we are involved, not only in the education of individuals, but also of communities. The problem is that if the competences required for the kind of religious growth and learning that we are after require competence above those presently available in the community, how can they be made available? One important answer, it seems to me, is the necessity of drawing on resources which range wider than one's own community. Fowler states the problem differently when he asks the question this way: "How can faith communities avoid the coerciveness of the modal developmental level, and how can they sponsor appropriate and ongoing lifelong development in faith?"[40] Fowler's answer is a focus on the nurturing of adult development. This focus would involve, one could infer, an emphasis on adult religious education, especially of a kind that would use experiential, relational methods. The nurturing of adult development would then foster, according to Fowler, a "climate of developmental expectation."[41]

There are, then, in Fowler's work some indications of the kind of religious educational process that would be important to employ. There is a clear indication that experiential, relational methods, rather than simply transmissive ones, would be given priority. Religious education would need to focus on and work imaginatively with the "contents" of faith that have the power to tap the imaginations of the learners and speak to their own lives and struggles. Educators will have to develop and provide structures that enable fairly intimate relationships of "sponsorship" to emerge, and, in order to provide adequate sponsors, may need to put significant energies into adult education. The question of *how* these processes can be put into effect, of what teaching methods to use and how to design curriculum, is something that faith development theory does not itself suggest answers to at all. This is a task for educators to accomplish themselves.

CONCLUSION

Faith development theory, as I have been trying to suggest throughout, is not a theory of religious education and should not be expected to be. In my view it does not give us direct answers to most of the questions that we, in our enterprise, must ask and answer. But it has been and can continue to be an important conversation partner for us. It can provide some leads and some clues which we may well want to follow up as we think through our aims, our understandings of who the participants are, and the educational processes in which we engage in religious education. Faith developmental theory can be most helpful to us, however, when we keep up our end of the conversation. We cannot just assume that the questions it tries to answer are *ipso facto* the right questions for us. We must ask our own questions first. If we do this, we are free to ask what it has to offer us. And we are also free to ask whether what it provides is what we need. In this essay I have attempted to articulate what some of our questions are and to find in faith development theory what is there that can be useful and stimulating to us.

NOTES

1. Thomas Groome, *Christian Religious Education* (San Francisco: Harper & Row, 1981), pp. 34, 35.

2. John H. Westerhoff III, *Will Our Children Have Faith?* (New York: Seabury, 1976), p. 50.

3. James W. Fowler, "Future Christians and Church Education," in *Hope for the Church,* ed. Theodore Runyan (Nashville: Abingdon, 1979), p. 105.

4. See ibid., pp. 105-106.

5. See ibid., p. 95.

6. Ibid., p. 96.

7. James W. Fowler, "Stages in Faith: The Structural-Developmental Approach" in *Values and Moral Development,* ed. Thomas Hennessy (New York: Paulist Press, 1976), pp. 203-204.

8. Ibid., p. 205.

9. James W. Fowler, "Faith Development Theory and the Aims of Religious Socialization," *Emerging Issues in Religious Education,* ed. G. Durka and J. Smith (New York: Paulist Press, 1976), p. 190.

10. Ibid., p. 189. A basic theme of this article is the inability of "intentional religious socialization theory" (of which John Westerhoff is the principle exponent cited) to provide the standpoint for this kind of critique, and to show how faith development theory can fill this vacuum.

11. Ibid., p. 192.

12. Ibid., p. 191.

13. Ibid., p. 192.

14. See ibid., pp. 197-99. The "categories" included in this essay were: form of logic, form of world coherence, role-taking, bounds of social awareness, form of moral judgment, and symbolic competence. In Fowler's later book on faith development theory, these "categories" came to be called "aspects," "role-taking" was changed to "perspective-taking," and "locus of authority" was added. See *Stages of Faith* (San Francisco: Harper & Row, 1981), p. 244.

15. Ibid., p. 202.

16. See ibid., pp. 196-97. The question of where these "qualitative" norms come from is a difficult one. It is not clear to me whether these derive primarily from the philosophical and psychological sources upon which Fowler builds his developmental theory, or from his own religious values drawn primarily from Christian faith. These sources are notoriously difficult to sort out, and it may be impossible to do so in our culture at the present time. But in the way I have laid out the relationship between faith development theory and the aims of religious education, this issue is not terribly important. Faith development theory does not provide norms for religious education so much as it offers some for consideration. Whatever the ultimate source, such help can be received with gratitude.

17. Ibid., p. 204.

18. Ibid. Fowler reiterates and extends this point a bit in *Stages of Faith* where he says that "the formal structural characteristics of faith stages can be employed to test the normative structuring tendencies of a given faith tradition. They can also be employed to evaluate a given faith community's *particular* appropriation of the content-structural vision of its tradition" (p. 302). Thus, "the structural-developmental perspective, with its formal descriptions of stage-like positions and styles of being in faith, has a contribution to make in clarifying what might be meant by *good faith*" (p. 203).

19. In a conversation at the "Faith Development Conference," Auburn Theological Seminary, March 5-7, 1982.

20. See *Stages of Faith,* p. 4, where Fowler says that what makes us different from other creatures is that "they do not struggle under the self-consciousness of shaping their lives through commitments they make or of searching for images of meaning by which to give sense to things." Fowler sometimes calls this the task of "meaning-making." I have difficulties with this way of phrasing it because it seems to connote that human beings are the source of all meaning rather than also (and, I would say, more fundamentally) appropriators of meaning. But the basic point that human beings require meaning in order to live, and actively search for it and even participate in its creation, is, I think, crucial and right.

21. For a further discussion of my agreements and disagreements with Fowler on this point, see my earlier essay in this volume, ch. 2.

22. See above, note 14, for a list of these aspects and a source reference.

23. See *Stages of Faith,* pp. 89-90, where Fowler sums up the *kinds* of changes he is dealing with and states why they need to be described in formal terms.

24. See, for example, "Stages in Faith: The Structural-Developmental Approach," p. 204, where Fowler explains that his faith stages are attempts to "take a life-span approach to understanding the person's readiness and capacities for nurture by particular ideological or spiritual traditions or approaches." See also, "Future Christians," p. 110, and *Stages of Faith,* p. 294, for similar comments. It is unfortunate, from my point of view, however, that when Fowler actually provides his stage descriptions he does not provide detailed, formal analyses of what these structural competences and capacities consist of. His formal statements are rather brief, while his descriptions tend to be impressionistic and anecdotal in character. This makes it difficult to use them for much more than general typological purposes.

25. The main elements of this discussion are found in *Stages of Faith,* ch. 23, but are not limited to that source. What follows is my own way of drawing out some of the significance of his work on these motifs for religious education.

26. *Stages of Faith,* pp. 275-76.

27. Ibid., pp. 282-83.

28. See ibid., pp. 285-86.

29. This latter, especially, is why Fowler says that "a given faith stage . . . is a structural *consequence* of [people's] exposure to the systems of belief and practice available in their environment as these intersect with the events and circumstances of their lives" ("Stages in Faith: The Structural-Developmental Approach," p. 205). It is unfortunate that Fowler nowhere, so far as I have been able to determine, discusses the stage transition *process* itself in any detail. The steps articulated here are my summary gleaned from allusions Fowler makes to this matter in various places and on the basis of my understanding of the main features of this process as articulated by developmental psychologists to whom Fowler is indebted.

30. A discussion of this process is not found in *Stages of Faith,* but rather in "Future Christians," pp. 103-104.

31. "Future Christians," p. 103.

32. Ibid., p. 104.

33. Ibid.

34. Ibid., p. 111.

35. Ibid., p. 110.

36. James W. Fowler, "Faith and the Structuring of Meaning," in *Toward Moral and Religious Maturity,* ed. J. Fowler and A. Vergote (Morristown, N.J.: Silver Burdett, 1980), p. 83.

37. See *Stages of Faith,* pp. 276-77.

38. Ibid., p. 287.

39. Ibid., p. 294.

40. Ibid., p. 295. The difference between our two ways of stating the question arise because for Fowler faith development is development in faith, whereas for me "faith development" is the development of competences and capacities that may (or may not) be necessary for growth in faith. On this disagreement, see my earlier essay in this volume.

41. Ibid., p. 296.

PART V

A Response by James Fowler

Chapter 12

Dialogue Toward a Future in
Faith Development Studies

JAMES W. FOWLER

The scholar-researcher who has focused a new area of theoretical discussion in a field is fortunate if that work attracts gifted critics and interpreters. In reading the essays that make up this volume, I feel fortunate indeed. Though it is tempting to engage each of the chapters on its own, I have decided instead to identify what seem to be the most important themes of critical engagement that link the chapters. I will make specific comments or responses to the different authors under the headings of the particular themes they pursue. In the closing section I will present some of the constructive lines of inquiry and activity that extend into the future of faith development studies.

STRENGTHS AND LIMITS OF
THE RESEARCH APPROACH

Faith development research had its methodological origins in my work as associate director of Interpreters' House in 1968-69. There, in co-leading seven three-week seminars with clergy, and some nine or ten intensive retreats with lay persons and clergy, I experienced the power of persons' telling their own faith stories in depth. I learned that, as Schleiermacher has taught us, conversation is a hermeneutical art. In focused, confidential, and sensitively probing listening we can enable others (and be enabled ourselves) to bring to word a great deal that is illuminative and which might otherwise remain unexamined. With receptive, active listening it became clear to me that people will tell their stories in sufficient depth and richness that both they and their listeners can begin to see patterns and connections which neither had seen before.

Upon returning to Harvard Divinity School to teach and lead continuing education in 1969, I began to teach a course I called "Theology as the Symbolization of Experience." From 1969 through 1971, before the more recent spread of interest in auto-biographical and narrative theology, that course provided students with an academic context in which intensive group experience modeled on Interpreters' House could be combined with lectures and readings on theological and developmental perspectives. In what David Tracy has since taught us to call a "mutually critical correlation," I attempted to involve my students in dialectical reflection upon their own experiences in relation to the developmental theories of Erikson, Freud, Jung, and eventually, Piaget and Kohlberg. Theological groundings from Tillich, H. R. Niebuhr, and later, Wilfred Cantwell Smith, rounded out the course. Under the impact of a 1972 postdoctoral year of study with Kohlberg in the Laboratory for Human Development of Harvard Graduate School of Education, this course turned in a more research-oriented direction. It seemed natural to take the experiences of small group storytelling as the basis for our research approach. It is important to stress, however, that from the first we have worked with a carefully structured interview protocol, and—in the structural developmental tradition of Piaget and Kohlberg—have trained interviewers to probe persistently for both comprehensiveness of content and adequate access to the underlying structures of faith.

Nelson and Aleshire are right when they point out the tensional unity of two (or three) divergent intents in the faith development interview protocol. From our interest in autobiography and life-story the interview has a narrative framework (Part I). This is followed by a more deeply probed narrative exploration of key relationships and experiences (Part II). From our interest both in the *content* of their ideation, beliefs, and their stories of meaning, on the one hand, and their *structuring* of experiences and interpretation, on the other, we pursue the life-issue oriented section of the interview (Part III). The goal of the interview to this point is to provide a kind of blank screen onto which the respondents can project their distinctive faith and autobiographical themes and patterns. To avoid some of the kinds of biases which concerned Nelson and Aleshire, we did not explicitly frame the introduction to the interview in terms either of *religion* or of *faith*. Rather, we spoke about values, beliefs, attitudes, and experiences that all persons have, and expressed our interest in *their* approaches, opinions, and feelings with regard to those matters. It was our belief (supported by our experience with the interview) that persons whose faith normally finds expression in religious terms would introduce religious language and material in their responses. Part IV focuses directly on religion as its central theme. We intended with this concluding section to provide a more direct opportunity to relate religious perspectives for those who, for whatever reason, might have avoided introducing religious matters earlier in the interview. We were also interested in the attitudes toward religion of those whose faith found expression in dominantly nonreligious modes.

On the whole, Nelson and Aleshire seem to have grasped the structure of the interview and the logic of its construction rather well. Broughton missed the mark, however, when he described the interview as "Rogerian" and "unprobed." The protocol has a definite structure and interviewers were trained to probe the statements and stories for both clarity and the limits of their respondents' statements. Also contrary to Broughton's understanding, interviewers were trained to probe for connections (or the lack of them) between espoused beliefs and attitudes and actual behavior and actions.

The issue of a possible lack of "full disclosure" brought up by Nelson and Aleshire requires clarifying comment. I have already mentioned that we did *not* describe the interview as a "faith development" interview. In that sense we did not "fully disclose" to the interviewees that we were studying "faith." As mentioned earlier, our reason for this was to avoid skewing the interview with the assumptions that it necessarily had to do with religion. (In this society, "faith" is popularly taken to be synonymous with "belief" or "religion.") We did describe faith *functionally* in our introduction but did not use the term. If this is nondisclosure it is surely a very mild form. The other reference in relation to this question about nondisclosure seems more problematic. We *did* say in our introductions to the interviews that we were interested in how persons of different ages across the life cycle look at and make sense of their lives' experiences. We did *not* say that, on the basis of the analysis of their language and imagery, we would identify the formal structuring underlying their ways of being in faith and would attempt to discern if their mode of faith corresponded with one or another of a hypothesized series of possibly developmentally related "stages." I do not believe we can justly be accused of nondisclosure in any injurious sense in this connection.

Nelson and Aleshire seem fair to me in their statements regarding the limits of our sample, the use of cross-sectional data, and their interpretation of the limits of the claims we can make on the basis of this research. I did find convoluted and confused, however, their discussion concerning religious and nonreligious faith. They write: "If the research is to gain information about the human universal dimension (of faith), interviewers must probe the answers to yield nonreligious equivalents so that such data could be compared with answers of respondents who do not use religious language." This proposal arises, in my judgment, out of a failure to grasp the distinction between the *content* and the *structuring* of faith. Nelson and Aleshire signal their misunderstanding of this distinction when they write: "The object of study is human faith unrelated to any religion." Nelson and Aleshire obviously fail to understand what I and Wilfred Cantwell Smith are proposing about faith. The following statement by Smith makes it clear that he does not speak of faith as necessarily "unrelated to any religion":

> Faith is deeper, richer, more personal. It is engendered by a religious tradition, in some cases and to some degree by its doctrines; but it is a quality of the person not of the system. It is an orientation of the personality, to oneself, to one's neighbor, to the universe; a total response; a way of seeing whatever one sees and of handling whatever one handles; a capacity to live at more than a mundane level; to see, to feel, to act in terms of, a transcendent dimension.[1]

The point is that faith—most frequently formed and expressed through religion—*can* be formed and expressed through other stories, allegiances, and dependencies. It has been our concern to try to understand the formal commonalities of the dynamics of faith in *both* these kinds of instance.

Broughton's discussion of our research method discloses a pattern one sees again and again in his chapter. On the basis of what I take to be an ideologically predetermined and limited reading of the faith development literature, he seems to have formed a "worst case" interpretation of the theory and its research base. In the next section of the present chapter I make an effort to interpret the framework of critical social theory which informs Broughton's approach to this work. As one example of the ways in which his effort to unmask the hidden interests and blind-spots of the theory lead him into distorting interpretations, consider this statement which concludes a paragraph of unsupported assertions: "The theory thus rests on the three assumptions: (1) that we know ourselves objectively, (2) that the actual self is identical with the self-image and self-presentation, and (3) that the interview situation itself is one without systemic constraint."[2] These "assumptions" have nothing to do with our understanding of the research approach and our confidence in it. The theory precisely is *about* a study of the process in which persons gradually disembed themselves from dominantly unconscious structurings of self-other, self-world relations, and through a series of stages develop the possibilities of more conscious and critical structuring of their worlds and meanings. Broughton chooses not to see that the interview method takes seriously the "sensuous" concreteness of the respondents' life-world and experience. He seems to ignore the possibility that faith development theory can be understood as providing a complementary hermeneutics—both of retrieval and of suspicion—to those of psychoanalysis and critical social theory.

In concluding these responses to the authors who principally addressed the strengths and limits of faith development research, I would like to focus for a moment on the question of the coding and analysis of interviews. Nelson and Aleshire fail adequately to understand what is involved in training coders to analyse structure-indicating passages of interviews. Analysts must become proficient in structural thinking and analysis; it is *not* simply a matter of people being "instructed to code black as red, and then reliably code red every time they see black."[3] In the three years since the Auburn seminar, my colleagues Romney Moseley, David Jarvis, and I have produced a two-hundrd page *Manual for Faith Development Research*.[4] There the kind of rigorous criteria employed in making structural judgments is delineated. Any person or group willing to work seriously with that manual can become proficient in analysing interviews. Tests of interrater reliability are yielding agreement in the 90 percent range. News of this manual and its availability does not settle the deeper issues underlying Nelson and Aleshire's questions regarding my analysis of the interview called "Mary's Pilgrimage" in *Stages of Faith*. Since that interview and the conflicts of interpretation to which it gives rise play a prominent role in a later part of this discussion, I will save my comments about those issues for that section.

CONCERN WITH THE CONCEPT OF "FAITH"

Virtually all of the essays in this collection address to some degree the appropriateness and adequacy of my use of the focal term "faith." In most instances the commentators manifest a desire to be both comprehensive and nuanced in their discussion of this aspect of the work.

Fernhout's carefully analytical contribution distinguishes what he takes to be three different ranges or levels on which I employ the term faith. One, which he characterizes as a "fairly narrow sense," has to do with faith as the investment of trust and loyalty in a center or centers of value and power. The second, he says, has to do with "forming an image of one's total environment." And third, he identifies a usage in which faith refers to that which integrates various dimensions of knowing, valuing, and committing in our lives. Having made his own analytic distinctions— which do not particularly correspond to or illumine my own— Fernhout then establishes a pattern of critique which he uses throughout the paper. He faults me for not indicating when I move from one of his levels or meanings of faith to another. In the course of his study he affirms and demonstrates the value of this multidimensional approach to faith. But he laments that I have not identified the center or the essential element that exerts ordering power on all the other dimensions of faith.

Two dominant reactions formed in my reading of Fernhout. First, he lacks musicality with the essentially metaphorical and evocative way in which I have written and spoken about faith. In addition to using the image of the cube, which I took from H. R. Niebuhr and on which Fernhout has largely built his case, I have frequently used the image for faith of a precious gem. The gem has many facets and in order to see faith whole we must turn the gem—or move ourselves around it. Its multiple facets cannot be seen from one angle of vision alone. And then there is another complicating factor as regards faith. Faith exhibits the qualities Gabriel Marcel associates with *mystery.* Faith, and our inquiry into it, is confounding because we are internal to the phenomenon under investigation. "Objectivity" about faith inevitably involves our "subjectivity." While I have tried at various points to pull definitions of faith together, I have never sought to over-systematize it into a manageable concept. Rather, I have tried to evoke a complex image and experience of faith in my reader's minds and then to operationalize it for research purposes through the aspects of the faith stages. Fernhout, influenced perhaps by linguistic-analytic philosophy, would like more conceptual crispness than my approach aims for. Second, Fernhout fails to see that the principle of cohesion, the centering power of faith, is *not* a structural feature. Rather, it is a function of the *concept* of faith. Ordering power, integrating power, meaning-making power in our lives, is exerted by that or those things on which we rest our hearts, or in which we trust most deeply. Fernhout's longing for a specification of the principle of integration in faith, therefore, is going to be frustrated so long as he looks for a formal or structural center. Here, as we saw in the essay of Nelson and Aleshire, we see a failure to grasp the interrelatedness of structuring and content, the interplay of the structural operations of faith and the animating *substance* of faith.

McLean's essay helpfully highlights the integral relation between my work and that of H. Richard Niebuhr. McLean, in contrast to Fernhout and others, sees the holistic and integrated character of the different dimensions of faith as the action by which we respond to and make sense of the force-fields of our lives. McLean gives a good account of my adaptation of Niebuhr's distinctions between polytheistic, henotheistic, and radical monotheistic faith. He sees, as Broughton does not, that each of these types represents *genuine* forms of faith. He also recognizes that each of these modes correlates with a pattern of identity which bespeaks either identity diffusion, integration around a narrow or idolatrous theme, or integration in the One-Beyond-the-Many. The latter, radical monotheistic faith, frees and empowers persons and groups to love many centers of value but prevents them from loving any of them excessively or making idols of them. McLean rightly stresses the grounding of faith in community and understands that the convenantal (triadic) pattern of faith is intrinsic to faith as trust and loyalty, and as the construction of an image of the ultimate environment.

McLean's sympathetic interpretation of what I have written about faith is balanced by Broughton's skeptical criticism. It is important to point out some of the background that Broughton brings to his reading of faith development theory. Broughton began his career as a psychologist in the laboratories of behaviorism and experimental research. Part of his tough-minded experimental rigor may derive from those early years. He became a convert, however, to structural developmental psychology, the field in which he did his doctoral research. His dissertation study culminated in the building of a rich structural stage theory of epistemological development. When Lawrence Kohlberg's research and theory on the development of moral reasoning came under sharp attack, Broughton wrote one of the most effective defenses of Kohlberg's work.[5] Even as he was defending Kohlberg, however, Broughton had already begun to take with great seriousness the perspectives on psychological theory developed by social psychologists immersed in critical social theory. I think it is not unfair to say that in Broughton's case a previously committed theorist and researcher in the structural developmental camp became a convinced and passionate critic of that approach. Many readers of this volume will know that the term "critical social theory" is associated with that group of social scientists called the Frankfurt School. (This group included Adorno, Horkheimer, Marcuse, among others, and more recently, Habermas.)[6] Since the 1920s, these figures have generated penetrating extensions of the insights of Karl Marx regarding the relation between ideology and the structures of economic and political privilege in societies. Powerfully affected by the rise of Hitler and of facism in the late forties, they originated the studies of authoritarianism which gave rise to the book *The Authoritarian Personality.* In the work of this school, especially under the leadership of Jürgen Habermas in the last twenty years, the critical legacy of Marx has been linked with the power of Freudian thought to unmask the hidden and interpenetrating dynamics which these theorists see as underlying both social and psychological processes—especially those rooted in patterns of social, economic, and political domination. Suggestively, the spirit and methods of critical inquiry generated in this tradition have been characterized as a "hermeneutics of suspicion."[7]

The preceding background may serve to give a context for the kind of interpretative reconstruction Broughton presses onto faith development theory. Manifestly, he brings two deep pools of suspiciousness to his readers. On the one hand, he resists the Kantian formalism and the thrust toward universalism he finds in the theory. His orientation leads him to suspect that formalism and normative abstractions always serve the interests of a particular class and their witting or unwitting ideological agents. On the other hand, he has grave misgivings about what he takes to be the inevitable linkage between radical monotheistic faith, as a normative endpoint of the theory, and political or religious absolutism and authoritarianism. Because of his own critical precommitments, Broughton seems unable or unwilling to see that faith development theory cannot be taken—nor does it offer itself—as a self-standing theology or an ideology. I have said consistently that the structural-developmental perspective on faith gives at best half of the picture—and as regards praxis it is surely the less important half. In the living faith of persons and communities, I have tried to make clear, the particular stories, myths, symbols, ethical teachings, and disciplines of their faiths provide the orienting and motivating directions. The structural stages describe the operations available to persons for varying degrees of critical self-reflection, responsible decision, and choice as regards their commitments.[8] As Habermas has seen, any adequate critical theory needs an account of how subjects become capable of disembedding themselves from the assumptive ideological ethos which form them so as to become critical participants in them. It is not a matter of splendid epistemological (or *pistuological*) solipsism, in which one leaves all particular cultural elements and affiliations behind, but rather a matter of critical and postcritical commitments which make one a more discerning participant in the dialogical unmasking and reconstruction of social ideology and reality. As regards my use of the concept "faith," therefore, perhaps our readers can understand my resistance to Table 1 in Broughton's article, where his analysis suggests that I am propounding faith development theory as a kind of self-standing formalistic, radical monotheistic ideology. In his effort to unmask the state as the hidden reference of radical monotheistic faith, Broughton unfortunately totally misses the critical power of an ethical approach which has the intent of radically relativizing *all* pretensions to absoluteness.

Dykstra's "thought experiment" on faith I find illuminating. His use of the hypothetical mode allows him to pursue a fair discussion of the implications and limits of my approach. His use of Lindbeck's category of the "expressive-experiential" approach to theology to describe my work is both helpful and misleading. Lindbeck's category—meant to be descriptive of most "liberal" approaches to the correlation of human experience with the symbols and stories of religious traditions—fails to take account of the grounding of H. Richard Niebuhr's theology, and of faith development theory, in the conviction of the sovereignty of God. "Sovereignty" derives from an admittedly troubled metaphor. But, as I have said elsewhere,[9] it intends to affirm and guard the reality, the objectivity, and the nonidentifiability of God with finite objects of our experience. It asserts and guards the priority in being and value of God. Thus Dykstra errs in interpreting me when he suggests that "meaning" need have no objective referrent in "reality" or in what *is*. (Ironically, as I read it, Lindbeck's "cultural-linguistic" approach, with which presumably Dykstra would identify himself, leaves the question of the ultimate status of the being referred to as God in Christian doctrine and its deep grammar far more to the relativity of evolving cultural language usage than does the theological grounding of my approach.) Further, Dykstra, in ways different than Broughton, has also failed to recognize my insistence on the "structuring power" of the *contents* of faith. He seems to have missed my effort, through the

discussion of conversion in Part IV of *Stages of Faith,* to indicate
that the formal structuring of faith—describable by the stages—
provides a very incomplete picture of a person's or group's faith if
it is separated from the stories, symbols, beliefs, and practice
which make it determinative. (In Dykstra's second essay, however,
this deficiency has been remedied.)

I have respect for the alternative view of growth in faith which
Dykstra offers. For the same reason that I honor the memory of
Karl Barth and love the works of Soren Kierkegaard and C. S.
Lewis, I appreciate Dykstra's compelling loyalty to the paradoxical logic of orthodoxy. Recently, in *Becoming Adult, Becoming
Christian,*[10] I sought to deal more frontally with the structuring
power of the Christian story. There I tried to bring developmental
theories, understood as contemporary presentations of a kind of
secular *ordo salutis,* into mutually critical dialogues with the
narrative structure of the Christian faith tradition. There I found
myself writing about the character of Christian community and
about the passions, affections, and virtues which it seeks to form
and call forth in its members. Dykstra and Hauerwas have emphasized more than I that certain "skills" are among the virtues
which communities of faith must model and call forth.[11] This is
an important contribution, not antithetical to faith developmental theory, but complementary to it, as Dykstra suggests in his
other essay in this volume. It is important to affirm that faith is a
"doing," a spiritual praxis that involves skills, intentionality, and
faithful action.

QUESTIONS OF THE THEORY'S
INTERNAL COHERENCE

I have always considered it a fair question whether the "aspects" which we have identified as categories for the structural
analysis of faith interviews adequately operationalize the rich and
multiform understanding of faith we have been discussing. There
is no need to insist that these seven aspects just as they are, and
no others, can operationalize faith for research. Indeed, as Fernhout points out, these aspects, in their present form, have
emerged from an ongoing process of refinement and reworking.
Moreover, I am prepared to acknowledge that the operational

structures underlying faith's knowing, believing, and acting have an *inferential* rather than a *demonstrable* status. This admission would, I think, apply to Piaget's operational structures of cognition as well, though his use of logico-mathematical structures as models gives his work—as is fitting for the study of rationality— far greater conceptual precision and exactitude.

One never has empirical access to "raw" or pure structures. Sharon Parks has put this well in her article in this collection:

> Piagetians have forgotten that the significance of stage structures is their capacity to receive, to hold, and to manipulate images. An understanding of the composing of "meaning" is insufficient without the recognition that meaning is composed by means of images which are inevitably particular, and as such contribute their own particular strength and weakness, adequacy, and inadequacy, to the dynamics of knowing.[12]

Parks recognizes that even Piaget never caught structures in the rough. They are *inferred* from behavior—both actional and linguistic. We begin to suspect we are in the presence of a structure when seemingly discrete samples of behavioral or linguistic action, involving different contexts and contents, disclose similar underlying patterns "in receiving, holding, and manipulating images."

The seven aspects we employ have proved to be windows or apertures by which we can go through and under linguistic accounts of faith as story, action, valuing, and worldview, and infer an operational set which constitutes, as it were, a structural dimension of what we might call the "intelligence" of faith.

No one seems to be satisfied with my distinction between the "logic of rational certainty" and the "logic of conviction." Let me try once more to be clear and then to relate this distinction to our discussion of the aspects. In a crude analogy we might say that the *logic of conviction* is to the *logic of rational certainty* as a tree trunk, with a wide spreading set of roots, is to one of its principal branches. Both ontogenetically and phylogenetically, I am proposing, the logic of conviction is more primitive, more holistic, more undifferentiated and inclusive than the logic of rational certainty. It is the sturdy trunk of the tree, nurtured by roots of experience, intuition, feeling, imagination, and judgment. It initially employs undifferentiated patterns of operation. The logic of rational certainty emerges as a narrowing and specialization of this broader knowing and reasoning and is the fruit of the development of reflexive capacities of thought. It begins with the contradictions that arise when what we experience fails to confirm the beliefs and images we have constructed. Our thought begins to become "self-conscious" and "critical" as we learn to use symbols and words to compare our believing and knowing, and our more inchoate images of the world, with those of others. Our knowing begins to develop a quality of "publicness."

The logic of rational certainty culminates in forms of self-critical inquiry and demonstration which are replicable by other suitably trained investigators and devoid of distortions arising from internal or external bias. As a form of knowing, this ideal constituted the goal of positivist philosophies of science. It also represented the form and limits of pure theoretical reasoning as depicted by Kant. Contemporary philosophy of science, however, is reasserting what the positivists tended to obscure: scientific knowing, in the interest of "objectivity," never succeeds in separating itself fully from the more holistic, emotive, intuitive, and imaginative forms of knowing which characterize the logic of conviction. Rather, it depends upon the motivated, interested leaps of intuition and the richly textured images of mind for the funding and orientation of the more focused and accountable process of critical, conscious, rational investigation and reflection.

We think by interrogating our images. Images hold together, in richly textured knowing, both our holistic awareness of a state of affairs and our guiding feelings and evaluative responses to it. As part of that interrogation we may design and pursue experiments and research designed to sharpen the conceptual accountability of our images and, indeed, to overturn, revise, or reground them. The participation of the logic of conviction in scientific knowing is, of course, what accounts for the resistance to paradigm relinquishment which Thomas Kuhn has noted, and for the conversion-like turn to new paradigms when they prove capable of giving rise to and of ordering a new convictional orientation.

Now what has all this to do with the seven aspects of faith

development theory? First, it suggests that the aspects were select-
ed and devised to represent faith as a holistic form of knowing
and committing. Second, it clarifies, I hope, that the inclusion of
Piagetian categories among the aspects corresponds to the ways
in which a logic of rational certainty "nests" in, or is funded by,
the more comprehensive processes of the logic of conviction. The
other aspects—moral reasoning, perspective taking, locus of authority, bounds of social awareness, and symbolic functioning—
focus on dimensions of that more inclusive knowing that is faith,
and serve the student of the dynamics of faith in the work of
inferring structures.

IMAGINATION AND INCLUSIVENESS

Reading Harris's essay in this collection led me to recall an
afternoon of revelatory experience. I had been teaching nonstop
throughout a difficult year of transition. My family and I had
recently moved to Atlanta. At the end of the first year they
accompanied me back to Boston to teach for an intensive two-
week summer session. When it was over we started back to
Atlanta. I was exhausted. On the return, we stopped for a visit to
Washington, D.C. On the first day, while our daughters toured the
Museum of Natural History on their own, my wife and I made
our first visit to the then new east wing of the National Gallery of
Art. On a magnificently sun-bright day we stepped into the soar-
ing spaciousness of that remarkable architectural environment.
Suffused in radiance, vivid against the graceful white framework
and high glass, vast mobiles, brightly colored, gently turned in
miraculous suspension. I felt transfixed. Then we moved into the
exhibit area. There we savored the most complete showing of
Picasso originals ever assembled. Bigger than life-size, and in
colors which the reproductions never could have duplicated, we
saw old visual friends we had learned to love. We realized that in
important ways those paintings had taught us to see and to be.

To that point in my life I had not experienced so consciously
an intense and concentrated recognition of "aesthetic hunger."
The hunger for beauty, yes. But more, the hunger for images and
forms that could touch deep places in the spirit, healing, energizing, and giving it new life.

In their essays on art and imagination, Harris and Parks remind us of the central role of spirit in faith and of the cruciality of symbols and imagination in the life of faith. It is not the case, I think, that faith development theory fails to take account of the roles of either spirit, aesthetics, or the imagination in faith. As a theory it affirms the centrality of image. It acknowledges the primary roles of symbol and story. It understands faith as the response of inspired imagination, forming into a unity of value and power our experiences of a world shot through with brokenness and chaos. It is the case, however, that the emphasis in the presentation and use of the theory, and in the research underlying it, has focused until recently mainly on the search for formal structures. In its search for what is common in the faiths of different persons, religious communities, and cultures, it has emphasized the formal at the expense of the symbolic, the structural at the expense of the aesthetic, and the abstract at the expense of narrative.

Moreover, insofar as the aesthetic and the imagination have been evoked and addressed in my writings on faith development, I think there is truth in Harris's claim that it has been, in large measure, done in a white male's mode. In Harris's gentle way, she makes a very forceful case for facing the curricular distortion and neglect of women's experiences and perspectives in education and research. But there is also something more. Behind and suffusing Harris's essay is an aesthetic formed in a religious tradition which, at its best, takes seriously all of the senses and sensibilities of worshipers. Catholic liturgy and spirituality take care to provide nurture for the eyes of faith and for the taste, feel, and smells of faith. In contrast, the aesthetic that dominantly formed me can best be symbolized in the dark bareness of Calvin's Genevan cathedral or the simplicity of Wesley's British chapels, where plain communion tables and lecterns with the Bible are the organizing images, and where the ear is the most sensual instrument.

IMPLICATIONS OF THE THEORY FOR COUNSELING AND EDUCATION

Three of the essays included here, the second by Dykstra and those by Schneider and by Lyon and Browning, make the valuable contribution of assessing the usefulness of faith development research and theory for the areas of educational and clinical counseling practice. Predictably, when a theory is employed and evaluated in the context of praxis, important theoretical as well as practical issues get focused.

Craig Dykstra has made a contribution of fundamental importance in his essay, "Faith Development and Religious Education." On the analogy that only when the identities of two persons are firm and clear can they have a genuinely intimate friendship, Dykstra's chapter creates the basis for an intimate relation between faith development theory and religious education. Taking his standpoint in his own field as an educator, he carefully distinguishes between the questions and aims of religious education and those of faith development theory. In a way that has to make an author grateful, Dykstra has carefully attended to what I have tried to say about religious education and faith development theory and has done us all the signal favor of putting his understanding of my position together in one place. The results make me happy, both professionally and personally, for there has been a fair amount of confusion and unnecessarily abrasive misunderstanding of my position in these matters.

Dykstra's essay makes it clear that the proper role for faith development theory in relation to religious education is that of conversation partner, hermeneutical aid, and source of fundamental categories for understanding the religious formation and transformation of persons. With regard to the first of these contributions, he writes:

> The constructive role for faith development theory in relation to aims for religious education, then, is to be a conversation partner with a religious community in its own critical inquiry into the norms embedded in its tradition. In this conversation, faith development theory has a particular role to play. It does not raise the question of *what* beliefs, attitudes, values, and ways of living are to be normative for a community, much less what (or who) the object of one's believing, knowing, trusting, and love is to be. Rather, it is to help us to discern the various ways in which such "contents" of faith are structured" and "processed" by various people in a faith community. As Fowler puts it, "The focus of our stages is on the 'how' of faith as a dynamic but structured process, as opposed to the 'what' of faith, i.e., that which is believed, known, trusted or loved in faith."[13]

In the intriguing section, "What Faith Development Theory Helps Us to Know About People," Dykstra points to three principal contributions: (1) the stress upon the fundamental and central human task of composing and responding to *meaning;* (2) the provision, through the seven aspects, of a "hermeneutical device" that intensifies and attunes our ways of attending to the faith articulations and meanings of others; and (3) the stage descriptions themselves as a kind of scaffolding for understanding. With proper cautions about superficial uses and misuses of the stages, Dykstra calls for a mutually critical correlation between the stage descriptions and the careful observations of real people by experienced educational practitioners.

Finally, Dykstra does a fine job of presenting the various perspectives of faith development theory on change and transformation. The sequence of the stages he characterizes as a "more or less natural" course of development which involve qualitative, though gradual, transformations. He provides a helpful compendium of what the theory offers as regards the dynamics of stage change. He notes the distinction the theory makes between stage transition and conversion, and handles well the event quality and content-orientation of conversion. He captures in a helpful way the dialectic between revelatory gifts from beyond us and human constructive response in the making of meaning.

Dykstra, in conclusion, provides an instructive synthetic summary of the implications for religious education that come to expression in my various writings. His highlighting of the interplay of experience-experiment with religious story and doctrine, his recognition of the role of dissonance and challenge in precipitating change, his attention to the need for "gifts to the imagination," and his acknowledgment of the importance of "sponsorship" gather into a unified statement some of the key elements of religious education for faith development. I have little or nothing by way of complaint about Dykstra's chapter. Instead, I have a great deal of gratitude for it.

Let us turn now to the helpful essays by Schneider and by Lyon and Browning. In both articles we have authors whose expertise lies in theory and practice at the intersection of theology and depth or dynamic psychology. Schneider's essay gives us a perspective on the relation of faith development theory to a tradition of diagnostic efforts in clinical pastoral care from Boisen to

Pruyser. I was particularly struck by the similarities between Boisen's interview protocols and our own, despite the fact that our group was unaware of his earlier work. Schneider, based on several months of discussions with colleagues and students in the clinical setting where he teaches, offers us a trenchant analysis and critique of my use and interpretation of "Mary's Pilgrimage" in *Stages of Faith*. Schneider's essay, which I have known in a different form for nearly four years now, has had a significant impact upon my understanding of "Mary's" case. I have been convinced by Schneider's argument and my own reflection that my published analysis of Mary's interview erred on the side of seeing her as more developed and equilibrated than the data and the theory warrant.

Schneider's reference to me as having some resistance to recognizing and dealing with elements of pathology in a frank way is on target. Retrospectively, I can see that I may have bent the analysis in the direction of seeing Mary's *present* functioning as developmentally more advanced than my candid assessment of most of the previous period (ages twenty-two to twenty-seven) now could sustain. In doing so, I failed to take seriously enough certain indications, which faith development categories actually make quite clear, regarding the limited and distorting capacities for perspective taking which Mary manifested. It is clear that at the time of the interview she was not consistently capable of mutual interpersonal perspective taking (synthetic-conventional stage) and that she has little reflective understanding of her own emotions and motivations, let alone those of others (i.e., her former husband or her parents). Coupled with the persistence of certain magical elements in her outlook, and the almost exclusively narrative quality of the interview, it is clear—by faith development criteria—that I assigned her interview a half to a whole stage beyond her functioning. My error came, in part, through my estimation during the interview that she was struggling to form the third-person perspective on herself and others that could have sustained the development of the executive ego and clearly bounded identity of the individuative-reflective stage. That hypothesis, formed during the interview and supported in part by the appearance of autonomous tendencies suggested by her reports of stubbornness and impulsiveness at many points in her stories, helps to explain my mistaken stage assignment.

I want to acknowledge my acceptance of Schneider's critique in such a way as to show that faith development theory itself is not without the resources for dealing with and identifying what, from traditional clinical perspectives, would be characterized as pathology. The excellent work of Robert Kegan in *The Evolving Self* has strengthened our ability to see and use faith development theory to deal with clinical issues. Nonetheless, both Schneider's essay and that by Lyon and Browning are right when they press us toward a more thorough theoretical and empirical examination of relations between faith development theory and the analytically oriented dynamic psychologies of object-relations and the "self-psychology" formulated by Kohut.

In their proposal, Lyon and Browning write:

> The idea here would be to acknowledge forthrightly that faith, as Fowler is studying it, *is* our object relations when viewed with respect to their implications for understanding the broader horizons of our experience as this is interpreted by one's particular level of cognitive developmental functioning. Or to say it differently, faith is our value knowing of what our object relations (our deeply felt and internalized interpersonal relations) seem to imply about the ultimate context of experience. . . . Faith is our comprehension of what these relations imply or suggest about things beyond themselves, particularly about the ultimate and enduring aspects of reality as a whole.[14]

Lyon and Browning press in the right direction here. But they must remember, as I must, that faith is a *response*—shaped of course (and sometimes misshapen) by our personal relations—to the transcendent. The actual character of the transcendent, however, is not determined by our primary object-relations. Moreover, there are strong reasons to believe that the language and symbols which mediate our relations to the transcendent have the power to give persons some degree of leverage and freedom over against the powerful and often distortive quality of their primal relations. Faith, mediated by truthful symbols, often becomes the means through which the consequences of intolerable primal relations are healed, overcome, or withstood. There is no one-to-one correlation between our primary object relations and the character we attribute to the ultimate environment. It is always a dialectical relation, one in which our object relations contribute to the shaping of our responses, but also in which they may be transformed in their content and effects through the response and relation of faith to its object.

While agreeing with Schneider, and with Lyon and Browning, that we need more comprehensive theoretical and empirical work on the structuring role of the unconscious in faith, I must disagree with the latter authors when they suggest that the essential core of what "develops" in faith is the *moral.* This is a typically post-Kantian way of approaching faith or religion—through an assertion of the autonomy (and, implicitly, the universality) of the moral. If we must identify the source or locus of criteria for development, I would have to urge that it is holistic and integrative. Here that part of Parks' essay in which she deals with Coleridge and the imagination is especially valuable. While the moral is important in faith development, it is neither central nor autonomous. It is grounded in a broader *aesthetic,* a knowing which, in H. Richard Niebuhr's language, gives us eyes to see "what is going on," and "what God is doing," and enables us to see how to make our lives—and our acts—"fitting" in relation to the larger action of which we are a part.[15]

TOWARD THE FUTURE

It has been my blessing and my burden to be the father of faith development theory. For thirteen years, in one way or another, it has been the principal concern of my academic activity and my ministry. Lectures, workshops, books, articles, with few exceptions, have been related to or inspired from the concern with an understanding of the patterns of responses—seemingly developmentally related—to God's call to partnership, which this theory and research have sought to illumine.

Since the time when I wrote the concluding sections of *Stages of Faith,* however, I have known that the next frontier of scholarly vocation for me lay in the direction of a deeper and more comprehensive approach to the understanding and *praxis* of faith development. The formalist description of structural stages provides, indeed, a "scaffolding for remembering"—the phrase

Dwayne Huebner used to characterize the stages in their value as hermeneutical and reconstructive aids to the understanding of children and youth, and of our own past "archeologies" of faith. We might also say that the stage theory represents a "scaffolding for anticipation"—a framework or model for looking ahead to times of crisis and transition, and to the shape of faith in periods in our futures. Perhaps, also, the descriptions of later stages enhance the possibility of our understanding better the faith of those whose lives of struggle and of grace have made them more developed than we in the shaping of their interpretations and responses to God's presence and work in the systems and powers of our common life.

But the lure for me, now, is to understand, explore, and try to bring to word in teaching and writing—as well as in my life—a broader and deeper version of faith development. My 1984 book, *Becoming Adult, Becoming Christian,*[16] took significant steps in this direction. The constructive parts of that book focused on the narrative structure of the Christian story, understood as a religious classic. I then focused on the themes of covenant and vocation as ordering concepts for Christian community and Christian personhood. I made an effort to write about the character of Christian community and to identify the passions, affections, and the virtues which the Christian community requires to form persons who are moved and oriented to be in partnership with God's work in the world.

In thinking through that book, in order to clarify substantive meanings for covenant and vocation, I returned to the teachings of H. Richard Niebuhr, in which he offered the three metaphors of God's *creative, governing,* and *liberative-redemptive activity* and set forth the correlated human responses in partnership to each of these modes. I also turned to the work of Walter Brueggemann, since his *The Prophetic Imagination* and an important article called "Covenanting as the Human Vocation" have been seminal for me.

Since writing *Becoming Adult, Becoming Christian,* the writings on doctrine of George Lindbeck[17] and Theodore Jennings,[18] among others, have begun to help me formulate new dimensions of my sense of calling to broaden and deepen my work toward a practical theology of faith development. Under the impact of

Lindbeck and Jennings I have begun to see in fresh ways the deep structure of an angular, inconvenient, but tough and resiliently integral truth at the heart of orthodox Christian faith. Lindbeck calls this structure the "grammar" of faith. With this he refers to the *regula fidei* which doctrine tries to express, by which we see the interconnectedness and holistic integrity of the life-giving truths which come to expression in what David Kelsey calls the "vast, loosely-structured, nonfictional novel" that is the Bible.[19]

Ted Jennings, reasserting the centrality and indispensability of the Trinity as the heart of Christian doctrine, helps us to see that there is a truth beneath the truths of doctrine. Doctrinal formulations are efforts to conserve and make accessible a certain interconnectedness of truths that constitute—in the lives where they have exterted formative influence—a rightly ordered and graceful faithfulness.

For Lindbeck, the analogy is that of learning to be "competent speakers" of the "Christian language"—that is, knowing (without necessarily having a theory) correct "grammatical usage," and more, having a sure sense and taste for that which fits as an expression of Christ in us and for resisting that which does not.

From the standpoint of Christian education and spirituality, the work of Paul Holmer, found in *Making Christian Sense,*[20] has proven helpful in trying to grasp more fully the implications of this confidence in the "structuring power of orthodoxy."

When I give myself over to the effort to understand and be formed by this testimony to the deep grammar of Christian faith, I find a deepened, even radicalized, apprehension of what I had earlier called the "structuring power of the contents of faith." And herein lies an interesting, even captivating insight: Lindbeck, Jennings, Holmer, et al. may be seen as doing something vis à vis the Christian classic[21] that is roughly analogous to what Freud, Jung, and depth psychologies have done for the dynamic unconscious and to what Piaget, Kohlberg, and I have done for the (also) unconscious operations of knowing and valuing underlying cognition, moral judgment, and faith. In all these instances, an effort has been made to bring to awareness and accountability an integral set of generative, dynamic patterns functioning at depth and in hidden ways to give character to aspects of persons' ways of seeing, being, acting, interpreting, and responding.

Lindbeck, Jennings, and Holmer, however, have primarily tried to honor and make visible the operating integrity of orthodox Christian faith. This operative integrity provides a formative and transformative matrix for persons and communities who— through proclamation, sacrament, public and private prayer, and through a kind of faith imitation of Christ and of others who have been rightly formed—will enter in and submit to it. Meanwhile, Freud, Jung, and others have tried to show how early primal relations (Freud), social experience, and perhaps even genetically transmitted archetypal symbols (Jung) impose channelings of interpretation, motivation, and defense which shape and misshape our characters. Piaget, Kohlberg, and, in a different way, I have sought, as it were, to bring to awareness underlying patterns of cognition, broadly understood, which account for the conscious leeway and responsibility we are able to develop so as to participate reflectively in the shaping and directions of our lives.

Any practical theology concerned with the formation and transformation of persons in Christian community will have to know and care about each of these angles of vision. Christian education and pastoral care, as practical theological disciplines, are precisely concerned about effective and faithful formation and transformation of persons in a living relation to God mediated through the shaping power of Christian faith. In this praxis they will encounter varying degrees of conscious awareness and need for a "theory" of what is going on. And they will encounter collisions and resistances of hearts twisted and bereft because of brokenness and distortions in the past relational histories of persons.

All three of these perspectives are *hermeneutical* in the sense that they enable us to see patterns underlying our responses to and compositions of the meanings that come to sustain and orient our lives. In a curious way all three are *structural,* in the sense that they try to make explicit certain "rules" or "patterned operations" that account for the ordering of meanings.

Each of these perspectives is indispensable—along with other disciplines such as critical social theory—to inform the praxis of Christian formation in such a period as our own. But what we lack, as yet, is a broad, variegated, and comprehensive theory of the kind of praxis that brings about the metanoia in which persons—of various developmental stages and of various personality histories and types—get access to and enter the praxis and disciplines of Christian faith so as to be deeply reformed. We are dealing here with mystery and with the domain of Spirit's activity. But we are not innocent anymore. Therefore, partnership—acknowledging mystery and the indispensable work of Spirit—must nonetheless work at understanding and creating conditions and experiences where the deep structural wellsprings of behavior and action can be decisively and ongoingly reshaped by the relation to God mediated in the deep structural wellsprings of Christian faith.

In addition to *Becoming Adult, Becoming Christian,* I have written two papers on practical theology in which I explored some of the methodological issues involved in the kind of undertaking the previous paragraphs suggest.[22] But the encounters, during the last year, with Lindbeck, Holmer, and Jennings, and behind them, with Soren Kierkegaard, C. S. Lewis, and Karl Barth, have lured and led me into what may have something of the character of a paradigm shift. This does not seem to mean a relinquishing of the structural developmental theory of faith development. Rather, it means a continuing broadening and deepening, as indicated above, of the purview of a practical theology of faith development.

This movement of mind and spirit seems both essential to and in some tension with the other "big idea" that has begun to use me since the publication of *Stages of Faith.* In that same year, 1981, Martin Marty[23] and Parker Palmer[24] published books concerned with faith and public life. Turning away from *civil religion* as adequate for a way of relating religion to public life, they proposed what Marty called the "public church." In different ways they focused for us visions of church—Evangelical, Catholic, and mainline Protestant—that combine deep, particular commitment to Christian faith with a principled and specific openness to dialogue and mutual work with other religious and nonreligious people on behalf of the common or public good. In this approach one senses a kind of celebration of pluralism and particularity. This is not because they lead to that kind of relativism where there is a grayness in which all cats are gray. Rather, it is because only when religious groups are deeply and fully formed by the particular stories and visions of their traditions do they have "character" enough to contribute richly toward public solutions to the challenges that threaten the common good. Yet we, and they, must learn the disciplines that are requisite for creating and maintaining public "space" and that make public discourse a means of judgment and grace. Marty says at one point in his book that "the most heroic task ahead for believers in the public church communions will be to bring their part of humanity to a whole new stage of faith, in which the God of prey is left behind and people can affirm what they believe without pouncing on others."[25]

Practical theology for the guidance of a public church will need a rich theory and praxis of Christian formation and transformation. The linkage between this need and my earlier discussion of the confluence of structural developmental, depth psychological, and Christian orthodox hermeneutics will be obvious.

Not so obvious, however, is the way in which concern for Christian formation for a public church has led me into a concern for religion and the education of the public. In a substantial 1984 article, entitled "Pluralism, Particularity and Paideia,"[26] I tried to formulate in a preliminary way the question whether it is possible to reground a *paideia* to inform public education for a contemporary American society which is radically pluralistic. In the constructive part of that essay I proposed that we consider a combination of faith development theory with root metaphor analysis to provide a basis for ethical education in public schools. From the deep structures of biblical faith, and built into the traditions that informed the United States Constitution, it has seemed to me that the root metaphor of *covenant* has an indispensable role to play in the present efforts to reconstruct public philosophy and an ethical foundation for public education. This work and the directions it proposes will be further tested conceptually and empirically in the Center for Faith Development's project on Ethics and Public Education. At this writing I am editing the papers from the Center for Faith Development's summer conference on Religion and the Future of Public Education. Including contributions by Marty, Palmer, Robert Bellah, Richard John Neuhaus, and others, it explores the possibilities of a reconstituted public *paideia*.

In conclusion, I should report that the Center for Faith Development is continuing empirical research. During the spring of 1986 we are reworking our interview approach with children, particularly of preschool age. During the coming year we will build on new pilot work in this area. In addition, we will devote particular attention to late-stage respondents in the attempt to enhance the empirical basis for the Conjunctive and Universalizing stages. Cross-cultural work in the Caribbean in the next year or so also seems to be a strong possibility. Moreover, work is pretty well advanced on the development and utilization of a computer program for the analysis and coding of faith development interviews. This program will enable us to carry out certain kinds of correlational studies which will advance considerably answers to the questions of construct validity and of the theoretical coherence of structural faith development theory.

NOTES

1. Wilfred Cantwell Smith, *Faith and Belief* (Charlottesville: University Press of Virginia, 1977), p. 12.

2. John M. Broughton, "The Political Psychology of Faith Development Theory," ch. 4 in the present volume.

3. C. Ellis Nelson and Daniel Aleshire, "Research in Faith Development," ch. 8 in the present volume.

4. James W. Fowler, Romney S. M. Moseley, and David Jarvis, *Manual for Faith Development Research* (Atlanta: Emory University, Center for Faith Development, 1986).

5. John M. Broughton, "The Cognitive-Developmental Approach to Morality: A Reply to Kurtines and Grief," *Journal of Moral Education* 7 (1978) 2, pp. 81-96.

6. For background and analysis of the Frankfurt School and the main lines of critical social theory, see David Held, *Introduction to Critical Theory: Horkheimer to Habermas* (Berkeley, Calif.: University of California Press, 1980), and Raymond Geuss, *The Idea of a Critical Theory: Habermas and the Frankfurt School* (Cambridge: Cambridge University Press, 1981).

7. See Jürgen Habermas, *Knowledge and Human Interests,* trans. Jeremy J. Shapiro (Boston: Beacon Press, 1971).

8. James W. Fowler, *Stages of Faith* (San Francisco: Harper & Row, 1981), pp. 269 ff.

9. James W. Fowler, *To See The Kingdom* (Lanham, Md.: University Press of America, 1985). Orig. Abingdon Press, 1974.

10. James W. Fowler, *Becoming Adult, Becoming Christian* (San Francisco: Harper & Row, 1984).

11. See Craig Dykstra, *Vision and Character* (New York: Paulist Press, 1981), and Stanley Hauerwas, *The Peaceable Kingdom* (Notre Dame, Ind.: University of Notre Dame Press, 1983).

12. Sharon L. Parks, "Imagination and Spirit in Faith Development: A Way Past the Structure-Content Dichotomy," ch. 6 in the present volume.

13. Craig Dykstra, "Faith Development and Religious Education," ch. 11 in the present volume.

14. K. Brynolf Lyon and Don S. Browning, "Faith Development and the Requirements of Care," ch. 9 in the present volume.

15. H. Richard Niebuhr, *The Responsible Self* (New York: Harper & Row, 1963).

16. Fowler, *Becoming Adult, Becoming Christian.*

17. George Lindbeck, *The Nature of Doctrine* (Philadelphia: Fortress Press, 1984).

18. Theodore W. Jennings, Jr., *Beyond Theism: A Grammar of God-Language* (New York: Oxford University Press, 1985).

19. David H. Kelsey, *The Uses of Scripture in Recent Theology* (Philadelphia: Fortress Press, 1975), p. 48.

20. Paul L. Holmer, *Making Christian Sense* (Philadelphia: Westminster Press, 1984).

21. I use the terminology framed by David Tracy in *The Analogical Imagination* (New York: Crossroad, 1981), but readers should attend to Lindbeck's footnote number 4 on page 136 of *The Nature of Doctrine* where he differentiates his use of the term classic from that of Tracy.

22. James W. Fowler, "Practical Theology and the Shaping of Christian Lives," in *Practical Theology: The Emerging Field in Theology, Church and World,* ed. Don S. Browning (San Francisco: Harper & Row, 1983), pp. 148-166, and James W. Fowler, "Practical Theology and Theological Education: Some Models and Questions," *Theology Today* 42 (April, 1985) 1, pp. 43-58.

23. Martin E. Marty, *The Public Church* (New York: Crossroad, 1981).

24. Parker J. Palmer, *The Company of Strangers* (New York: Crossroad, 1981).

25. Marty, *Public Church,* pp. 136-37.

26. James W. Fowler, "Pluralism, Particularity and Paideia," *Journal of Law and Religion* 2 (1984) 2, pp. 263-307.

Contributors

JAMES W. FOWLER is Professor of Theology and Human Development and Director of the Center for Faith Development at Candler School of Theology, Emory University. He is the author of *To See the Kingdom: The Theological Vision of H. Richard Niebuhr* (1974), as well as of *Stages of Faith: The Psychology of Human Development and the Quest for Meaning* (1981) and several other books on faith development theory, including his latest, *Becoming Adult, Becoming Christian* (1984).

CRAIG DYKSTRA is Thomas W. Synnott Professor of Christian Education at Princeton Theological Seminary and Associate Editor of the journal, *Theology Today.* His previous writings include *Vision and Character: A Christian Educator's Alternative to Kohlberg* (1981).

J. HARRY FERNHOUT is Senior Member in Philosophy of Education at the Institute for Christian Studies, Toronto, Canada. The focus of his work is in the area of foundations of moral and religious education.

JOHN M. BROUGHTON is Associate Professor of Psychology and Education at Teachers College, Columbia University. He is the editor of two books, *The Cognitive-Developmental Psychology of James Mark Baldwin* (1982) and *Critical Theories of Development* (1986). He is also founding editor of the two journals, *Psych Critique* and *New Ideas in Psychology.*

MARIA HARRIS is Howard Professor of Religious Education at Andover Newton Theological School. She is author of six books in the field of religious education, the most recent of which is *Teaching and Religious Imagination* (1986).

SHARON PARKS is Associate Professor of Developmental Psychology and Faith Education at The Divinity School, Harvard University. Her recent book is entitled, *The Critical Years: The Young Adult Search for a Faith to Live By* (1986).

STUART D. McLEAN is Associate Professor of Christian Ethics and Christian Education at The Graduate Seminary, Phillips University. He is the author of *Humanity in the Thought of Karl Barth* (1981), and is currently preparing a new book entitled, *Rites of Passage Youth Ministry: An Alternative.*

C. ELLIS NELSON now teaches at Austin Theological Seminary. Formerly President and Professor of Christian Education at Louisville Presbyterian Theological Seminary, and Skinner and McAlpin Professor of Practical Theology at Union Theological Seminary in New York, Nelson is author of many publications including *Where Faith Begins* (1967), and editor of a collection on *Conscience: Theological and Psychological Perspectives* (1973).

DANIEL ALESHIRE is Associate Professor of Psychology and Christian Education at The Southern Baptist Theological Seminary. Formerly a research scientist at the Search Institute in Minneapolis, he has conducted numerous empirical research efforts in the areas of psychology and religion. He is the author of *Understanding Today's Youth* (1982).

K. BRYNOLF LYON is Assistant Professor of Pastoral Care at Christian Theological Seminary. The focus of his work is in religious and ethical issues in human development. He is author of *Toward a Practical Theology of Aging* (1986).

DON S. BROWNING is Alexander Campbell Professor of Religion and Psychological Studies at The Divinity School, the University of Chicago. He is the editor of the *Theology and Pastoral Care* series published by Fortress Press, and author of several books including *The Moral Context of Pastoral Care* (1976), *Religious Ethics and Pastoral Care* (1983), and the forthcoming *Religious Thought and the Modern Psychologies.*

CARL D. SCHNEIDER is Senior Staff Pastoral Psychologist at the Pastoral Psychotherapy Institute, Parkside Human Services Corporation, a part of the Lutheran General Health Care System in Park Ridge, Illinois. He is also Director of the Divorce Mediation Service and of the Divorce Mediation Institute, a mediation group practice and an educational and training institution, respectively. Schneider is the author of *Shame, Exposure, and Privacy* (1977).

Index of Names

Index of Subjects

310